THE DISTRICT GAZETTEER OF
UTTARANCHAL

THE DISTRICT GAZETTEER OF
UTTARANCHAL

Editor
S.C. Bhatt

GYAN PUBLISHING HOUSE
NEW DELHI-110 002

THE DISTRICT GAZETTEER OF UTTARANCHAL

Rs. 490

ISBN : 81-212-0775-4

Published in 2003 in India by
Gyan Publishing House
5, Ansari Road, New Delhi-110002
Phones : 3261060, 3282060, Fax : (011) 3285914
E-Mail : gyanbook@del2.vsnl.net.in
Website: http:\\www.gyanbooks.com

Lasertypesetting by : Varsha Graphics, Delhi
Printed at : Mehra Offset Printers, Delhi

CONTENTS

PREFACE

India is a vast and diverse country. Some of its 28 states are bigger in size and population than a few of the countries in the world. Uttaranchal is the 27th state of India with 13 districts, it is in the north of Uttar Pradesh. It is a matter of deep satisfaction that the work on Uttaranchal has been accomplished. Detailed information about all the districts is presented here with a concise but exhaustive history, the people inhabiting it, its geography, its present development and administrative set-up and much more.

The British, ruled over India for about two centuries and had tremendous impact on the thinking, education, and culture of our people and mainly on the people of high altitude areas. It is a well known fact that the district is a very important administrative unit for a state Government or the Union Territory Administration in India. As part of the administrative control, all the planning and developmental activities whether concerning its towns or villages is planned, implemented and monitored at the district level by the bonafide district authority.

I hope that this publication will serve as a useful reference and become an invaluable companion to all researchers and scholars, administrators, planners, tourists, librarians and all those who want to know about a particular district. This work is beneficial to all people who are interested in the history, developments and future of the new state.

My grateful thanks are due to the Resident Commissioner, Uttaranchal, professors, librarians, the state information centres and those connected with the government for valuable material they made available to me. I have consulted a large number of published works and thus I could fill up several gaps in the draft drawn from them. I owe a debt of gratitude to all those publishers, authors, editors and compilers, who helped me in the process.

S.C. Bhatt

INTRODUCTION

Uttaranchal came into existence on 9th November 2000 as the 27th state of the Republic of India. It is one of the most beautiful, well preserved and enchanting regions located in the northern part of India. The state comprises 13 districts of the erstwhile Uttar Pradesh, namely Almora, Bageshwar, Chamoli, Champawat, Dehradun, Hardwar, Nainital, Pauri Garhwal, Pithoragarh, Rudraprayag, Tehrigarhwal, Udham Singh Nagar and Uttar Kashi. The state of Uttaranchal is spread over an area of 55,845 sq. km. and the population is 84,79,562.

The Himalayas are an integral part of the mother earth in the mountain ecosystem formed by almost parallel tertiary ranges, which constitutes a gigantic arch, separating the Indian planes from North Tibet and Central Asia. The Western Himalayas having length approximately 320 km., is the smallest among the four Himalayan regions and lies between river Kali and the great defile of river Sutlej and comprises the Garhwal and Kumaun hills. In the heart of this majestic mountains lies the state of Uttaranchal. The mountainous region offers a wonderful panorama of high snow clad peaks. The unparallel beauty, mystic surroundings and breath taking views make one fall in love with the Himalayas and feel closer to God.

Nature has endowed this region with so much beauty and spiritual bliss that the land is also known as Dev Bhumi (Land of Gods). It includes the Chardhams, the four most sacred and revered and significant Hindu shrines of Badrinath, Kedarnath, Gangotri and Yamunotri. This is the land where Vedas and Shastras were composed and the great Indian epic—the Mahabharata was written. The region has always been the source of inspiration for nature lovers and seekers of peace and spirituality. The Ganga, the Yamuna and scores of other rivers originate from Uttaranchal. Among them, the Ganga is the most holy and prominent among them. It represents the soul of India, her rich culture, history and civilisation. The credit of weaving the country into one religious entity goes to the unique thread of the holy Ganga. The source of the Ganga is at Gaumukh (the shape of the ice formation is like a cow's mouth), where the mighty river emerges from the depth of Gangotri glacier. Here the river is known as 'Bhagirathi' after the name of king Bhagirath. Rising in the icy caves of Gangotri glaciers, the gushing, tossing and gurgling Bhagirathi starts its long journey downwards where it joins rivers 'Alaknanda' and Ganga.

Panch Kedar. The Kedarnath shrine, one of the 12 jyotirlingas of Lord Shiva, is a scenic spot situated against the backdrop of the majestic Kedarnath Range. There are about 200 shrines dedicated to Lord Shiva in Chamoli district itself and the most important is Kedarnath.

According to a legend, the Pandavas after having won over Kauravas in Kurukshetra war, felt guilty of having killed their own brothers and sought the blessings of Lord Shiva for redemption. He eluded them repeatedly and while feeling took refuge at Kedarnath in the form of a bull.

The arms appeared at Tungnath, the face at Rudranath, the belly at Madmaheshwar and his locks (hair) with head of Kalpeshwar. Kedarnath and these four shrines are treated as Panch Kedar.

Panch Badri. Badrinath is situated in the lap of Nar-Narayan Parvat with the towering Neelkanth Peak in the background. Badrinath is one of the most revered Hindu shrines of India.

Badrinath is devoted in the worship of Lord Vishnu who according to an amusing tale, usurped this place from Lord Shiva. For Vishnu had come here as the gods once did, to offer penence. He loved the place so much that he plotted to unseat Lord Shiva from his meditation here. He took on the form of a beautiful child and began to wail. Shiva's wife, Parvati picked him up but could not calm the child. Since his wailing continued to disturb Shiva, he shifted to Kedarnath in exasperation, leaving the spot free for Vishnu to occupy. But remainder of Shiva's stay continued to linger, most visibly in the name Badri, a kind of berry that Shiva was most fond of and the gigantic tree, invisible to the mortal eyes, that served Shiva. Badrinath's four subsidiary badris include Bhavishya Badri, Yogdhayan Badri, Birdha Badri and Adi Badri. These are called the PANCH BADRI.

Panch Prayag. Panch Prayag, confluence of the most sacred rivers, is considered the epitome of immortal piety. River confluences in India are considered very sacred especially since rivers themselves are extolled as goddesses.

Deoprayag is situated at the confluence of Alaknanda and Bhagirathi rivers. It is commonly believed to be the birth place of river Ganga, 70 kms. from Rishikesh on Rishikesh Badri-Kedar route. The famous Raghunath and Shiva temple are situated here.

Five Prayag are—Vishnu Prayag (at the meeting point of Vishnu Ganga and Dhauliganga rivers), Nand Prayag (at the meeting point of Alaknanda and Mandakini rivers), Karan Prayag (situated at the joining point of Pindari and Alaknanda rivers), Rudra Prayag (is located at the meeting point of Alaknanda and Mandakini rivers), Deo Prayag (at the joining point of Alaknanda and Bhagirathi rivers). These five prayags are called PANCH PRAYAG.

Kumaun, was the northern most Division of the former United Provinces, situated almost entirely in the Himalayas, and extending from the border of Tibet to the damp submontane tract known as the Terai. In 1901 there were three districts under the Kumaun division, namely, Nainital, Almora and Garhwal. Nainital lies on the outer ranges of the Himalayas but most of it is included in the waterless tract at their feet known as the Bhabar, and the moist country below called the Terai. The other two districts are situated mainly in the Himalayas, and include the highest peaks. Garhwal was the western district of Kumaun Division of the then United Provinces. It extends from the submontane plain across central axis of the Himalayas to the watershed between the drainage systems of the Sutlej and the Ganges. It consists of the most part of rugged mountain ranges which appear to be tossed about in the most intricate confusion. They can however, be ultimately traced to the great watershed, and by their general direction from north-east to south-west they determine the course and direction of the drainage channels. The greater part of the Garhwal is included in the basin of the Ganges, the principal tributary of which is Alaknanda. This stream is formed by the confluence of the Bishanganga with the Dhauliganga, both rising near the watershed and flowing south-west, their upper courses being divided from that of Mandakini, which joins the Alaknanda at Rudraprayag, by a massive spur of mountains. At Devaprayag, on the border of the then Tehri state, the Alaknanda meets the Bhagirathi, their valleys being separated by another lofty range.

The combined stream assumes the name of Ganges and from the point of confluence separates Garhwal from Tehri and subsequently from Dehradun. The great central axis of the Himalayas, lying about 50 km. south of the water-shed, includes two ranges of lofty snow-clad hills on either side of the Alaknanda. From the eastern range, which culminates in the giant peak of Nanda Devi, a series of spurs divides the valleys of the Birehi, Mandakini, and Pundar, all tributaries of the Alaknanda, from each other. Farther south the Dudatoli range forms the boundary between the Ganges basin and the Ramganga, which drained the south-east of the district. The principal peaks are Trisuli, Dunagiri, Kamet, Badrinath and Kedarnath. The river flows in narrow valleys which may rather be described as gorges or ravines and in their lower courses some of them are used for rafting timber. There are a few small lakes in Garhwal but the Gohna lake is the only one of importance. A narrow strip of Bhabar or waterless forest land some 3 to 5 miles in breath, intervening between the southern base of the hills and the alluvial low lands of Rohilkhand forms the only level portion of Garhwal.

The early history of Garhwal is extremely obscure. A part of it was probably included in the kingdom of Brahmapura referred to by the Chinese traveller in the seventh century. The earliest dynasty of which records exist was that of the Katuris. According to tradition, they had their origin at Joshimath in the north of the district, and then spread to the south-east and upto Almora. The country was subsequently divided among a series of petty chiefs. Local tradition states that a Raja, named Ajaya Pala, reduced the petty chiefs about the middle or close of the fourteenth century and settled at Dewalgarh but a successor, named Mahipal Shah, who lived early in the seventeenth century and founded Srinagar, was possibly the first of the line to establish real independence. The Garhwal Rajas first came into conflict with their neighbours, the Chands of Almora, about 1581, when Rudra Chand attempted, but without succcess, to invade Garhwal. Subsequent attempts were also resulted. In 1654, Shah Jahan launched an expedition to coerce Raja Pirthi Shah, which ended in the separation of Dehradun from Garhwal. The same Raja, a few years later, robbed the unfortunate refugee, Sulaiman Shikoh, son of Dara Shikoh, and delivered him up to Aurangzeb. Towards the close of the seventeenth century the Chand Rajas again attempted to take Garhwal, and Jagat Chand (1708-20) drove the Raja from Srinagar, which was formerly bestowed on a Brahman. Pradip Shah (1717-72), however, recovered Garhwal, and held the Dun till, in 1757, Najib Khan, the Rohilla, established his authority there. In 1779 Lalat Shah of Garhwal defeated the usurper who was ruling in Kumaun and allowed his son, Praduman Shah, to become the Raja of that territory. A few years later, on the death of his brother, Parduman Shah held both Garhwal and Kumaun for a year, but he then preferred secure tenure of his own dominions from the intrigue of Almora and retired to Srinagar.

The Gurkhas conquered Almora early in 1790 and made an attempt on Garhwal, but withdrew owing to trouble with the Chinese in Tibet. Internal dissensions prevented an other advance for some years but in 1803 the Gurkha overran Garhwal and also took Dehradun. Parduman Shah fled to the plains and collected a force, but perished near Dehra with most of his Garhwali retainers in 1804. The Gurkha rule was severe and when the British conquered Kumaun in 1815, in consequences of aggressions by the Gurkhas, the change was felt with delight by the hill-men. The whole division was administered directly by a Commissioner. But in 1837 Garhwal became a separate subdivision under an Assistant Commissioner, and in 1891, was constituted a district.

Dehradun was in Meerut Division in former United Provinces. The district consists of two distinct portions. The greater part of it forms a gently sloping valley between the Himalayas and the Siwalik Hills. It is divided into two parts by a connecting ridge, from which the Eastern Dun slopes down to the Ganges and Western Dun to Jamuna. The scenery of these mountain dales can hardly be surpassed for picturesque beauty even among the lovely slopes of the massive chain to which they belong. On the north, the outer range of Himalayas rises abruptly to a height of 7,000 feet or 8000 feet, with the hill station of Mussoorie and the cantonment of Landour and Chakrata. The Siwaliks rise with a more gentle slope on the south west of the valley, but fall away suddenly to the great plain of the Doab. The other portion of the district is the Jaunsar-Bawar pargana or Chakrata tehsil, which strikes north from the outer range of the Himalayas between the valleys of the Tons and Jamuna, and consist of a confused mass of ridges and spurs clothed with forest. The draïnage of Jaunsar-Bawar into the Tons or the Jamuna, which unites where they penetrate the outer range. The Western Dun is drained by the Asan, which falls into the Jamuna, and the eastern Dun by a network of small channels which meet and diverge, again and again before they join the Ganges. Both the Jamuna and Ganges are here rapid rivers pouring over beds of boulders in several channels with island between.

The Siwalik range is composed in its lower and southern most parts of middle Siwalik soft sandstone or sand-rock with a few thin mammalian fossil-bearing conglomerates, and along its crest of thick upper Siwalik conglomerates. These are all of fresh-water origin, and dip at low angles below the flat surface of the valley. The latter is a broad expanse of recent gravels and consolidated ferns of scree derived from the higher ranges. On the north of the valley the middle and upper Siwalik again emerge, bent into sharp reversed folds by faulting against the older Himalayan series. The much consorted outer Himalayan rocks include the slates and dark-grey limestones or dolomites of the mussoorie ridge, the Jaunsar series of dark slates, quartzites, fine volcanic ashes, and basic traps, the Deoban massive lime stone which comes above the latter and forms much of the rugged elevated country north of Chakrata and finally the Mandhata conglomerates and Bawar quartzite schists, which lie flatly above both of the latter series. All these older rocks have proved unfossiliferous and are probably very ancient. Lead and sulphur mines are found on the Tons river and gypsum in the lime-stones below Mussoorie.

The arboreal vegetation of the Siwaliks consist largely, of species occurring both on the lower slopes of the Himalayas and in the hilly districts of central and southern India. Epiphytic orchid are absent, and ferns are but few. The Himalayan long-leaved pine is found, and the sal is here near its western limit and appears only in a stunted form. In the valley a rich vegetation is kept green throughout the whole year. The prevailing forest tree is sal, and the flora is an interesting mixture of species found in the plains and species from the lower hills. In the Himalayas, the vegetation gradually changes at higher elevations to European genera, and the deodar, silver spruce, and weeping pine are found. The district is singularly rich in animal life, though the game has been shot down lately. Wild big animals are found in the Siwaliks and tigers, leopards, sloth bears, spotted and other deer, and monkeys in the forests. Among game-birds may be mentioned the black and grey partridge, peafowl, florican, snipe, wood cock, and pheasant. The rivers abound in fish.

Extremes of heat in the valley are unknown. The proximity of the Himalayas cools the atmosphere. The hot blasts from the plains do not reach so far, while the heavy rains of the monsoon bring an abundant downpour, and even in May and June occasional showers refresh the country. The Eastern Dun is malarious in the extreme and is entirely deserted during the rainy seasons.

In the earliest ages of Hindu legend, Dehradun formed part of the mythical regions known as Kedarkhand, the abode of the great god Siva, whose sovereignty is still commemorated in the name of Siwalik Hills. Many generations later, according to the most ancient myths of the Aryan settlers, the valley became bound up with the two great epics of the Ramayana and Mahabharata. Either came Rama and his brother, to do the penance for the death of the demon king, Ravana, and here sojourned the five Pandavas brothers on their way to the inner recesses of the snowy range, where they finally immolated themselves upon the sacred peak of Mahapanth. Another memorable legend connects the origin of the little river Suswa with the prayers of 60,000 pigmy Brahmanas, whom Indra, the rain god, had laughed to scorn when he saw them vainly endeavouring to cross the vast lake formed by a cow's footprint filled with water. The indignant pigmies set to work, by means of penance and mortifications, to create a second Indra who should supersede the raining god, and when their sweat had collected into the existing river, the irreverent deity, alarmed at the surprising effects of their devotions, appeared their wrath through the good offices of Brahma. Traditions of a snake Bamun, who becomes lord of the Dun on the summit of the Nagsidh Hill, seems to point towards a period of Naga supremacy. The famous Kalsi stone, near Haripur on the right bank of the Jamuna, inscribed with an edict of the Buddhist emperor Ashoka might mark the ancient frontier of Northern India. It consists of a large quarters boulder, standing on a ledge which overhangs the river, and is covered with the figures of an elephant, besides an inscription in the ordinary characters of the period. Hiuen Tsiang does not mention any cities which can be identified as lying within the present district, and tradition asserts that it remained without inhabitants until the eleventh century, when a passing caravan of Banjaras struck with the beauty of the country, permanently settled on the spot.

Authentic history, however, knows nothing of Dehradun till the seventeenth century, when it formed a portion of the Garhwal kingdom. The town of Dehra owes its origin to the Sikh Guru Ram Rai, who obtained from the emperor Aurangzeb from the Raja of Garhwal, Fateh Shah. His presence in the Dun shortly attracted numerous devotees, and the village of Gurudwara or Dehra grew up around his abode. The Raja endowed his temple, a curious building of Muhammadan architecture with the revenue of three estates. The Guru possessed the miraculous power of dying at will, and returning to life after a concerted interval, but no one occasion, having mistaken his reckoning, he did not revive. The bed on which he died still forms an object of reverence to the devout worshippers at his cenotaph. Monuments of earlier date, erected by one Rani Karnavati, still exist at Nawada. Fateh Shah died soon after the arrival of Ram Rai, and was succeeded (1699) by his infant grandson, Pratap Shah, whose reign extended over the greater part of a century. But the flourishing condition of his domain attracted the attention of Najib-ud-daula, governor of Saharanpur, who crossed the Siwaliks with a Rohilla army in

1757, and occupied the Dun without serious opposition. Under Najib-ud-daula's benevolent and enlightened administration, the district rose to an unexampled degree of prosperity. Canals and wells irrigated the mountain-sides, Mohammadan colonists brought capital to develop the latent resources of the soil, and mango groves. Still standing among primaeval forest, bear witness even now to the flourishing agriculture of this happy period.

But Najib-ud-daula's death in 1770 put an end to the sudden prosperity of the Dun. Henceforth a perpetual inundation of Rajputs, Gujars, Sikhs and Gurkhas swept over the valley, till the once fertile garden degenerated again into a barren waste. Four Rajas followed one another on the throne but the real masters were the turbulent tribes on every side, who levied constant blackmail from the unfortunate cultivators.

Meanwhile, the Gurkhas, a race of mixed Nepalese origin, were advancing westward, and had reached at the last the territories of Garhwal. In 1803, Raja Parduman Shah fled before them from Srinagar into the Dun and then to Saharanpur, while the savage Gurkha host overran the whole valley unopposed. Their occupation of Dehradun coincided in time with British entry into Saharanpur, and the great earthquake of 1803 proved the miraculous harbinger of either event. The Gurkhas ruled their new acquisition with a rod of iron, so that the district threatened to become an absolute desert. Under the severe fiscal arrangements of the Gurkha governors, slavery increased with frightful rapidity, every defaulter being condemned to lifelong bondage, so that slaves became far cheaper in the market than horses or camels. From this unhappy condition, the advent of the British rule rescued the feeble and degraded people.

The constant aggressions of the Gurkhas against the frontier compelled the British Government to declare war in 1814. Dehra was immediately occupied, while seige was laid to the hill fortress of Nalapani or Kalanga, which fell after a gallant defence, with great loss to the besieging force. The remnant of its brave garrison entered the service of Ranjit Singh, and afterwards died to a man in the battle with the Afghans. A resolution of Government, dated November 17, 1815, ordered the annexation of the new occupied territories to Saharanpur, while the Gurkhas, by a treaty drawn up in the succeeding month, formally ceded the country. The organisation of the district on the British model proceeded rapidly, and in spite of an ineffected rising of the disaffected Gujaras and other predatory classes led by a bandit named Kalwa, in 1824, peace was never again seriously disturbed. Under the energy and perseverance of its first British officials, the Dun rapidly recovered its prosperity.

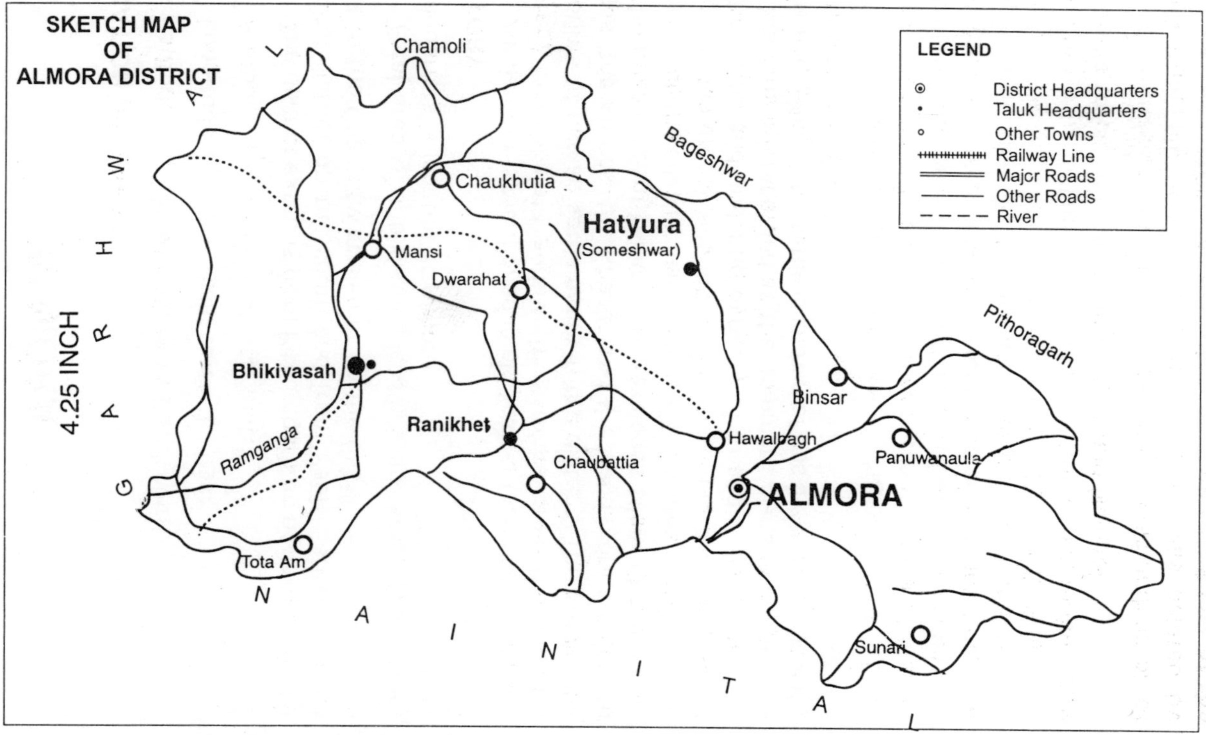
SKETCH MAP
OF
ALMORA DISTRICT
4.25 INCH
G A R H W A L
Chamoli
Chaukhutia
Mansi
Dwarahat
Hatyura
(Someshwar)
Bageshwar
Bhikiyasah
Ranikhet
Ramganga
Chaubattia
Hawalbagh
Binsar
ALMORA
Panuwanaula
Pithoragarh
Tota Am
Sunari
N A I N I T A L
LEGEND
District Headquarters
Taluk Headquarters
Other Towns
Railway Line
Major Roads
Other Roads
River

ALMORA

LOCATION AND AREA

Latitude : 29.45° North to 29.9° North

Longitude : 79.1° East to 80.1° East

Altitude : 1829 m at Ranikhet.

The district extends from Pithoragarh on north-east to the Nainital district on the south and from Pauri Garhwal on the west to the Champawat district on the east.

Total area of the district is 3075 sq. kms. The district headquarters is located at Almora.

HISTORY

Ancient lores mentioned in old Sanskrit Classics of Vishnu Purana, Mahabharata and Varita-Samhita present primordial accounts of human settlements in the district. The Sakas, the Nagas, the Kiratas, the Khasas and the Hunas, are credited to be the most ancient tribes. The next ages silent of them may probably be the ones signalling many petty states, rivalling each-other for supremacy and ultimately chartering the inauguration of the noted and enduring dynasty of Chand's. Earlier to this, the Katyuris are recorded as the dominant clans in copper and stone engravings. Very little is known of this dynasty, particularly relating to this district.

The Chand's dynasty from their inception in 953 A.D. to their ouster in the late 18th century present a saga of sterife, with horrifying series of wars with rulers of Garhwal culminating in the destruction of this prosperous land and establishment of inglorious Gurkha rule. This dynasty was peculiar in that it made Almora the seat of strongest hill power in 1563 A.D. From that time onwards, the limits of Kingdom of Kumaon extended over the entire tracts of districts of Almora and Nainital.

A notable contribution of these rulers was unification of entire Kumaoni land, though, the process was belated by centuries by hostility of the rulers of Garhwal. Some of the kings of this line were of supremely religious temperament and their inclination fruited in maintenance and erection of many of temples in the district. These peacetime pursuits were possible because of diplomatic patronages procured by Chand rulers from Emperors at Delhi by tact and shrewdness with a view to foiling the horrendous attacks of hostile governors of Delhi bordering southern frontiers of Kumaon.

The decline of the dynasty started from the reign of Debi Chand (1720-1726 A.D.) and the process rapidly invited an anxious attacker from across the eastern borders. The enemy were Gurkhas and their swift blow to internally strifed and dissension-ridden dynasty was fatal. The district passed under them in 1790 A.D. In due course, Gurkhas came in contact with frontiers of ever-expanding mighty British Raj and invited hostility of it by the time of Lord Hastings only to be humilitated and defeated. The Britishers hailed the victory over Gurkhas in 1815 A.D. as heralding the era which was more in spirit of self-aggrandisement than in reality. The struggle for freedom liberated the district from the alien rule.

POPULATION (2001)

Total population of the district according to 2001 Census is 630446 persons, comprising 293576 males and 836870 females. Rural population of the district is 576497 persons (263144 males and 313383 females) and urban population is 93949 persons (30462 males and 23487 females).

The decennial growth rate of population of the district as a whole in relation to the state between the period 1991-2001 is presented below:

State/ District	*Decennial growth rate of population (per cent)*	
	1981-1991	*1991-2001*
Uttaranchal	24.23	19.20
Almora	9.43	3.14

LANGUAGES AND RELIGION

Main language spoken in the district is Hindi.

Main religion of the district are Hindus, Muslims, Christians, Sikhs, Buddhists, and Jains.

GEOGRAPHY AND PHYSICAL FEATURES

Amazing varieties of wild species find habitats in this hilly district. Jungles are full with birds and wild animals. Varied terrain accompanied by uneven climate and thanks for scarce human settlement produce a splendid environment for these creatures in these lands. Various types of flora in the district are common depending upon the climate and topography. Upto a height of 1200 mts. the Sal is of common occurrence in the forests. The same elevation is shared by less common the haldu, the dhasusi, the tun sain and the kharik the last two being of occasional occurrences. The trees of the plains too-the mango, pipal, banyan and shisham are common upto about 900 mts. The chir are common in forests occurring upto about 1800 mts. The forest found between 1800 and 2400 mts. consist of the banjoak. The same elevation is shared by Rhododendron and ringal-bamboo, but sometimes these two occur upto about 3050 mts. Above 2400 mts., the tilonj and the kharsu forests occur. The most daring of the trees are the horse-chestnut and the syeamore occupying the heights upto 3050 mts.

Wild apple, pear, meldar, cherry, apricot, plum, peach, fig, barberry, Kaphal, rasp-and blackberry are the chief fruit trees found upto about 910 mts. Much higher altitudes are occupied by the currents and the gooseberry. Only the hazel (called the Bnotia badam) is common beyond the snowlines.

Forests occupy more than half of the area in the district containing pine, sal, oak, surai, deodar, panger etc. Lessa made from pine trees is an important economic commodity of the district. It's yearly production is about eighty two thousand quintals. The forest-based business of the district is of more than ten crores of rupees. Herbs of medicinal value are in plenty in the forests of the district. A cooperative drug factory at Ranikhet uses these herbs to make Ayurvedic medicines. Departments of forests and soil conservation are jointly pursuing an afforestation drive in Ramganga catchment area, of which about fifteen thousand hectares is in this district.

RIVERS, CANALS AND WATERWAYS

The district is drained by the western Ramganga and the Kosi alongwith their tributaries. The other important streams are Gagas and Suwal.

TOWNS, VILLAGES AND AMENITIES

The district at present comprises of 3 tehsils. It has 4 towns.

The urban population of the district as percentage of total population in the census year 2001 is indicated below. It also shows the sex ratio (females per 1000 males) and density (population per sq. km.) in the urban population of the district in relation to the State:

State/ District	*Urban population as percentage of total population*	*Sex ratio, (Females per 1000 males)*		*Density (Population per sq. km.)*	
	2001	*1991*	*2001*	*1991*	*2001*
Uttaranchal	25.54	936	964	133	159
Almora	8.55	1099	1147	198	205

Amenities

Number of villages having one or more amenities in the district are Education, Medical, Drinking Water, Post and Telegraph, Market and Hat, Communications, Approach by Pucca Road, and Power Supply.

COMMUNICATIONS

The figure of 312 kms. of pucca roads per thousand sq. km. in the district in contrast to 201 kms. for the state of looks impressive but its impressiveness wanes in the context that interiors of the district which are lacking roads are connected by the communication line based on ancient modes and also that in the absence of rail communication, the roads, solely bear the brunt of swift movement of men and material. No National Highway passes through this district and the total length consists of State Highways, main districts roads and small roads. Roads are basic to augment fully the potential of tourism and this will certainly have a good prospect in this hilly district.

AGRICULTURE AND IRRIGATION

Primary economic activity in the district is agriculture. The terrain permits mainly terrace-cultivation. The sloping hill side that does not lend itself for agricultural operations is also occasionally used for cultivation by burning the shrubs and sowing the seed with the help of a hoe. Natural forces are the sole arbiter of crop-prospect in this Kumaoni land. Cultivation is rainfed in nine-tenth of cultivable land. The agriculture suffers from poor economic prospect. The fields are very small, agriculture seasons are shorter and weather extreme that make cultivation difficult and unremunerative. Under these conditions an Almoran is averse to engage himself in the pursuit and prefers migrating to plain in search of more remunerative and less taxing job. Therefore, the increasing number of women are having the stakes in agriculture of this district.

Good yielding lands are in the vicinity of the valleys of rivers Ramganga, Sarju, Kosi and their numerous tributaries. Rabi and Kharif are the two harvests in district.

More efforts are under way to speed up the production of such commercial crops as are suited to terrain and yield high returns. Such crops are soyabeen, potato etc. Hurdles in marketing are to be tackled so as to make economy of the cultivation of these crops viable. There is a good prospect of opening industries based on these crops. A cold-storage for potato near a train-head in places like Kathgodam of Haldwani will help tremendously for the tillers of the district.

Fruit production has an enviable growth potential in the district. Fruit based industries and commercial activities have an immense scope in this district. A large quantity of fruit is wasted for want of outlets. Kosi unit of fruit protection is almost idle and Lamgara or Shitalkhet are the suitable places for location of the unit. These abound in fruits. Other setback to fruits business is the dearth of fruits market in the district. Setting up of fruit processing units at Ranikhet will cast a catalystic effect on fruit cultivation. The district keeps more than six-thousand orchards spreading in twenty-two thousand hectares. The yearly production of fruits is about twenty-eight thousand tonnes. Apple, pear, peach, apricot, plum, walnut, mango, lichi, small orange, lime etc. are the chief produce.

ANIMAL HUSBANDRY

Apart from agriculture another important allied occupation is rearing of livestock especially for small and marginal farmers. Income supplemented thus is important for the reason of meagre income from cultivation. German aid is being sought for increasing better breeds. About fifteen artificial insemination centres are opened under this programme. Pataldevi liquid nitrogen plant and Bhainswada semine laboratory are doing tremendous job in this sphere. Hawalbagh poultry unit with birds of one thousand stout breeds is making fowl rearing a beneficial occupation. Poultry development programme is under implementation in Hawalbagh, Takula, Dwarahat and Tarikhet development blocks. Karmi and Leeti sheep rearing units are providing marino breeds to the needy. Fodder research centre at is doing yeomen's service in cultivation and propagation of nutritious fodders in this district.

INDUSTRIES

The district has some large deposits of magnesite and soft-stones. A survey could authenticate the exact quantity of copper around kharai-patti, limestone near Jhiroli area and iron in places like Deotoli, Moram etc. The minerals exported from the district are magnasite and soft-stone. Jhiroli magnasite factory is producing twelve thousand tonnes of dead-burned magnesite annually. The production of bronze powder by a factory at Tarikhet is about forty tonnes a year. The magnasite produced by the factory is of worth rupees one and a half crores. Seven hundred persons are working in the factory. Production of bronze powder is of seven lakhs of rupees and factory employment accounts sixty persons.

Apart from these other concerns in medium sector are Ranikhet Cooperative Drug Factory: Chanauda Gandhi Ashram, wool processing and finishing factory, Almora; Agro Canning and Bottling factory, Kosi; Sarswati, Woollen Mills, Ranikhet, and Alps Pharmaceuticals. The factories registered under Factories Act. 1948 are number eleven employing on an average 618 persons. Worth rupees three crores of goods are produced in these factories. Goods produced per head amounts to rupees forty-five. Goods produced by a worker of these concerns amounts to rupees 47573. In every lakh of people in the district, 82 persons are working in these registered factories.

Small units are more than six hundred in district. About three thousand of persons are pursuing these activities. Registered units with Director of Industries number about two hundred. About eight hundred workers of these units are producing goods worth rupees 219 lakhs. Cottage industries that include woollens, wood-craft, soap-making, leather-work etc. are being assisted by about thirty-four cooperative societies.

HANDICRAFTS

Cane and Bamboo works and carpets

TRADE, COMMERCE AND EXPORT

The important commodities manufactured in towns of the district are copper utensils, woollen garments, wooden goods and sweetmeats. The chief commodities exported are copper utensils, woollen garments, potatoes and resin. The most important commodities imported are copper, wool, food grains and food stuff.

The table given below presents most important commodities manufactured, imported into and exported from each town of the district.

Name of the towns	*Most important commodity*		
	Manufactured	*Exported*	*Imported*
1	*2*	*3*	*4*
Almora	Cooper Utensils	Copper Utensils	Copper
Almora Cantt.	Woollen Garments	Woollen Garments	Wool
Dwarahat	—	—	Food stuff
Ranikhet Cantt.	Sweetmeats	Resin	Foodstuff

TOURISM

The district of Almora occupies a glittering place in the mountainous terrain of the State. Nature's serenity awsomeness and beauty mingle in the misty heights of the glacier clad peaks. Picturesque valleys and sky-scraping mountain ranges. From tops a crest and the narrow valleys seem like ravines. Wild vegetation swaying to the gusts of wind besides boulders and rocks present a majestic spectacle to the connoissuers of nature. Vast caverns and chasms side by side with meadows and orchards evoke a majestic fantasy spinned with myths and traditions of this ancient district. The district is full of lush valleys of rivers Ramganga, Sarju, Kosi, Ganga and other streams, the valleys where soft ruttle of breeze splash the ripples of piquant charm capable of echoing without an end in the minds of visitors. The savage grandeur of the district is obvious everywhere. Though the most frequented places are as under.

Almora. This mofussil town is the head-quarters of the district administration. Main attraction is the place Bidsar, eighteen miles away from the town. Himalayas are under clear view from this place.

Ranikhet. The place is shrouded in the forest of chir, banje and deodar. The areas covered by these forests are fascinating to the trekkers. Himalayas could be glimpsed in their full glory from this place. The added attraction is its golf course, one of the best in the world.

Kausani. It is undoubtedly the most famous place in the district. The tract is ridden with marvellous forests of chir and deodar. A visitor harried from the hustle and bustle of ordinary life should pay the visit to this place.

Baijnath. A museum of ancient sculptures is located at this place. The huge Parvati idol is the rare collection of the museum.

Other Sectors. Tourism offers tremendous scope in the district. Tourist attractions other than the abundance of historical religious and cultural places. The expansion of tourist infrastructure will generate employment avanues apart from earning of valuable foreign-exchange. The sixth five year plan has set to increase the tourist amenities at places like Kausani, Ranikhet, Almora, etc.

ZOO

Deer Park, Narain Tewari Dewal

HOTELS

Corret Rataganga Resort (Government approved) 2 star, Marchula.

Access: 35 kms. from Ramnagar Railway station and Bus stand. Rooms: 29

Snow View Resort, (Government approved), Snow View Estate, Pappersallie.

Access: 122 kms. from Airport, 94 kms. from Railway station and 5 kms. from Bus stand. Rooms: 15.

FAIRS AND FESTIVALS

Important fairs and festivals organised in different parts of the district are mentioned below:

Vaisakhi Purnima, Mar, Kot Bharamri, Nanda Devi, Uttaryini, Shivratri, Bikhoti, Syalde, Somnath, Poornagiri, Harela, Devi Dhura.

EDUCATION

According to 2001 Census the population of total literates (excluding the population in the age group of 0-6 years) is 398391 persons. Of these, 219784 are males and 178607 are females. In the rural areas of the district 353392 persons (193399 males and 159993 females) are literates and in urban areas 44999 persons (26385 males and 18614 females) are literates. The rate of literacy of this population, to the total population excluding 0-6 years age group according to 2001 Census is shown below:

	1991			*2001*		
	Persons	*Males*	*Females*	*Persons*	*Males*	*Females*
Total	59.83	80.78	41.32	74.53	90.15	61.43

There are 5.88 Primary Schools for every ten thousand of population in urban areas of the district. The highest ratio of 17.15 primary schools is observed in Dwarahat against the lowest of 3.85 in Ranikhet Cantt. A ratio of 1.05 Junior Secondary Schools obtains in the urban areas of the district. There are 1.68 school of Matriculation Standard per ten thousand of urban population of the district. There are no schools in Cantt. area of Almora. The educational facilities are availed by the inhabitants of this town from the adjacent town of Almora.

COLLEGES

Almora Campus College, Almora (Established 1940) (campus college). Enrolment 3286, Teachers 112.

Arya Kanya Degree College, Almora (Established 1975). Enrolment 65, Teachers 7.

Government Degree College, Syalde, Enrolment 120.

Government Degree College, Jainti (Established 1996).

Government Postgraduate College, Ranikhet, (Established 1973). Enrolment 1010. Teachers 20.

Government Degree College, Dwarahat, (Established 1983) Enrolment 229, Teachers 6.

Government Degree College, Mainila (Established 1989). Enrolment 125, Teachers 6.

Kumaon Engineering College, Dwarahat (Established 1989). Enrolment 125, Teachers 6.

(Above named colleges belong to Kumaun University, Established 1973).

MEDICAL

There are 1078 beds in hospital and other medical institutions for every thousand of population in the urban areas of the district. Almora town is served by the largest ratio of 13.15 beds while Dwarahat is served by the lowest ratio of 1.71 beds. There are no medical institution in Almora Cantt. with bed facility. The population of the district of this town avails themselves these facilities from the adjacent town of Almora.

MEDIA

Air Station. All India Radio, Almora.

ADMINISTRATION

(i) Administrative Division

Tehsils: Bhikia Sain, Ranikhet, Almora.

Towns with their Population, Urban Status and Literates (2001)

City/Town	*Urban Status*	*Population*			*Literates*		
		Person	*Male*	*Female*	*Person*	*Male*	*Female*
Almora	MB	30613	16,443	14,170	25,745	14,206	11,539
Almora	CB	1744	1126	618	1388	975	413
Dwarahat	NP	2543	1347	1196	2084	1156	928
Ranikhet	CB	19049	11546	7503	15782	10048	5734

(ii) Parliamentary Constituencies along assembly segments:

No. & Name of Parliamentary Constituency.

3-ALMORA

No. and Name of Assembly Segments of Almora Parliamentary Constituency which lies within the Jurisdiction of Almora District.

Assembly Constituency: 45. Dwarahat

TEHSIL—RANIKHET

Chaukhuttia—50. Chaukhuttia; 51. Dhansyari; 52. Dhudhaliya; 53. Jaitisera; 54. Naugaon Akhoria; 55. Mahakaleshwar; 56. Dhanan; 57. Puniyabagarh; 58. Farika; 59. Adigaon; 60. Dipakote; 61. Bhagoti. ***Dwarahat***—30. Dwarahat; 31. Dunagiri; 32. Binta; 33. Rana; 34. Chhatena; 35. Malli Mirai; 36. Dhyari; 37. Kafara; 38. Chhabisa; 39. Saili Sunoli; 40. Chhana Golu; 41. Kama; 45. Chhatgula; 49. Faldwari. ***Jalali***—42. Kande; 43. Asgoli; 47. Paithani. **Urban Area:** Dwarahat (NAC).

Assembly Constituency: 46. Bhikiasain

TEHSIL—BHIKIASAIN

Bhikiasain—1. Bhikiasain; 2. Dob; 3. Bauli; 4. Singoli; 5. Batula; 6. Binoli; 7. Sanara; 13. Bangora; 14. Masi; 15. Kanoni; 35. Rotapani. ***Manila***—31. Manila; 32. Kunidhar; 33. Kwairalla; 34. Nainwalpali; 41. Amkhet. ***Syalde***—43. Syalde; 44. Udepur; 45. Basai; 46. Kotshari; 47. Bharsoli; 48. Deghat; 49. Payalgaon; 50. Khalyun; 51. Khalduwa; 52. Kumaleshwar; 53. Chachroti; 54. Chauna.

TEHSIL—RANIKHET

Jalali—44. Baban; 62. Jalali; 63. Jaitoli; 64. Takulti; 65. Chaura; 66. Bheti Kama.

Assembly Constituency: 47. Salt

TEHSIL—BHIKISASAIN

Machhor—8. Raparh; 9. Sinoura; 10. Adboura; 11. Majhera; 12. Basot; 26. Panuwadokhan; 27. Baret; 28. Harara; 29. Machhor; 30. Jakh. ***Manila***—36. Bisarakhet; 37. Gajar; 38. Ghanyal; 39. Chakkargaon; 40. Gumati; 42. Dhaneta. ***Salt***—

16.Dabhra; 17. Kafalta; 18. Dangula; 19. Painsiya; 20. Jhimar; 21. Dewikhal; 22. Bangidhar; 23. Dewayal; 24. Tukura; 25. Kupi.

Assembly Constituency: 48. Ranikhet

TEHSIL—RANIKHET

Jalali—21. Sagneti; 46. Irha; 48. Kuna. ***Ranikhet***—1. Ranikhet Sadar; 2. Pantkotuli; 3. Karchuli; 4. Chaukuni; 5. Dugaurha; 6. Pankhurha; 7. Suri; 8. Garshari; 9. Shaharo; 27. Riyuni; 28. Malli Riyuni. **Tarikhet**—10. Maharkhola; 11. Bamsyu; 12. Uparari; 13. anyali; 14. Ganiyadheoli; 15. Mawara; 16. Timila; 17. Tarikhet 18. Jaina; 19. Tana; 20. Dewalikhet; 22. Naphan; 23. Billekh; 24. Syalikhet. **Urban Area:** Ranikhet (Cantt.)

Assembly Constituency: 49. Someshwar

TEHSIL—ALMORA

Hawalbagh—16. Daulaghat; 17. Khauri; 18. Govindpur; 19. Katarmal; 20. Kwerali; 21. Kathpuriya; 22. Shitalakhet; 23. Sainj; 24. Doba; 25. Khunt; 26. Dhamas; 27. Jyoli. ***Someshwar***—1. Chhani; 2. Bhainsarhgaon; 3. Baigniya; 4. Tana Sajoli; 5. Someshwar; 6. Dhoungarh; 7. Amkholi; 8. Jhijar; 9. Bhainsou; 12. Bhagtola; 13. Gwalakote; Tehsil—Ranikhet ***Ranikhet***—25. Kunwali; 26. Naini; 29. Dida.

Assembly Constituency: 50. Almora

TEHSIL—ALMORA

Almora—28. NT Dewal; 29. Almora; 30. Chitai; 31. Falseema; 32. Dewali; 33. Khatyari; 34. Raikholi; 40. Petshal; 41. Chirala; 42. Naini; 43. Pandeytoli; 74. Dhaura; 75. Chaumu. ***Hawalbagh***—14. Hawalbag; 15. Pankhura. ***Lamgarha***—47. Naura; 48. Lamgarha; 70. Jalna; 71. Satyu; 72. Ujyoula; 73. Thanamatena; 76. That; 77. Dharkhola; 78. Gutholi. ***Panuwanaula***—35. Lingunta; 36. Trinaili; 37. Nyoli; 38. Palyoun. ***Someshwar***—10. Bhetuli; 11. Patlibagarh; **Urban Area:** Almora Cantonement; Almora MB.

Assembly Constituency: 51. Jageshwar

TEHSIL—ALMORA

Dariya—57. Barakuna; 58. Dhura; 59. Mayoli; 60. Dhyari;

61. Basoli; 62. Pali; 63. Dasauli Badyar; 64. Bhanoli; 65. Rangori; 66. Kafalani; 67. Danya; 68. Chausala; 69. Kote Mahar Bind.

Lamgarha—39. Dalakote; 46. Nakot; 49. Maharagaon; 50. Selakot. ***Panuwanaula***—44. Panuwanaula; 45. Toli; 51. Bhagartola; 52. Kafli; 53. Kotuli; 54. Gairarh; 55. Tapani; 56. Kheti. ***Shahar Pathak***—79. Motiapathar; 80. Bakswar; 81. Naugaon; 82. Gandaun; 83. Jainti; 84. Binaula; 85. Pubhaun; 86. Kanara Chaukhuttia; 87. Sangarh; 88. Fatkwaldungra; 89. Futa; 90. Shahar Phatak; 91. Mornaula.

MINERAL AND ORES OCCURRENCES

Building Stone

Good building stone is to be obtained almost everywhere in the district. Fine grained evenly bedded quartzites are used for purpose at Almora (29.6, 79.71) itself and a pale coloured gneiss at Ranikhet (29.65, 79.5) close to Almora of a prophyritic grey granite, suitable for ornamental work.

Copper

Numerous old open cast working are present along a mineralised quartz reef and associated talc-schist near the Dewal Dhar, Shishkhani, and Khanigar on the Baldeo hills. Deposits occur in crystalline dolomites at Bono Agar, Bafila, Thela, Tama, Khani, Dhiranli.

Occurrence of copper-ore are also reported from Phadyari, Bhalugarha, Bajura and Rithait.

Lead

Lead are occurs along a belt in small scattered patches between Chhanapani and Bilaun sera, where galena occurs as small stringers and dissiminations in dolomitic lime stones.

It is found along a belt in small scattered patches between Chhanapani (29°47':79°45') and about 500 metre S.W. of Bilaun Sera (29°49':79°46'), Rai (29°43': 80°03') Shishakhani (29°48': 79°45'), Girith Valley (30°40': 80°07')

Limestone

Very large deposits of limestone interbedded with states occur along the southern boundary of Almora crystalline zone in the valley of Kosi River. Dolomitic lime stone occurs in a large belt about 3 kms. wide over a distance of more than 65 in Dhanpur of Garhwal district up to Dwarahat in Almora.

Large deposit of limestone underbedded with states occur along the southern boundary of the Almora crystalline zone in the valley of the Kosi rivers, and Manwa Devi (29°52':79°25')

Dolomite

At DWARAHAT (29°47':79°26'), BHURAGAON (30°05':79°06')

Magnesite

Occurrence of crystalline magnesite at Bozagar (29.7, 80.1), Ganai (20.71, 79.95), Rithait (29.7, 79.99), Tachhri (29.79, 79.85) Chandog (29.6, 80.2) etc. in the Kumaon Hills.

Magnesite—Magnasite deposits as narrow bands of variable thickness in massive dolomite of the Krol series at AGAR (29°48':79°41'), CHAHANA (29°47':79°47'), NAIL (29°46':79°47'), BORAGAR (29°43':80°03') GANAI (29°43':79°57'), RITHAIT (29°42':79°79')

Pyrites

Small pockets of pyrites occur in talc-schists near Pagna (29.8, 79.8) and Pagnakhol (29.8, 79.8).

Steatite

A deserted steatite mine is situated about 7 km. south of Bageshwar. The mineral is said to occur in large detached masses. Another occurrences of steatite is recorded near the summit of Thakil Hill (29.5, 80.26) near Pithoragarh. The steatite is said to be of good quality. Occurrence of steatite in dolomite at Greechhina (29.8, 79.7) Badolisera (29.7, 79.9) Chuma (29.86 79.8). Some of the deposits are large enough to warrant development.

Alum

The occurrence of Alum as an afforescence on pyritous slates in the bed of the Kosila River and in the same manner on pyrites shales near the village of JAKH.

Arsenic

It is found at two or three places on the DHARMA and JUWAR or NITI GHATS (passes), orpiment is collected in small quantities near MANSIARI also found at SHANKALPA glacier.

Quartzites

Fine-grained evenly bedded at Almora and a pole coloured genesiss at RANIKHET.

At Dewal Dhar (29°48':79°55'); Shishkhani (29°48': 79°45') and Khanigar (29°47': 79°46') on the Baladeo Hill in the Chhanapani area. Also at Bonoagar (29°43': 80°03'), Bafila (29°49': 79°58'), Thela (29°48':79°55'), Bhalugarha (29°41':79°59') near Kurli (30°13': 79°06')

Ralam (30°48': 79°45'), Girith Valley (30°40': 80°07')

Ralam (30°18': 80°20'), Bainskal (29°55': 80°13')

Galena

At Kapuri (29°48':79°59')

Graphite

It was found in nodules from 1 to 3 inches in Diametre, weathered out from a band of mica-schist on the ridge between Almora and KALIMATTI, 5 km. to the north. Graphite of poor quality occurs in Schist at BULT and SIRAR. Graphite of good quality has been noticed at PATON and PHALSIMI. Small and minor occurrences of graphite have been reported from DIURI, UKKA KOT and CHIRA.

Iron

At DWARAHAT—SAMALKHET, veins of compact red hematite occur in clay slate, varying from 2 to 30 ft. in width. Beds of massive brown hamatite also occur in clay slate, varying from 1.5 to 3 ft. in thickness in the PONAR valley. A small deposit of lateritie iron-ore occurs at SUTARGAON.

OBSERVATIONAL ORGANISATION

Agricultural Meteorological Stations

This facility is available in the district at Chaubatia. The instrument lies in.

Chaubatia

Latitude	:	29.75° North
Longitude	:	79.60° East

Altitude : 1962 m

Date of starting : 24-2-1960

Hydrometeorological Stations for Climatological Purposes

This facility is available in the district at three places. Bageshwar, Loharkhet, Ranikhet, Sama. This instrument lies in

Ranikhet

Latitude : 29.63° North

Longitude : 79.43° East

Altitude : 1876° m

Date of starting : 30-4-1984

DIASASTROUS WEATHER EVENTS

Snowfall

On 5th January, 1991, there was heavy snow-fall, more than 10 persons died due to snowstorm.

On 27-31 December 1991, it was severe and several people died.

From 28-30 December, 1996, it was severe and several person died due to it.

Floods and Heavy Rains

During August (4th week) and September (1st week) 1982 it was heavy rains, several housed collasped, standing kharif crops damaged, vehicular traffic from Almora to Pithoragarh and Dharchula—Sahar Pathak closed due to heavy landslides.

On 22nd July 1983, it was heavy rains, 37 people died and 38 cattle heads perished in a landslide, Karmi, Patti, Malda and Danpur villages completely cut off from rest of the state.

On 2nd July 1984, it was heavy rains, 9 persons killed in a landslide in Jagthana village, several housed damaged.

During 4th week of July to September 2nd week, 1986, there was flood in the river and its tributary, several hectares of cropped area submerged under flood water.

During 16-17 August 1991, it was heavy rains, one person died, 14 cattleheads perished, 38 hectares of croped area submerged. In July 1993, it was flood, people died cattleheads and crop damaged.

DISTRIBUTION OF *SCHEDULED CASTE* POPULATION BY SEX (1991)

	POPULATION Total	Males	Females
ALMORA			
	1,84,237	91,303	92,934
Agariya	15	7	8
Badhik	26	16	10
Badi	149	77	72
Baheliya	3	3	0
Baiga	236	135	101
Baiswar	110	65	45
Bajaniya	3	3	0
Bajgi	15	8	7
Balahar	15	10	5
Balai	6	5	1
Balmiki	2,441	1,342	1,099
Bangali	86	43	43
Banmanus	5	4	1
Bansphor	4	3	1
Barwar	12	11	1
Basor	8	4	4
Bawariya	8	5	3
Beldar	2	2	0
Beriya	109	49	60
Bhantu	6	3	3
Bhuiya	9	2	7
Bhuyiar	8	4	4
Boria	2	1	1
Chamar, Dhusia, Jhusia, Jatava	356	213	143
Chero	96	63	33
Dabgar	129	83	46
Dhanuk	14	10	4
Dhobi	153	96	57
Dom	646	353	293
Domar	17	10	7
Gharami	2	1	1
Ghasiya	19	14	5
Gond	19	11	8
Gual	4	4	0
Hela	1	1	0
Kalabaz	2	1	1
Kanjar	39	25	14
Kapariya	3	2	1
Khairaha	23	10	13
Kharwar (excluding Benbansi)	3	1	2
Khatik	18	13	5
Kol	120	57	63
Kori	164	72	92
Korwa	13	9	4
Lalbegi	17	7	10
Majhwar	2	2	0
Mazhabi	18	7	11
Musahar	23	9	14
Nat	105	54	51
Pankha	1	1	0
Parahiya	28	12	16
Pasi, Tarmali	9	4	5
Patari	20	11	9
Rawat	54	31	23
Saharya	112	47	65
Sanaurhiya	59	31	28
Sansiya	19	15	4
Shilpkar	1,78,367	88,080	90,287
Turaiha	79	46	33
Unclassified	205	95	110

DISTRIBUTION OF *SCHEDULED TRIBE* POPULATION BY SEX (1991)

	POPULATION		
	Total	Males	Females
	ALMORA		
	2,739	1,405	1,334
Bhotia	2,335	1,174	1,161
Buksa	10	7	3
Jaunsari	1	1	0
Raji	382	214	168
Tharu	8	8	0
Unclassified	3	1	2

SKETCH MAP
OF
BAGESHWAR DISTRICT
CHAMOLI
PITHORAGARH
PITHORAGARH
ALMORA
Phurkia
Dwali
Khati
Loharkhet
Shama
Kapkot
Pajena
Baijnath Temple
BAGESHWAR
LEGEND
District Headquarters
Taluk Headquarters
Other Towns
Railway Line
Major Roads
Other Roads
River

BAGESHWAR

LOCATION AND AREA

Latitude : 28.8° North to 30.3° North

Longitude : 79.6° East to 80.1° East

Bageshwar is one of the mountainous district of the state lies in Cascading chains of the Himalayas. It is bounded on the north by Chamoli district, on the north-east and east by Pithoragarh district and on the south, south-west and west by its parent district, i.e., Almora. Total area of this district is approximately 2311 sq. kms. and its headquarters is located at Bageshwar town.

HISTORY

The district of Bageshwar has been carved as a separate district vide State Government Notification No. 2796/1-5/97-327/97-R.5 dated 15th September, 1997. According to the said notification two tehsils namely Bageshwar and Kapkot (created as a tehsil on 12-9-1997), except that of Kaosani Patwari area were taken out from the then existing Almora district to form a new district called Bageshwar.

As stated above, prior to its formation as a separate district, Bageshwar constituted a part of Almora district which was ruled by the Chand's dynasty from their inception in 953 A.D. to their ouster in the late 18th century, and thereafter this region was ruled by the Gurkha. In due course of time, the Gurkhas came in contact with frontiers of ever-expanding mighty British Raj and invited hostility of it by the time of Lord Hastings only to be humilitated and defeated. The Britishers hailed the victory over Gurkhas in 1815 A.D. as heralding the era which was more in spirit of self-aggrandisement than in reality. The struggle for freedom liberated the district from the alien rule.

POPULATION

The total population of the district according to 2001 Census is 294453 persons, comprising 118,202 males and

131251 females. Rural Population of the district is 241650 persons (113896 males and 127754 females) and urban population is 7803 persons (4306 males and 3497 females).

The decennial growth rate of population of the district as a whole in relation to the state between the period and 1981-1991 and 1991-2001 is presented below:

State/District	*Decennial growth rate of population (per cent)*	
	1981-91	*1991-2001*
Uttaranchal	24.23	19.20
Bageshwar	14.92	09.21

The Community Development Blockwise population distribution of this district alongwith rural-urban breakup and also those of the Scheduled Castes and Scheduled Tribes population is presented in the table given below:

Community Development Block	*Total/ Rural/ Urban*	*Total Popu-lation*	*SC Popu-lation*	*ST Popu-lation*
Kapkot	T	70407	14528	1306
	R	70407	14528	1306
	U	—	—	—
Bageshwar	T	73158	18213	450
	R	67386	16942	225
	U	5772	1271	225
Garud Baijnath	T	5700	14484	60
	R	5700	14484	60
	U	—	—	—

LANGUAGES AND RELIGIONS

Kumaoni is the main dialect spoken by the people of this district. However, in urban areas as well as for inter-group communications Hindi is generally used.

Major religion of the district are Hindus, Muslims, Christians, Sikhs, Buddhists and Jains.

GEOGRAPHY AND PHYSICAL FEATURES

The area ccomprising the present district constitutes

mountainous terrain. A ridge of vast magnitude with heights exceeding 5550 metres above the sea runs almost parallel to the line of water-parting along the Tibetan frontier and forms a dividing line with the district adjoining to western border. Elevation casts special effects in conditioning of climate in a hilly tract as that of the district of Bageshwar. The two chief elements that determine the changes in the climate are rains and temperature. Both are subject to severe changes in this hilly tract, giving a quite varied climate. Amazing varieties of wild species find habitats in this hilly district. Jungles are full with birds and wild animals.

RIVERS, CANALS AND WATERWAYS

The district is drained by the river Pinder, Revti Ganga, Kosi and Sarju alongwith their tributaries. The other important streams are Gumti, Punga, Lolgon.

TOWNS, VILLAGES AND AMENITIES

The district has two tehsils and three Community Development Blocks. It has only one town and 798 villages (754 inhabited villages and 44 uninhabited villages).

The urban population of the districtt as percentage of total population in the census year 2001 is indicated below. It also shows the sex ratio (females per 1000 males) and density (population per sq. km.) in the urban population of the district in relation to the state.

State/ District	*Urban Population as percentage of Total Population*	*Sex Ratio (Females per 1000 males)*		*Density (Population per sq. km.)*	
	2001	*1991–2001*		*1991–2001*	
Uttaranchal	25.59	936	964	133	159
Bageshwar	3.12	1055	1110	99	108

Amenities

Number of villages having one or more amenities in the district are Education, Medical, Drinking Water, Post and Telegraph, Market and Hat, Communications, Approach by Pucca Road, and Power Supply.

COMMUNICATIONS

Being a hilly terrain, the district is deprived of any railway tract. Similarly, no National High-way passes through this district. The roads, mostly the district roads or other pucca roads solely bear the brunt of swift movement of the people and the material. Thus, a lot more is required to be done for the improvement of roads and road-transport in this region, including the present district.

AGRICULTURE AND IRRIGATION

Cultivation is primary activity in this district. However, the fields are very small, agriculture seasons are shorter and weather extreme that make cultivation difficult and unremunerative. Under these conditions, the people of Almora (in general) is averse to engage himself in the pursuit and prefers migrating to plain in search of more remunerative job. Therefore, the increasing number of women are having the stake in agriculture of this district. Rabi and Kharif are the two harvest in the district, except the north tract of Kapkot Community Development Block. The main kharif crops are Madua, Paddy, Sawan (Thungra), and maize. The principal Rabi crops are wheat, barley, masoor and rape mustard. The cultivation is rainfed in nine-tenth of cultivable land. Guls (channels) and houses (reservoirs) are the main sources of irrigation.

ANIMAL HUSBANDRY

Rearing of livestock is another important allied occupation apart from agriculture, particularly for small and marginal farmers. Main livestock of the district are milch animals which include cows and buffaloes, apart from sheep and poultry birds. A number of schemes are underway in the district for the development of poultry and sheep rearing. Veterinary institutions like hospitals and Pashu Sewa Kendra are looking after the welfare of animals wealth.

INDUSTRIES

Industrially, the district is backward as there is no major or medium scale industrial unit existing in it. There are, however, many cottage industries that include woollens, wood-craft, soap-making, etc.

TRADE, COMMERCE AND EXPORT

The table given below presents most important commodities manufactured in, exported from and imported in the town of this district.

Name of the town	Most important commodity		
	Manufactured	*Exported*	*Imported*
1	*2*	*3*	*4*
Bageshwar	Wooden goods Woollen garments, mats	Potatoes onion, wool	Food-grains, vegetable ghee, tea

TOURISM

Tourism offers tremendous scope in the district. Tourist attractions other than the historical or religious places includes the ice-created chains of the Himalayas. The expansion of tourist infrastructure will generate employment avenues apart from earning of valuable foreign-exchange.

Some of the important places of tourist interest in the district and also at a distance, though in the adjoining district a.e Almora, Ranikhet, Kausani, Baijnath and Pindari. The other places of religious importance are Jogeshwar, Doonagiri and Pandukholi.

Baijnath which is situated in the district, has a museum of ancient sculptures. The huge Parvati idol is the rare collection of the museum.

Pindari glacier is remote and hardly accessible but once visited is hard to forget for its sylvan beauty. Majestic ascends of Himalayan chains starts from this place.

FAIRS AND FESTIVALS

Important fairs and festivals organised in different parts of the district are mentioned below:

Vaisakhi Purnima, Kot Bhramari, Nanda Devi, Uttaryini, Shivratri, Bikhoti Syalde, Somnath, Poornagin, Harela, Devi Dhura.

EDUCATION

According to 2001 census, the population of total literates (excluding the population in the age group of 0-6 years) is 249453 persons. Of these 118202 are males and 131251 are females. In the rural areas of the district 241650 persons (113896 males and 127754 females) are literates and in urban areas 7803 persons (4306 males and 3497 females) are literates. The rate of literacy of this population, to the total populaton, excluding 0-6 years age group according to 2001 census is as follows:

1991			2001		
Persons	*Males*	*Females*	*Persons*	*Males*	*Females*
54.54	76.52	34.22	71.94	88.56	57.45

The table given below furnishes information on educational institutions, stadia and public libraries available in the town of the district:

Name of the town	*Educational Institutions*	*Stadia*	*Public libraries including reading rooms*
1	*2*	*3*	*4*
Bageshwar	Arts College (1), Higher Secondary Intermediate School (1), Secondary/Matriculation Schools (2), Junior Secondary and Middle Schools (2), Primary Schools (5)	—	PL : 1

MEDICAL

The following table provides information on medical institutions (alongwith beds facility) available in the town of this district:

Name of the town	*Medical institutions (including beds facility)*		
1	*2*		
Bageshwar	Hospital (1)	:	5
	Dispensary (1)	:	—

COLLEGE

Government Postgraduate College, Bageshwar (1974), Enrolment 491, Teachers 18 (Kumaun University), established 1973.

ADMINISTRATION

(i) Administrative Division:

Tehsils: Bageshwar, Kapkot.

Community Development Blocks: Bageshwar, Kapkot, Garud, Baijnath.

Town with its Population, Urban Status and Literates (2001)

City/Town	*Urban Status*	*Population*			*Literates*		
		Person	*Male*	*Female*	*Person*	*Male*	*Female*
Bageshwar	MB	7803	4306	3497	5863	3398	2465

(ii) Parliamentary Constituency and Assembly Segments

No. and Name of Parliamentary Constituencies:

3-ALMORA

No. and Name of Assembly Segments of Almora Parliamentary Constituency which lies within the jurisdiction of Bageshwar district.

Assembly Constituency: 42. Kapkot

TEHSIL—KAPKOT

Danpur—41. Ason; 43. Karmi; 44. Kanyalikot; 45. Kapkot; 46. Golana; 47. Namtichetabagarh; 48. Patiyasar; 49. Farasali; 50. Badiyakot; 51. Bharari; 54. Majkhet; 55. Liti; 56. Loharkhet; 58. Shama. ***Kanda***—42. Udiyar; 52. Bhantola; 53. Mahroori; 57. Simagadi; 59. Horali; 60. Diyali;

Assembly Constituency: 43. Kafligair

TEHSIL—BAGESHWAR

Bageshwar—8. Khunouli; 10. Ghinghartola; 11. Choara; 14. Tuper; 18. Banlekh; 19. Vastoli; 20. Bilakhet. ***Kafligair***—1. Amserkot; 5. Kandey; 6. Queralli; 9. Gurana; 12. Jethai; 24. Ason; 25. Nandigaon; 26. Baidibagar; 27. Khankar; 28. Choagounchina;

29. Bilori. ***Kanda***—3. Kameri Devi; 4. Kanda; 7. Khatigoun; 16. Patoanja; 17. Wajeena; 22. Rawatsera; 23. Saniudiyar.

Assembly Constituency: 44. Bageshwar (SC)

Bageshwar—2. Aare; 13. Talla Katyur; 15. Dug Bageshwar; 21. Rawaikhal. ***Kausani***—30. Kausani; 31. Garur; 32. Galaie; 33. Gagarigol; 34. Jakhera; 35. Dangoli; 36. Darshani; 37. Naugoun; 38. Patali; 39. Pinglon; 40. Wajyula. ***Urban Area***—Bageshwar NP

OBSERVATIONAL ORGANISATIONS

Hydrometerological Stations for Climatological Purposes

Latitude	:	29.8 North
Longitude	:	79.7
Alttitude	:	900 (m)
Date of Starting	:	21-10-1982

Loharkhet

Latitude	:	30.1° North
Longitutde	:	79.95° East
Altitude	:	1750 m
Date of starting	:	31-10-1982

Sama

Latitude	:	29.96° North
Longitude	:	80.1° East
Altitude	:	2000 m
Date of starting	:	12-11-1981

DISASTROUS WEATHER EVENTS

Snowfall

From 28-30 December, 1996, it was severe and several people died due to it.

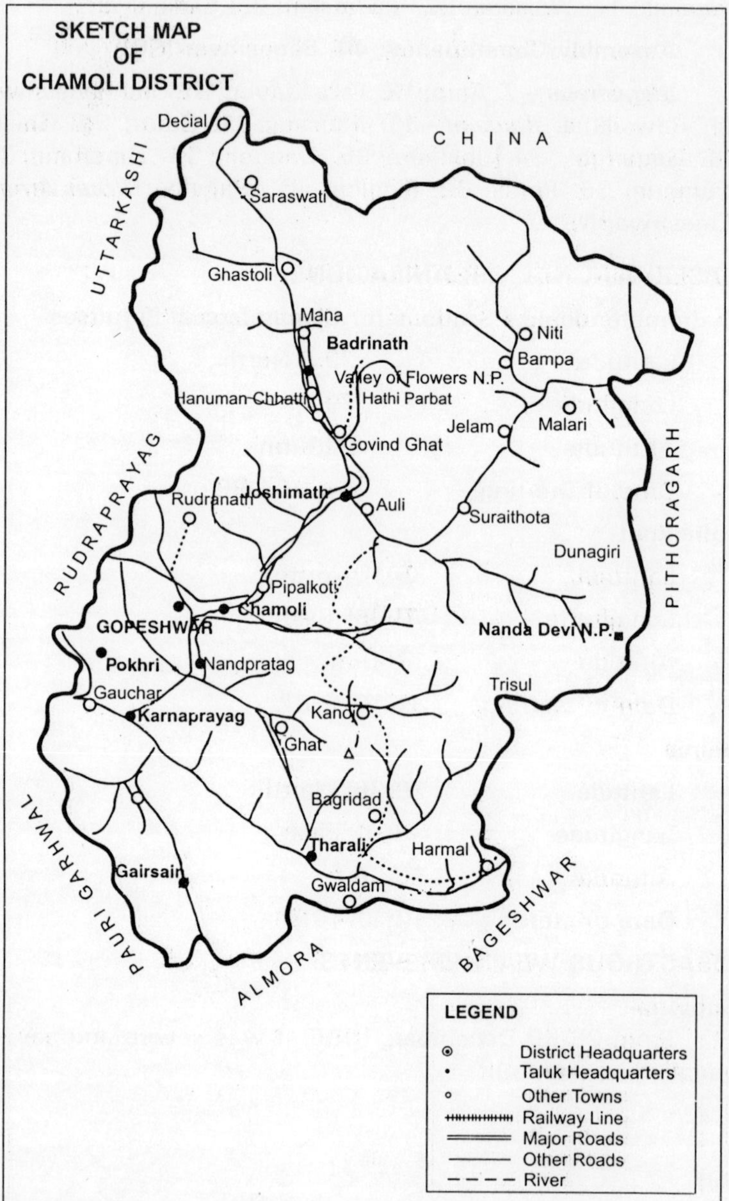
SKETCH MAP
OF
CHAMOLI DISTRICT
CHINA
UTTARKASHI
RUDRAPRAYAG
PAURI GARHWAL
ALMORA
BAGESHWAR
PITHORAGARH
Decial
Saraswati
Ghastoli
Mana
Badrinath
Niti
Bampa
Valley of Flowers N.P.
Hanuman Chhatti
Hathi Parbat
Malari
Jelam
Govind Ghat
Joshimath
Rudranath
Auli
Suraithota
Dunagiri
Pipalkoti
Chamoli
GOPESHWAR
Nanda Devi N.P.
Pokhri
Nandpratag
Gauchar
Karnaprayag
Trisul
Kand
Ghat
Bagridad
Tharali
Harmal
Gairsain
Gwaldam
LEGEND
District Headquarters
Taluk Headquarters
Other Towns
Railway Line
Major Roads
Other Roads
River

CHAMOLI

LOCATION AND AREA

Latitude	:	30.0° North to 31° North
Longitude	:	79° East to 80° East
Altitude	:	1160 m.

The district came into existence in 1960. It is in north-east corner of the state, the area being 7691 sq. kms. in the rugged terrain of the mystic Himalayas. On its north lie Tibet, while on its south touch the districts of Garhwal Almora and Bageshwar. Districts of Bageshwar and Pithoragarh bound it in the east and the territory of districts of Uttarakashi and the Rudraprayag in the west.

The districts is named after its tehsil or sub-division Chamoli, which was in district of Garhwal prior to 1960. It was the part of Uttarakhand division till December 20, 1968 when that division was abolished and the district was included in the newly formed Garhwal division.

HISTORY

The district lies in awesome crests of the Himalayas, undaunted by the cruellest sufferings inflicted by nature, this land was inhabited by hill tribes namely *Kiratas, Nagas, Kharas, Tanganas and Kulindas.* The land of Chamoli was spiritual centre of Hinduism, Jainism, Buddhism and Sikhism. Seers and sages of yore found here the concrete opportunity to realise the 'Moksha' (salvation). This land of *'Kedar' Kshetra* and *'Badri-Kshetra'* was of grave importance to Devas, to Brahma who took the solemn pledge to create the world, to Vishnu who resided in the *'Panch-Badri,* to Siva who resided in *'Panch-Kedar'* to Manu and Narad, to Kuber and Ravana, to Pandu, to Pandavas who disposed their destinied here during their last sojourn in this district. Gautam, Vyas, Jaimini, Garga, Varrachi, Badra-yan etc. are also associated with this district.

The piercing horders of *Sakas, Kushanas* and *Hunas* sundered the silence of this region as ages rolled by. From eighth to tenth century, the *Katyuri* dynasty modified the destiny of this district. During the *Katyuri* reign, Adi-Shankara-charya established his *'Matha'* in this district. The *Katyuri* dynasty was succeeded by the 'Pal' dynasty of Garhwal, which was changed to *'Sah'* during the 15th century. During this reign the bloodstained history of conflict with *Chand* dynasty of Kumaon was a ghastly tragedy. In 1804, Amar Singh Thapa, the Gurkha took over the suzerainty of this district and assumed the Governorship. Anxious to foment an uprising, the Gurkhas, after their defeat by the British, signed the treaty of Sigauli in February 28, 1816. With the annexation of Garhwal in British territory, it was split up into eastern and western Garhwal, the former retained by the British government. In 1839, Kumaon was divided into the district of Garhwal. In 1947, like the rest of the country this district was also liberated from British rule.

POPULATION (2001)

Total population of the district according to 2001 Census is 369198 persons, comprising of 183033 males and 186165 females. Rural population of the district is 319613 persons (154461 males and 165152 females) and urban population is 49585 persons (28572 males and 21013 females).

The decennial growth rate of population of the district as a whole in relation to the state between the period 1981-1991 and 1991-2001 is presented below:

State/ District	*Decennial growth rate of population (per cent)*	
	1980-1991	*1991-2001*
Uttaranchal	24.23	19.20
Chamoli	21.97	13.51

LANGUAGES AND RELIGION

Main language spoken in the district is Hindi.

Main religion of the district are Hindus, Muslims, Christians, Sikhs, Buddhists and Jains.

GEOGRAPHY AND PHYSICAL FEATURES

Perched in the breath-taking loveliness of upper Himalayas divided by the ranges as venerable as the Pyramids, the district of Chamoli stretches across the snow free valleys to the sky-scraping peaks with perpetual snow and glaciers. The terrain consists of the ridges of Nanda Devi range and Badrinath range which are the dominant features and leaves only the narrow and precipitious valleys such as on the banks of Alakhananda and at Lohta plateau. The adjacent ridges of the valleys are the homes of dense forests. Between the dense fringe of the forest occur the scarcely populated tracts, the inhabitants of which subsisting on terrace-cultivation.

The nature is at its best in expressing its flora and fauna in the district of Chamoli. The serrated snowy peaks and high ridges are interspersed with a variety of vegetation, amidst which the streams brooks and rivers provide ideal habitat for an amazing variety of wild life. Various types of seasons and lands culminates into a breeding ground for a diverse species of wild-life and vegetations. The environ is constantly punctuated by the huge dimensions of the forests in the large areas of the district and contains a plethora of plants and amounts to more than 54 per cent of the land. Very big area of the land is covered under the forests. The rest of the land is in use for cultivation or being covered by snow-clad peaks and nude rocks. The forests consist of Himalayan subtropical pine between the heights of 910 m. and 1825 m. moist temperate seral forest between the altitude of 1200 m. and 1500 m., Banj Oak forests between the height of 1825 metres and 2450 metres at places the limit of Banj Oak forests ascend upto 2600 metres; Oak scrub forests also occur in the localities of Banj Oak forests, Tilonj forests between the same altitude as that of the Oak forests; Blue Pine forests between the heights of 1825 metres and 2600 metres, Dry Coniferous forests between the altitude of 1825 metres and 2600 metres, Moist Temperate Diciduous forests upto the heights of 2750 metres, Cypress forests between the heights of 2125 metres and 2600 metres, Kharasu forests between the heights of 2450 metres and 2600 metres and Dry Temperate Diciduous forests at further higher altitudes. Alpine pastures occur between the heights of 3500 metres to 4877 metres above the sea level, *Deodar* forests are not common in this district. During June to September rich varieties of grass, shrubs and herbs of great medicinal importance come up in areas of Alpine pastures. In other parts of the year the alpine areas are covered with snow. Over 120 species of ferns inhabit in damp ravines on mossy rocks and tree-trunks. The monsoon months are the best times for ferns. The common trees abounding in the area are wild cherry, wild apple, spindle wood, oak, fig, poplar, holluy, rhododendron, Himalayan maple, wild cinnamon, masuri berry, dogwood, horse chestnut, hill tun, Himalayan cypress, *deodar* blue pine, fir and long leafed pine.

RIVERS, CANALS AND WATERWAYS

Alakhananda alongwith its tributaries, the Nandakini and Pindar are the chief rivers of the districts. The former merges in Alakhananda and Nandaprayag while the later at Karnaprayag and thus embodying these places an aura of spiritual pilgrimage and great reverence. Dhauliganga and its tributaries has the network in the north-eastern part of the district.

TOWNS, VILLAGES AND AMENITIES

The district at present comprises of 6 tehsils and 6 towns.

The urban population of the district as percentage of total population in the census year 2001 is indicated below. It also shows the sex ratio (females per 1000 males) and density (population pr sq. km.) in the urban population of the district in relation to the state:

State/ District	*Urban population as percentage of total population*	*Sex ratio, (Females per 1000 males*		*Density (Population per sq. km.)*	
		1991	*2001*	*1991*	*2001*
Uttaranchal	25.59	936	964	133	159
Chamoli	13.43	982	1017	43	48

Amenities

Village having one or more facility in the district are Education, Medical, Drinking water, Post and Telegraph, Market and Hat, Communications, Approach by pucca road, and power supply.

COMMUNICATIONS

Railways are conspicuous by their non-existence in this district leaving the communications solely dependent on roads and pathways. In remote areas transportation is done through pack animals like horses, ponies, she-goats, etc. National highway no. 58 touches Karnprayag, Nandprayag, Chamoli, Joshimath and Badrinath.There is about 64.0 kms. of state highway and a total length of 231 kms. of roads fall under the management of D.G.B.R. and M.E.S. On an average, an area of 1000 sq. kms. is served by 100 kms. of pucca road against a ratio of 201 kms. obtaining at the state level while the ratio of pucca roads per lakh of population works out to 201 kms. The district thus lacks communications facilities.

AGRICULTURE AND IRRIGATION

Kharif and *rabi* are the two harvests of the district. Paddy small millets and potato are the main *kharif* crops and wheat and barley the main *rabi* crops. Almost 80 per cent of cropped area is claimed by these crops. The potato yield of a hectare of land could be doubled by adopting the package of improved agricultural practices suitable to the terrain. The improved methods are not much in vogue. The area under improved seeds is to be increased. The increase is expected in the use of fertilizers. While the stage average of use of fertilizer in a hectare is 47.35 kgs. for the district, it is merely 4.60 kgs.

The terraces made on sloping hill sides are the main fields of cultivation. The steep hills do not lend themselves to terracing and are used for shifting cultivation after burning the scrubs and bushes. Hoe is the main instrument for rowing.

ANIMAL HUSBANDRY

Animal husbandry including sheep rearing and village industries mainly wool spinning and weaving play an important role in sustaining the population of the area. As a constraint the availability of cultivable land is chief obstacle. The low fertility of soil, short cropping season, low temperature, high altitude, soil erosion and small holdings mar the prospect of agriculture. Therefore, instead of cultivation, the sheep rearing for production of wool and meat, spinning, weaving of wool and other cottage industries based on forest produce offer good scope.

Animal husbandry is an important source of supplementing the income in the country side. The quality of stock is poor and the milk yield per milch animal is very low. Measures are being taken to improve the breed of the livestock. Production of silk cocoon is almost 717.3 kgs. annually. About 1526 kgs. of tusser cocoon is being produced.

INDUSTRIES

Deposits of dolomite iron ore, limestone and markable magnesite sulphur are known to occur in the district. However, these deposits are not considered at present important from the point of view of their exploitation and there are no mineral based industries in the district. There are no factories registered under Factory Act 1948 except one medium scale concern in Augustmuni in Public Sector. About 850 small scale factories are registered with Directorate of Industries. Wool and woollen goods occupy prominent place in the industry. *Namdas*, tweeds and blankets are the chief products upto the height of 1525 metres. Basket making, mat-weaving and wood-crafts are other important cottage industries.

Forest and horticulture based industries have much avenues in the district. Transportation and marketing facilities are to be created to develop these industries.

Tourism can provide jobs and is yet to be fully exploited for this purpose. Cottage industries will find a new stimulus in development of tourism, specially in the vicinity of Kedar and Badri temples. The district deserves to be provided with adequate infrastructural facilities so that its serene beauty and host of sacred places of pilgrimage are fully exploited for tourist development.

TRADE, COMMERCE AND EXPORTS

The commodities manufactured are carpets, woollen cloth, fruits and wooden furniture. The commodities exported are potato, *thulma* (a sort of woollen blanket), canned fruits and wooden furniture. The most important commodities imported are salt, woollen cloth and rice.

The table given below presents most important commodities manufactured in, exported from and imported into the towns of the district.

Name of the towns	*Most important commodity*		
	Manufactured	*Exported*	*Imported*
1	*2*	*3*	*4*
Badrinathpur	Carpets	Potato	Salt
Chamoli Gopeswar	Woollen cloth	Thulma	Salt
Gauchar	—	—	Woollen cloth
Joshimath	—	Potato	Salt
Karnaprayag	Fruit preservation	Canned fruits	Woollen cloth
Kedarnath	—	—	Rice
Nandprayag	Wooden furniture	Wooden furniture	Rice

TOURISM

Badrinath (Tehsil Josimath). One of the four chief pilgrimage centres of Hindu mythology, the temple is situated on the right bank of Alakhananda river and is equi-distant from to mountains of Nar and Narayan in the east and west sides. The temple lies at an altitude of 3122 metres above the level of sea. The temple is dedicated to Badri Naryan, an incarnation of Vishnu. However, the Jains and Buddhas differ from the traditions of the Hindus about the nature of the temple. According to the former the temple is dedicated to a Tirthankar while the latter asserts that the temple is a shrine of Lord Buddha. *Namboodiri-pad Brahmins* of the south are the head priest to the temple for generations. The temple is covered with snow from November to the middle of May and the establishment retires down to Joshimath, the winter headquarters. The view of Neelkanth, a snow-clad peak, is clearly visible from Badrinath. Opposite to the temple, on the other side of the Alakhananda river is situated the *Tapa Kund* (literally a tank of hot water) besides this, the other worth seeing places are *Vasudhara* water fall and *Vyas-gupha* the latter of which is ascribed as the place where the sage Vyas compiled the Mantras and Chhandas of the Vedas.

Valley of Flowers (Tehsil Joshimath). For the nature lovers, the district contains a paradise of flowers in the full riot of colours, especially during the month of August at valley of flowers when the surrounding wilderness looks like a painting against the sheer dazzling whiteness of the snows. More than a thousand varieties of flowers, shrubs and orchids in various shades and textures makes the valley a gorgeous hue of brighting colours looking like an artistic creation. The valley is located at the heights of 3352 metres to 3658 metres. The valley is almost 19 kms. from Govind Ghat where a Gurudwara of the Sikhs is located.

Hem Kund Saheb (Tehsil Joshimath). It is sacred lake situated at the heights of 4320 metres and is a pilgrim centre of Sikhs, due to its association with Guru Govind Singhji, who performed the penances at this place. The place can be visited from Govind Ghat through the valley of flowers.

The other worth seeing sacred places are the *Karanaprayag* (tehsil Karnaprayag) which is situated on the confluence of Pindar and Alakhananda rivers and is famous for Uma Devi and Karna temples. *Nanda prayag* (tehsil Chamoli) situated on the confluence of Alakhananda and Mandakini rivers are famous for Gopal Ji Ka Mandir, Joshimath (tehsil *Joshimath*) is sacred because of the temple of Jagat Guru Shankar Acharya Ji, *Sonprayage* (tehsil Ukhimath) which is the confluence of the rivers Son Ganga and Mandakini and is in the pathway to *Trijuginarayan* (tehsil Ukhimath) which is almost three kilometres away from Sonprayag, Gauri Kund (tehsil Ukhimath) where the temples of Parvati Ji and Krishna Ji are located and there is a hot water spring, *Ukhimath* (tehsil Ukhimath) famous for the temples of Usha, Shiva, Parvati, Anirudha and Mandhata and is the most important Shiva Pith after Kedarnath, is the residence of Rawal priests and also it is an important halting place on way to Kedarnath: *Gopeshwar* (tehsil Chamoli) which is the seat of the district administration and famous for its Shiva temple and other temples. Besides, above places, the other sacred places in the district are Pandukeshwar Tungnath, Rudranath, Kalpanath Augustmuni, Kalimath and Guptakashi.

ZOO

Musk Deer Breeding centre, Joshimath, Chamoli.

FAIRS AND FESTIVALS

Important fairs and festivals organised in different parts of the districts are mentioned below:

Kishan Mela, Bishwat Sankranti, Nautha, Naumi, Nanda Devı, Gaucher, Shivratri, Bishwat Sankranti, Ansi Shivratri, Nagnath, Bikhot, Madmeshwear, Makrayan.

EDUCATION

According to 2001 Census, total literates excluding the population in the age group of 0-6 years) is 163,501 persons. Of these, 107016 are males and 56485 are females. In the rural areas of the district 145787 persons (95958 males and 49829 females) are literates and in urban areas 17714 persons (11058 males and 6656 females) are literates. The rate of literacy of this population to the total population, excluding 0-6 years age group according to 2001 census is shown below:

1991			*2001*		
Persons	*Males*	*Females*	*Persons*	*Males*	*Females*
60.40	80.85	39.66	76.23	89.89	63.0

A ratio of 8.91 Primary Schools is obtained in the urban areas of the district per 10000 of population. It varies between the maximum of 18.56 Primary Schools in Karnaprayag and the minimum of 6.09 Primary Schools in Gauchar. Nandprayag shows the highest ratio of 9.07 Middle Schools while Chamoli Gopeshwar is served by 1.03 Middle Schools per 10000 of their population. The ratio of schools of Matriculation Standard varies between the maximum of 9.07 in Nandprayag and the minimum of 1.03 schools in Chamoli Gopeshwar. The urban areas of the district are served by 2.06 schools in Matriculation Standard per 10000 of their population. A ratio of 2.40 Inter Colleges is obtained for the urban population of the district. It ranges between the maximum of 9.07 in Nandprayag and the minimum of 1.16 in Joshimath.

COLLEGES

Government College, Talwai (Established 1993)

Government Degree College, Joshimath (Established 1963)

Government P.G. College, Gopeshwar (Established 1968). Enrolment 2500, Teachers 60.

Government Degree College, Karanprayag (Established 1979), Enrolment 200, Teachers 7.

(Above named colleges belong to Hemwati Nandan Bahuguna Garhwal University, (Established 1973).

MEDICAL

There are 6.72 beds in medical institutions of the urban areas of the district. The highest ratio of 15.45 beds is observed in Chamoli Gopeshwar. The second largest ratio of 3.18 beds is observed in Karnaprayag. Gauchar with 1.22 beds per thousand of its population shows the least ratio.

ADMINISTRATION

(i) Administrative Division:

Tehsils: Joshimath, Gauasen, Rudraprayag, Chamoli, Karnaprayag, Tharali Pokhari.

Towns with their Population, Urban Status and Literates (2001)

City/Town	*Urban Status*	*Population*			*Literates*		
		Person	*Male*	*Female*	*Person*	*Male*	*Female*
Badrinath-puri	NP	841	543	298	716	501	215
Chamoli	MB	19855	11126	8729	16000	9488	6512
Gochar	NP	7278	4196	3082	5918	3578	2340
Joshimath	MB	13202	7993	5209	10152	6661	3491
Karn Prayag	MB	6976	3910	3066	5273	3152	2121
Nand Prayag	NP	1433	804	629	1009	625	384

(ii) Parliamentary Constituency and Assembly Segments (2001)

No. and Name of Parliamentary Constituency: **2-Garhwal**

No. and Name of Assembly Segments of Garhwal Parliamentary Constituency which lies within the Jurisdiction of Chamoli district.

Assembly Constituency: 38. Badrinath

TEHSIL—CHAMOLI

Chamoli. 1. Papriyana (Gopeshwar); 2. Saikot; 3. Chhinka; 4. Bairagana; 5. Gauna; 6. Chamoli; 7. Kauriya. ***Nandprayag.*** 1.

Nandprayag. **Forest Area:** Forest Area. **Urban Area:** N.P. Parishad; Chamoli-Gopeshwar

TEHSIL—JOSHIMATH

Joshimath. 1. Malari; 2. Tapovan; 3. Pandukeshwar; 4. Joshimath; 5. Helang; 6. Langsi; 7. Tangni. **Urban Area:** Joshimath N.P. Parishad; Nagar Panchayat; Badrinath

Assembly Constituency: 39. Karanprayag

TEHSIL—GAIRSEN

Adibdri—1. Adibadri; 2. Kanswa; 3. Dewalkot; 4. Mathar. **Gairsen**—1. Panchali; 2. Rohira; 3. Maithan; 4. Pajiyana; 5. Gairsen; 6. Maihalchori; 7. Kunigad; 8. Latugair; 9. Silpata. **Forest Area:** Forest Area.

TEHSIL—KAMPRAYAG

Adibadri—1. Sirosain; 2. Bainoli; 3. Thapli; 4. Koti. ***Karanprayag***—1. Karanprayag; 4. Gauchar; 5. Kolipani; 6. Simli; 7. Shrikot. **Forest Area:** Forest Area. **Urban Area:** Nagar Panchayat; Gauchar; Nagar Panchayat; Karanprayag

Assembly Constituency: 40. Pindar

TEHSIL—THARALI

Dewal—1. Gwaldum 2. Mundoli; 3. Naldhura; 4. Talwadi; 5. Jainbisht; 6. Dewal. ***Narayan Bagar***—1. Narayan Bagar; 2. Panti; 3. Ased Simli; 4. Chhekuda; 5. Nalgaon; 6. Jakh Patiyun. ***Tharali***—1. Tharali; 2. Dungri; 3. Devrana; 4. Kulsari; 5. Harmani; 6. Gadkot. **Forest Area:** Forest Area

Assembly Constituency: 41. Nandprayag

TEHSIL—CHAMOLI

Nandprayag—2. Gandasu; 3. Mankhi; 4. Mokh; 5. Ghat; 6. Farkhet; 7. Bura. **Urban Area:** Nagar Panchayat; Nandprayag. ***Adibadri***—5. Kandara; 6. Kankhul.

TEHSIL—KARNPRAYAG

Karanprayag—2. Langasu; 3. Mangroli. ***Pokhari (Nagpur)***—1. Pokhari; 2. Raduwa; 3. Dewar; 4. Thalabair; 5. Trishula; 6. Masoli; 7. Girsa; 8. Bamoth; 9. Simlasu. **Forest Area:** Forest Area.

MINERALS AND ORES OCCURRENCES

Arsenic. A small vein of arsenic has been recorded near Maku (30.5, 79.1). The occurrence appears to be very small. The sample on assaying yielded 0.67 Ozs of silver per long ton.

Asbestos. Occurrences of asbestos have been reported from Rarwa (30.4, 79.2). At Joshimath (30.5, 79.6) Stephen mentions the occurrence of veins of asbestos some tmes 4 to 5 inches in width, traversing serpentinous rocks in this neighbourhood.

At Ukhimath (30.5, 79.1). A discovery of asbestos, considered to be of good quality, is recorded by Atkinson in a hill situated a little to the north of Ukimath. It is said to be used by the villagers as a dressing for wounds, and as a wick for oil lamps.

Copper. Numerous occurrences of copper formerly mind at Pokhri (30.3, 79.2) and at Dhanpur (30.2, 79.1). Occurrence of copper-ore have been recorded at (30.4, 79.2), Danda Khan (30.4, 79.2), Khanni (30.4, 79.2) Khandara (30.4, 79.1). At Dhangadh a six foot wide copper bearing zone is located.

Lead. At Dhanpur (30.2, 79.1). Lode is over 12 ft. in width consisting of brownish quartz thickly impregnated with galena. The yield is said to be about 6.5 per cent of metal.

At Jhak (30.1, 79.4). Quartz lode occurs in clay slate with pockets of galena, yielding 33 per cent of lead with some silver.

Limestone. Limestone belonging to the Garhwal series is exposed between the villages of Tila (30.2, 79.1) and Gawar (30.23, 79.11).

Mica. Greenish coloured mica with cracks and heavy stains occurs in pegmatites near Badni Khal, Kunet and Majholi.

Mineral water. At Tapoban, discharge is fairly copious. Water is chalybeate, deposit a yellow incrustation.

Pyrites. A small deposit of pyrites occurs near Sirgid (30.4, 79.2). The mineral occur disseminated over a distance of 400 ft. in cholorite-schists. Pyrites occurs in ferrogenous slate near Masaun (29.9, 79.1).

Sulphur. Sulphur is deposited in small quantities by hot springs in the bed of Ramganga and Garjia Rivers, at the mouth of the Jowar or Niti pass, near Tatra (30.2, 79.6) and at Nand Prayag (30.6, 79.4).

OBSERVATIONAL ORGANISATION

Surface Observatories

The Chamoli district lies under Meterological sub-division, Hills of Uttar Pradesh, West (now Uttaranchal). This facility is available at three places in the district, these are Chamoli, Joshimath and Ghangaria. These places lies in,

Chamoli

Latitude	:	30.4° North
Longitude	:	79.3° East
Altitude	:	1160 m
Date of starting	:	18-4-1976

Joshimath

Latitude	:	30.5° North
Longitude	:	79.6° East
Altitude	:	1875 m
Date of starting	:	4-7-1958

Ghangaria

Latitude	:	30.7° North
Longitude	:	79.6° East
Altitude	:	3077 m
Date of starting	:	3-10-1949.

Hydrometeorological Stations for Climatological Purposes:

This facility is available at Tharali and Gourikund. This instrument is for the study of Rainfall snow Hydrology and Glaciology of Himalayas. These places lies in:

Tharali

Latitude	:	30.1° East
Longitude	:	79.5° East
Altitude	:	1250 m
Date of starting	:	30-10-1981

DISASTER WEATHER EVENTS

Snowfall

From 28-30 December, 1996, it was severe and several people died due to it.

Floods and Heavy Rains

During August 2nd week there was flash floods in *nullah* several persons drowned, many houses washed away in Admala village.

During 17-18 July, 1986, it was severe, several persons died and several hectares of cropped area damaged and again repeated on 4th week of July to 2nd week of September 1986.

During 15 and 16 August 1991, it was heavy rains, 32 persons died and about 90 cattleheads perished, several hectares of agriculture land submerged.

During 3 to 20 September 1992, there was floods in Ganga and its tributaries, cropped area affected, several roads blocked.

On 14 August 1995, it was heavy rains, persons died and 3 others injured, large number of houses washed away.

DISTRIBUTION OF *SCHEDULED CASTE* POPULATION BY SEX (1991)

	POPULATION Total	Males	Females
CHAMOLI	79,572	40,249	39,323
Agariya	652	347	305
Badhik	71	44	27
Badi	29	15	14
Baiga	21	8	13
Baiswar	32	17	15
Bajaniya	271	146	125
Bajgi	191	97	94
Balahar	1	0	1
Balai	35	18	17
Balmiki	816	542	274
Bangali	3	2	1
Banmanus	2	1	1
Bansphor	32	17	15
Barwar	5	2	3
Basor	3	2	1
Bawariya	28	14	14
Beldar	44	36	8
Beriya	89	50	39
Bhantu	1	1	0
Bhuiya	25	14	11
Bhuyiar	3	2	1
Boria	273	146	127
Chamar, Dhusia, Jhusia, Jatava	1,731	1,032	699
Chero	9	4	5
Dabgar	4	2	2
Dhangar	5	2	3
Dhanuk	3	1	2
Dharkar	4	2	2
Dhobi	282	161	121
Dom	373	199	174
Domar	36	22	14
Dusadh	1	1	0
Gharami	3	2	1
Ghasiya	29	14	15
Gond	2	0	2
Gual	2	2	0
Habura	1	1	0
Hari	67	38	29
Hela	7	2	5
Kalabaz	1	1	0
Kanjar	3	3	0
Karwal	5	4	1
Khairaha	42	25	17
Kharwar (excluding Benbansi)	6	4	2
Khatik	8	4	4
Kol	230	122	108
Kori	226	100	126
Korwa	40	14	26
Lalbegi	21	10	11
Majhwar	83	55	28
Musahar	14	9	5
Nat	10	5	5
Pasi, Tarmali	76	52	24
Patari	35	20	15
Rawat	17	10	7
Saharya	57	11	46
Sanaurhiya	13	11	2
Sansiya	44	32	12
Shilpkar	73,426	36,734	36,692
Turaiha	22	15	7
Unclassified	7	2	5

DISTRIBUTION OF *SCHEDULED TRIBE* POPULATION BY SEX (1991)

	POPULATION		
	Total	Males	Females
	CHAMOLI		
	10,273	4,982	5,291
Bhotia	9,549	4,636	4,913
Buksa	543	260	283
Jaunsari	12	8	4
Raji	152	71	81
Tharu	9	1	8
Unclassified	8	6	2

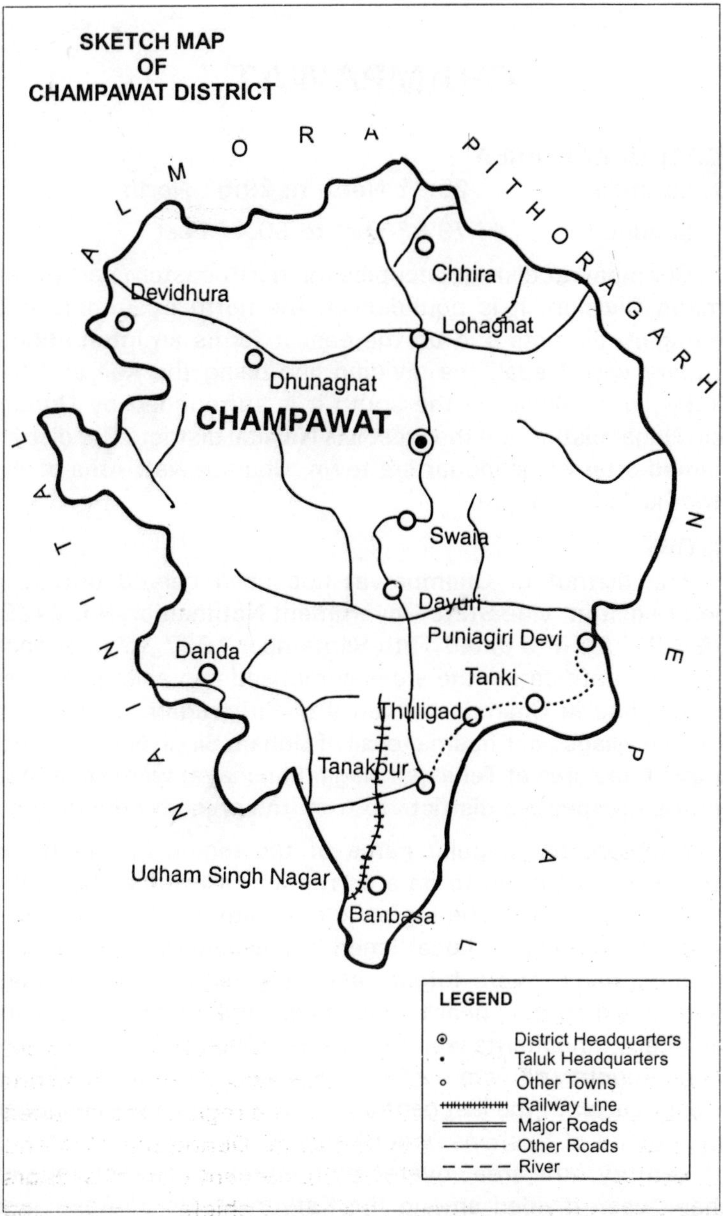
SKETCH MAP
OF
CHAMPAWAT DISTRICT
ALMORA
PITHORAGARH
NAINITAL
NEPAL
Udham Singh Nagar
CHAMPAWAT
Chhira
Devidhura
Lohaghat
Dhunaghat
Swala
Dayuri
Puniagiri Devi
Danda
Tanki
Thuligad
Tanakpur
Banbasa
LEGEND
District Headquarters
Taluk Headquarters
Other Towns
Railway Line
Major Roads
Other Roads
River

CHAMPAWAT

LOCATION AND AREA

Latitude : 29.1° North to 29.5° North

Longitude : 79.8° East to 80.4° East

Champawat district occupies the north-eastern part of the Kumaon Division. It is bounded on the north by Almora and Pithoragarh districts and on the east it forms an international boundary with Nepal, the dividing line being the Kali and the Sharda rivers. While on the south it is surrounded by Udham Singh Nagar district, on the west lies Nainital district. The district is named after its headquarters town, Champawat. Area of the district is 1781 sq. km.

HISTORY

The district of Champawat has been carved out as a separate district vide State Government Notification No. 2799/1-5/97-327/97-R-5 dated 15th September 1997. In pursuance of the said notification the areas comprised immediately before the said date in Champawat tehsil of Pithoragarh district and thirty five villages of Khatima tehsil of Udham Singh Nagar district alongwith the area of Tanakpur Nagar Panchayat were separated from their respective districts to form the present new district.

Kumaon, the popular name of the region in which the district lies is believed to be a corruption of Kurmanchala, the name of a mountain. The region is associated with many tales of gods and demons. Local legends are generally associated with mountains, rivers forests and other sites of the region. Parts of the district appear to have been inhabited since ancient times. Early inhabitants were the Asuras, Nagas, etc. who were perhaps fought and won by Kirats, Khasas and Kuninds. About the last quarter of the last century A.D. the region was included in the empire of Kushans under Kanishka. During the 11th and 12th century,/ the area covered by the present district appears to have been divided among the Katyuri chiefs of Askot and Darma and Chands of Champawat, all of whom were probably subordinate to the Maharajas of Doti. Tohar Chand (1261-1275 A.D.) was the first Chand Raja to start the Chand Dynasty on the entire Kumaon region. The Chand Dynasty ruled over the Kumaon until 1790 when Gurkhas invaded Kumaon. The later history of this district is more or less the same as of Pithoragarh district which has narrated in brief in that district.

POPULATION

Total population of the district according to 2001 Census is 224461 persons, comprising 110916 males and 113545 females. Rural population of the district is 191,727 persons (93,238 males and 98,489 females) and urban population is 32734 persons (17678 males and 15056 females).

The decennial growth rate of population of the district as a whole in relation to the state between the period 1981-1991, and 1991-2001.

State/District	*Decennial growth rate of population (per cent)*	
	1981-91	*1991-2001*
Uttaranchal	24.23	19.20
Champawat	34.22	17.56

The Community Development Blockwise population distribution of this district as per 1991 census, alongwith rural-urban breakup and also those of the Scheduled Castes and Scheduled Tribes population is presented in the table given below. Since separate population figures in respect of thirty five villages and the areas of Tanakpur Nagar Panchayat, which were taken out from the Khatima tehsil of Udham Singh Nagar, are not available, the total population of Khatima Community Development Block (rural) alongwith the population of Tanakpur town are shown below which will provide idea of its population concentration:

Community Development Block	*Total/ Rural/ Urban*	*Total Population*	*SC Population*	*ST Population*
Kapkot	T	23897	5081	2
	R	23897	5081	2
	U	—	—	—

Lohaghat	T	40275	7366	23
	R	36384	6810	17
	U	3891	556	6
Champawat	T	42488	5784	116
	R	39963	5309	95
	U	2525	475	21
Khatima*	T	148057	19705	40191
	R	134947	18150	40150
	U	13110	1555	41

* While under the urban area the population of Tanakpur (MB) has been shown, the rural population includes the population of 35 villages *viz.,* Chandani, Manihar Goth, Fagpur, Sailani Goth, Bichai, Bagdora Hansi, Bagdora Khas, Deupur (Sitapur), Uchola Goth, (Bhajanpur, Anandpur, Naik Goth, Bastiya, Mohanpur, Gyan Khira, Baramdev, Gainda Khali No. 1, Gainda Khali No. 3, Gainda Khali, No. 4, Thawal Khera, Suwa Goth, Khet Khera, Banbassa, Panchpakaria, Bamanpuri, Bhainsha Khal Mundeli, Devipura, Takanpur, Chhennai Talli, Cheni Malli, Bela Goth, Chenni Goth, Almiya, and Katuwa Patti.

LANGUAGES AND RELIGIONS

Kumaon dialect is generally used by the local people for intra as well as inter-group communications. Hindi is, however, the main language spoken in the district, particularly in urban areas.

Separate religionwise breakup of population of this district is not available as it was the parts of Pithoragarh and Nainital (Udham Singh Nagar district carved out from Nainital district) districts at 1991 census. Combined figures in this regard are shown in its parent districts.

GEOGRAPHY AND PHYSICAL FEATURES

The district is sprawls over in the rugged terrain of the mystic Himalayas. The considerable area is rocky and barren and therefore, cultivation is limited to the river valleys and gently sloping hills. Most of the soil in the district is poor, shallow and stony. Taking into consideration the differences in the altitudes and the climatic conditions the flora of the district can be divided into four divisions (1) the sal forests, (2) chir forests, (3) oak forests and (4) coniferous forests. In the sal forest, the chief tree sal is found upto a height of about 1220 mts. The other associated trees in these forests are haldu, sain, and tun kharik. The mango and pipal trees are also frequently found in these forests. Chir trees are found upto the altitude of about 1800 mts. Different varieties of oak are found in different altitude zone between the altitude of 3250 mts. and 4000 mts., the dominant species are the conifers. The main species are chil, thaner, ragha and surain.

RIVERS, CANALS AND WATERWAYS

Sarda, Kali and Lohawati are the main rivers of this district. The other rivers are Ladhiya and Kalauna.

TOWNS, VILLAGES AND AMENITIES

The district is initially formed with one tehsil and three Community Development Blocks. It has three towns and 688 villages (644 inhabited and 44 uninhabited villages).

The urban population of the district as percentage of total population in the census year 2001 is indicated below. It also shows the sex ratio (females per 1000 males) and density (population per sq. km.) in the urban population of the district in relation to the state:

State/ District	*Urban population as percentage of total population*	*Sex ratio, (Females per 1000 males)*		*Density (Population per sq. km.)*	
	2001	*1991*	*2001*	*1991*	*2001*
Uttaranchal	25.59	936	964	133	159
Champawat	14.58	945	1024	107	126

Amenities. Villages having one or more amenities in the district are Education Medical, Drinking Water, Post and Telegraph, Market and Hat, Communications, Approach by Pucca Road and Power Supply.

COMMUNICATIONS

Most part of the district, (except for a very short distance in the south-eastern portion is deprived of railway facility and thus, the communication solely depends on roads. A small metre gauge tract runs upto Tanakpur town and linked this district with Udham Singh Nagar and Pilbhit districts. National highway does not pass through this district. State highway no. 29 passes through the district which connects with National Highway No. 24 at Bareilly. The tehsil headquarters, Community Development Blocks headquarters and all the towns are connected by roads.

AGRICULTURE AND IRRIGATION

Cultivation in the district is limited to the river valleys and gently slopping hills. There are few places where soil is fertile but cultivation is rich in those land where perennial water supply for irrigation is available. About 67 per cent of the total area of the district is available for cultivation but less than three per cent of the total cultivable area is irrigated. Kharif and rabi are the two crops of this district. While main kharif crops are paddy, jhangora, maize, mandua, pulses and tomatoes, the rabi crops are wheat, barley, masur, peas, linseed and mustard. Ginger and pepper are also grown in the district. Sugarcane is grown in the southern valley. The cultivation of wheat is carried on the largest area followed by paddy, barley and maize. Irrigation facilities in the district include canals, gool (channels) and hauz (tanks).

ANIMAL HUSBANDRY

Animal husbandry is an important source of income for the rural people. Most of them spin and weave the wool of their indigenous sheep. The livestock population include cows, buffaloes, sheep and goats. Horticulture is another field that can boost up the economy of the district.

INDUSTRIES

The district is backward in terms of industrial development. There is one cement factory at Lohaghat. Wool spinning and weaving are old cottage industries. Another old time handicraft of this district is basket and matting manufactured out of ringal.

TRADE, COMMERCE AND EXPORT

The following table presents information on most important commodities manufactured in, imported into and exported from the towns of this district. It also indicates the number of banks available in the towns:

Name of the towns	*Most important commodity*			
	Manufactured	*Exported*	*Imported*	*Banks*
1	*2*	*3*	*4*	*5*
Champawat	—	Potatoes, fruits, chillies	Wheat, rice, pulses	3

Lohaghat	—	Potatoes, fruits, chillies	Rubber, cloth, edible oil	3
Tanakpur	—	Stone, wood, herbs	Gur, food-grains, salt	2

TOURISM

Tourism possesses tremendous possibilities of development. However, for the development of tourism intra district road connection is utmost necessary. Following places are important for tourism:

Champawat: Situated on the 1615 metres high, Champawat was at one time capital of Chand Rajas of Kumaon. The ancient fort at the place now houses headquarters of the district office. A historical place, Champawat has many well known temples of high artistic value.

Lohaghat: At an elevation of 1706 metres, Lohaghat is a centre of historical and mythological importance.

FAIRS AND FESTIVALS

Important fairs and festivals organised in different parts of the district are mentioned below:

Nanda Ashtmi, Shivratri, Chifala, Milkutia, Lhamsel, Jauljibi, Kartika Purnima, Tamanauli Mahakali, Kotgari, Thal, Bikhuwat Sankranti, Kalinag, Durbashtimi, Sanai Khola, Nag fair, Berinag, Dychochla, Dyochla, Tania, Tania Nauli, Atathu, Deokali, Tripura Devi, Baraun, Rameshwar, Pandan, Sonar Khola, Koteshwar, Bashuki Nag, Dasauli Mool, Sirakot, Panch March, Shera Ghat, Thal Parao, Kedar Sila Deity, Patal Bhubneshwar, Lory, Chauka, Chharaudeo, Mostmanu, Thelke-dar, Dhaj, Daulaikh, Lechara, Chaupakhiya, Bhadrika, Chandrika Ghat, Hanshaishwar, Pancheswar.

EDUCATION

According to 2001 Census the population of total literates (excluding the population in the age group of 0-6 years) is 131627 persons. Of these 79928 are males and 51699 are females. In the rural areas of the district 109194 persons (66822 males and 42372 females) are literates and in urban areas 22433 persons (13106 males and 9327 females) are literates. The rate of literacy of this population to the total population (excluding 0-6 years age group) according to 2001 census

1991			2001		
Persons	*Males*	*Females*	*Persons*	*Males*	*Females*
55.81	77.63	32.62	71.11	88.13	54.75

Information on educational institutions, stadia and public libraries including reading rooms available in the towns of this district is provided in the table given below:

Name of the towns	*Educational Institutions*	*Stadia*	*Public Libraries including reading rooms*
Champawat	Higher Secondary/ Intermediate School (1), Secondary/Matriculation School (1), Junior Secondary and Middle School (1), Primary Schools (2)	—	—
Lohaghat	Arts, Science and Commerce College (1), Higher Secondary/ Intermediate School (1), Secondary/Matriculation School (1), Primary Schools (2)	—	PL:1
Tanakpur	Arts, Science and Commerce College (1), Polytechnics (1), Higher Secondary/Intermediate School (1), Primary Schools (2)		

COLLEGES

Government Degree College, Lohaghat (1979), Enrolment 431, Teachers 9.

Government Degree College, Champawat (1996), Enrolment 148.

(Above Named Colleges belong to Kumaun University, Established 1973).

MEDICAL

The following table gives information on medical institutions (alongwith beds facility) available in the towns of this district:

Name of the town	*Medical institutions (including beds facility)*		
1	*2*		
Champawat	Primary Health Centre(1)	:	—
	Hospitals (2)	:	8
	Family Planning Centre (1)	:	—
Lohaghat	Hospital (1)		4
	Dispensary (1)	:	—
	Primary Health Centre (1)	:	—
Tanakpur	Hospitals (3)	:	18

ADMINISTRATION

Administrative Division:

Tehsils: Champawat.

Community Development Blocks: Barakot, Lohaghat, Champawat.

Towns with their Population, Urban States and Literates (2001)

City/Town	*Urban Status*	*Population*			*Literates*		
		Person	*Male*	*Female*	*Person*	*Male*	*Female*
Banbasa	CT	7138	3710	3428	4786	2778	2008
Champawat	NP	3958	2273	1685	2908	1778	1130
Lahaghat	NP	5828	3242	2586	4494	2565	1929
Tanakpur	CB	15810	8453	7345	10245	5985	4260

Name of Parliamentary Constituency: Almora

No. and Name of Assembly Segments of Almora Parliamentary constituency which lies within the jurisdiction of Champawat district.

Parliamentary Constituency and Assembly Segments:

Assembly Constituency: 64. Purnagiri

TEHSIL—CHAMPAWAT

Amauari—1. Swala; 2. Bhanuli; 3. Khatoli; 4. Buram; 5.

Sukhidhang; 6. Kotkendri; 7. Dhaun; 8. Tanakpur; 9. Banbasa; 10. Chandani. ***Bhingrara.*** 1. Parewa; 2. Mangallekh; 3. Chaurapita; 4. Saal; 5. Balatari; 6. Bhumwari; 7. Raulmale; 8. Dhunaghat. ***Champawat.*** 1. Champawat; 2. Mudiyani; 3. Phungar; 4. Palsnou; 5. Sipty; 6. Garhkot; 7. Kalukhan; 8. Bhaginakhet. ***Manch.*** 1. Duberjainal; 2. Birgola; 3. Simiyauri; 4. Riyansibamangaon; 5. Bakora; 6. Ruiyana; 7. Maunpokhari.

Forest Area: Forest area Amori; **Urban Area:** Tanakpur NP

Assembly Constituency: 65. Lohaghat

Barakot. 1. Barakot; 2. Bardakhan; 3. Raighaon; 4. Bisrari 5. Gallagaon; 6. Bapru; 7. Maoo; 8. Dyartoli; 9. Valson.

Devidhoora. 1. Devidhoora; 2. Paniyan; 3. Paty; 4. Gagar; 5. Anarpa; 6. Reethakhal; 7. Chaurakot; 8. Moolakot; 9. Patangaon. ***Lohaghat.*** 1. Lohaghat; 2. Patanpatni; 3. Karnkarayat; 4. Dhernath; 5. Khetikhan; 6. Jankandey. 7. Irakot; 8. Khunabora 9. Mangoli. ***Manch.*** 8. Dungrabora. ***Pulla.*** 1. Pulla; 2. Manlak; 3. Chaupata; 4. Jakh; 5. Khilpati; 6. Dudpokhara; 7. Khatera; 8. Raunsal; 9. Digalichaur.

DISASTER WEATHER EVENTS

Snowfall

From 28-30 December, 1996, it was severe and several person died due to it.

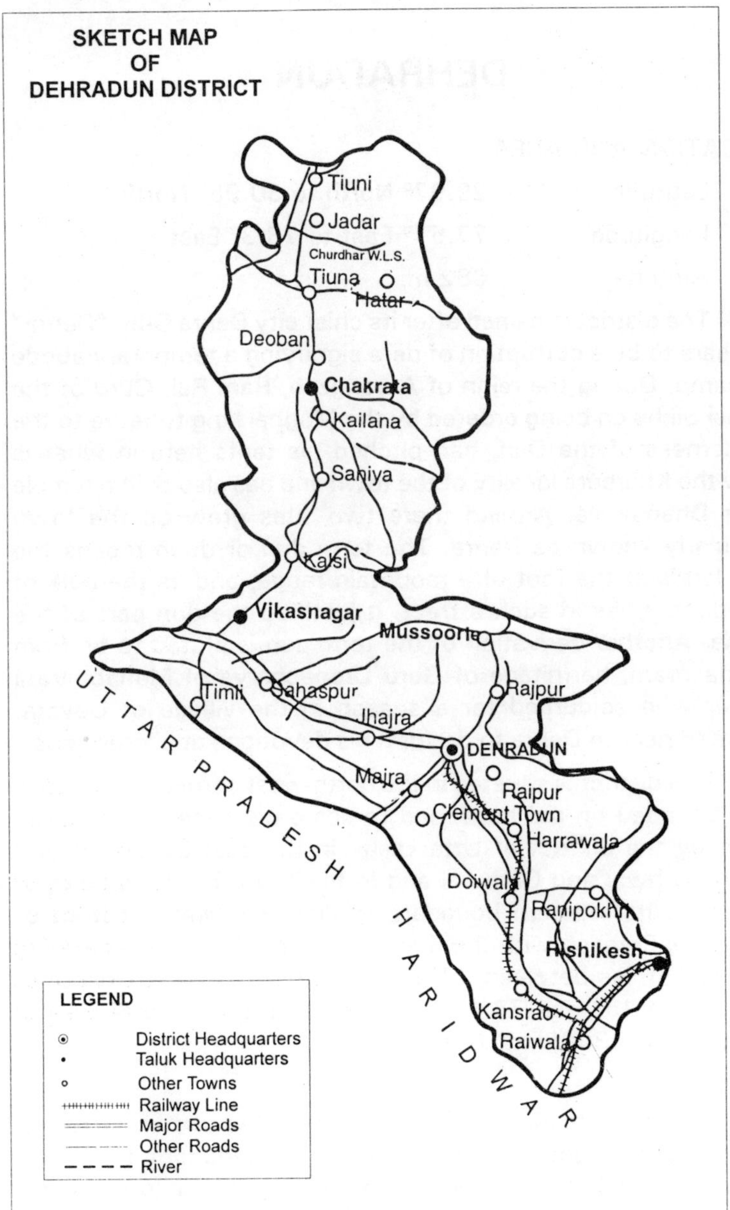
SKETCH MAP
OF
DEHRADUN DISTRICT
Tiuni
Jadar
Churdhar W.L.S.
Tiuna
Hatar
Deoban
Chakrata
Kailana
Saniya
Kalsi
Vikasnagar
Mussoorie
Timli
Sahaspur
Rajpur
Jhajra
DEHRADUN
Majra
Raipur
Clement Town
Harrawala
Doiwala
Ranipokhri
Rishikesh
Kansrao
Raiwala
UTTAR PRADESH
HARIDWAR
LEGEND
District Headquarters
Taluk Headquarters
Other Towns
Railway Line
Major Roads
Other Roads
River

DEHRADUN

LOCATION AND AREA

Latitude	:	29.97° North to 30.95° North
Longitude	:	77.57° East to 78.3° East
Altitude	:	682 m.

The district is named after its chief city Dehra Dun. "Dehra" appears to be a corruption of dera signifying a temporary abode or camp. During the reign of Aurangzeb, Ram Rai, Guru of the Udasi Sikhs on being ordered by the Mughal king to retire to the wilderness of the Dun, had pitched his tents here in what is now the Khurbura locality of the town and has also built a temple near Dhanawala. Around there two sites grew up the town popularly known as Dehra. The term dun or doon means the low lands at the foot of a mountain range, and as the bulk of the district lies in such a tract, it justified the dun part of the name. Another derivation of the term dun is stated to be from Dronashram, hermitage of Guru Dronacharya of Mahabharata fame, who sojourned for a season in the village of Devara, situated near to Dehra to perform his devotions at a lonely spot.

The district is situated in the north-west corner of the state. It is bounded on the north and to some distance in the north-west by the district of Uttarkashi, in the east by the district Tehri Garhwal and Garhwal and in the south by the district of Hardwar. Its western boundary adjoins the Sirmur district of Himachal Pradesh with the rivers Tons and Yamuna separating the two. It lies between 29°58' and 31°2' 30" north latitudes and 77°34'45" and 78°18'30" east longitudes. Total area of the district is 3088 sq. kms.

HISTORY

According to *Skanda Purana,* Dun formed part of the region called Kedar Khand. It was included in the kingdom of Ashoka by the end of 3rd century B.C. It is revealed by history that for centuries the region formed part of the Garhwal kingdom with some interruption from Rohillas. For about two decades till 1815 it was under the occupation of the Gorkhas. In April 1815 Gorkhas were ousted from Garhwal region and Garhwal was annexed by the British. In that year the area now comprising tehsil Dehra Dun was added to district Saharanpur. In 1825, however, it was transferred to the Kumaon Division. In 1828, Dehra Dun and Jaunsar Bhabar were placed under the charge of a separate Deputy Commissioner and in 1829, the Dehra Dun district was transferred from the Kumaon Division to the Meerut Division. In 1842, Dun was attached to Saharanpur district and placed under an officer subordinate to the Collector of the district but since 1871 it is being administered as a separate district. In 1968 the district was taken out from Meerut division and included in the newly formed Garhwal Division.

POPULATION (GENERAL, SC/ST)

Total population of the district according to 2001 Census is 1279083 persons, comprising 675549 males and 603534 females. Rural population of the district is 601965 persons (314296 males and 287669 females) and urban population is 677118 persons (361253 males and 315865 females).

The Scheduled Castes and Scheduled Tribes population of the district as per 1991 Census is 137464 persons and 84076 persons respectively. The rural-urban breakup of this population is indicated below:

Rural	(i)	Scheduled Castes	: 77287
	(ii)	Scheduled Tribes	: 81005
Urban	(i)	Scheduled Castes	: 60177
	(ii)	Scheduled Tribes	: 3071

The decennial growth rate of population of the district as a whole in relation to the state between the period 1981-1991 and 1991-2001 is presented below:

State/District	*Decennial growth rate of population (per cent)*	
	1981-91	*1991-2001*
Uttaranchal	24.23	19.20
Dehradun	34.66	24.71

LANGUAGES AND RELIGION

Main languages spoken in the district are Hindi, Sindhi, Punjabi and Urdu.

Religion-wise breakup of population as per 1991 Census (At District Level)

Hindus: 874760, Muslims: 98748, Christians: 8949, Sikhs: 30417, Buddhists: 8345, Jains: 4159, Other religions and persuasions: 225, Religion not stated: 76.

GEOGRAPHY AND PHYSICAL FEATURES

Dehra Dun can be divided into two distinct tracts i.e. the montane tract and the sub-montane tract.

The montane tract covers whole Chakrata tehsil of the district and consists entirely of a succession of mountains and gorges and comprises Jaunsar Bhabar. The mountains are very rough with steep slopes. The most important features of this tract is the ridge which separates the drainage area of Tons on the west from that of Yamuna on the east.

Below the montane tract follows the sub-montane tract, which is the famous Dun valley bounded by Siwalik hills in the south and outer scarp of the Himalayas in the north.

Dehra Dun is distinguished from most other districts in the state by the existence of very large forests chiefly stocked with sal. Forest products play an important role in the economy of the district. Besides, supplying fuel, fodder, bamboos and medicinal herbs, they also yield a variety of products like honey, lac, gum, resin, catechu, wax, horns and hides. The forests account for 221796 hectares of area, giving a percentage of 43.70 of the total area of the district.

Owing to the variation in altitudes and other aspects, the flora of the district vary from tropical to alpine species. Different types of forests and varying species of shrubs, climbing plants and grasses, depending upon the aspect, altitude and soil condition are found in the district.

Sal forests and coniferous forests are predominant in the western part of tehsil Dehra Dun. Chir is the only coniferous species in the old reserved forests of Dehra Dun. Besides other associates of a Chir, a few Deodar trees are also seen in the district. Wide ranges of Sal forest occur in this part of the tehsil. Sal is the main timber species and is generally pure towards the Siwalik ridges. A mixture of miscellaneous species are found in the lower parts.

In the eastern part of tehsil Dehra Dun, the flora may be divided into a number of Botanical divisions mentioned below:

Moist Siwalik Sal Forests. These forests are found in the Motichur and Thano forest ranges. Low quality of Sal is found in these forests. The main associates of sal are bakli and sain.

Moist Bhabar Doon Sal Forests. These forests are found in a large areas in Thano and Barkot forest ranges. Sal is pure in the overwood and its typical associates are sain and dhauri. The underwood growth includes karaunda and chameli.

West gangetic Moist Deciduous Forests. These are found in the Kansro, Barkot, Motichur and Thano forest ranges. These are closed forests from medium to good height. The main associates of sal are safed siris, jhingan, bahera and dhauri.

Sub-montane Hill Valley Forests. These forests are found in Motichur, Barkot and Lachhiwala forest ranges and consist of evergreen species viz. gular, jamun, safed siris etc.

Dry Siwalik Sal Forests. These forests are found on the higher slopes of Siwaliks. In Chakrata tehsil they occur near the junction of the Tons and the Yamuna rivers in the neighbourhood of Kalsi. Sal is the predominant species mixed with other associates viz. bakli, sain, haldu, jhingan etc.

Besides the above many other types of forests occur in small belts in the plains of the district.

RIVERS, CANALS AND WATERWAYS

The Siwalik (outer and lower ranges of Himalayas) lies at its feet, the outer-scarp of the Himalayas bound it on the north and the sacred Ganga and the Yamuna skirt it on the east and west respectively. The Ganga enters the district in the eastern Dun at Japoban and meandering south-west goes to Hardwar via Raiwala near Rishikesh. The Yamuna enters the district in Jaunsar and flows southwards for about 32 kms. on the south-east border of the district. Besides Ganga and Yamuna, the other rivers that flow in the district are Asan, Suswa, Tons, Rispana, Bindal and Amalava.

TOWNS, VILLAGES AND AMENITIES

The district, at present comprises of four tehsils and six Community Development blocks. It has 14 towns and 764 villages (746 inhabited villages and 18 uninhabited villages).

The urban population of the district as percentage of total population in the census 2001 is indicated below. It also shows the sex ratio (females per 1000 males) and density (population per sq. km.) of the district in relation to the State:

State/ District	*Urban population as percentage of total population*	*Sex ratio, (females per 1000 males)*		*Density (Population per sq. km.)*	
	2001	*1991*	*2001*	*1991*	*2001*
Uttaranchal	25.59	936	964	133	159
Dehradun	52.93	843	893	332	414

Amenities

Number (with percentage) of villages having one or more amenities in the district as per 1991 Census is given below:

Sl. No.	*Amenities*	*Number of inhabited villages*	*Percentage*
1.	Education	367	72.96
2.	Medical	491	97.61
3.	Drinking Water	498	99.01
4.	Post and Telegraph	87	17.30
5.	Market/Hat	22	4.37
6.	Communications	175	34.79
7.	Approach by Pucca Road	406	80.72
8.	Power Supply	431	86.69

COMMUNICATIONS

The district is served by roads and to some extent by rails. Dehra Dun and Rishikesh are the two railway termini of the northern railway. The length of railway line in Dehra Dun district is 64.50 kms. A National Highway does not pass through this district. The district is served by a total length of 1211.71 kms.

of roads giving a ratio of 39 kms. of road per 100 sq. kms. of area. Of the total road length the State Public Works Department manages 943.00 kms. of which State Highway accounts for 154.06 kms. main district roads 148.45 kms. other district roads 516.43 kms. and village roads 124.06 kms. Besides, 268.71 kms. of roads are managed by the local bodies.

AGRICULTURE AND IRRIGATION

Agriculture in the Dun Valley is carried on the same way as in the plains, but in the hill areas, it requires hard labour and skill. The facilities for irrigation from canals and rivers are abundant but there is great deficiency of manure. Cultivation in the hill tract of Dehra Dun tehsil and throughout the Jaunsar Bhabar area is of two descriptions regular and intermittent. The hills, however, contain very little level ground and terraced cultivation is therefore, the rule. Intermittent cultivation consists of small patches of hill sides cleared of shrubs and grass usually by fire. These patches are cultivated for a year or so and then left fallow both to recuperate and also to enable the coarse grass to grow. In the district there are two harvests, the kharif sown in June or little earlier in the hills and reaped in September and October and the rabi sown in October-November and reaped in March in the plains and in April and May in the hills. Paddy is one of the most important kharif food crops in the district. Many kinds of rice are sown in this area, both superior and inferior. The district is famous for its basmati rice. Other important kharif crops are maize, mandua jhangora, sonk, urd, kulath, tor (arhar) and sugar cane. Wheat is the principle crop of rabi and is grown in almost all parts of the district. Barley and mustard are other important rabi crops.

The important fruits grown in the district are the mango, guava, peach, grape, strawberry, pear, lemon and litchi. Dehra Dun is famous for its litchi. Among vegetables, potato is the most important crop. Potato cultivation in the Mussoorie hills is an old and established industry. Besides, catering to the needs of the town of the district, a considerable portion of the production of potato is exported to other districts of the state.

ANIMAL HUSBANDRY

Live stock plays an important role in rural areas in raising the income of small scale farmers. Cows and buffaloes are the main sources of milk, while male cattle are used for ploughing the fields. Sheep and goats are also reared in great number, both for meat and wool. Wool is of immense importance and is used for making home-spun woollen cloth and blankets. The production of milk per milch animal is very low. Action is being taken for the improvement of breed of the cattle.

There is ample scope for poultry development in the district. As per livestock census there were 53455 fowls and 24630 other birds in the district.

INDUSTRIES

Tourist Industry possesses tremendous possibilities of development. On the one hand, there are beautiful hill resorts like 'Queen of Hills-Mussorrie', Chakrata there are places like Sahasra Dhara, famous for its sulphur springs, religious and ancient places like Rishikesh and Lakhmandal, Dak Pathar-ideal picnic spot and Kalsi—place of historical importance of Ashoka's edict. Many institutions of national importance like the Forest Research Institute; Oil and Natural Gas Commission; Indian Military Academy; Indian Petrol Research Institute and Survey of India etc. are located in Dehra Dun which makes it a place of national importance attracting tourists in large numbers.

In this district, geology and mineral development work is done by the Uttar Pradesh State Mineral Development Corporation and Directorate of Geology and Mining.

The district has 97 registered factories. There are two heavy industries in the district. The Indian Drugs and Pharmaceuticals Ltd., a Government of India Undertaking was established with Soviet collaboration at Virbhadra for manufacturing antibiotics. The Sturdia Chemicals Ltd., which produces carbonate, another heavy industry in the private sector was established in 1963. Woollen and synthetic tops, woollen cltoh, sugar, cotton yarn, wheat products, medicines and miniature bulbs are manufactured in seven large scale units. They are Sri Janki Sugar Mills Co. Ltd.; Amitash Textile Mills Ltd.; Miniature Bulb Industries of India Ltd; Bengal Immunity Ltd.; Doon Valley Combers (P) Ltd.; India Woollen Textile Mills (P) Ltd. and Raj Narain Floor Mills Ltd.

A variety of items are produced in small scale units of industries like dairy, canning and preservation, bakery, chocolate, khandsari, tea, malt, textiles, card board boxes, printing, timber goods, steel furniture, liquor, ayurvedic medicines, resin and turpentine, tubes, leather products, musical instruments, optical lenses, miniature bulbs, medicinal instruments automobile industry, agricultural implements, utensils and hospital equipments, weigh bridges, sewing machines, metal goods and plaster of paris etc.

In the rural areas of the district a number of cottage and village industries like wool industry, handloom cloth, powerloom, durries, tailoring, oil, gur, rice, apiary, baskets, cots and mats, walking sticks, pottery, brick kilns, smithy, leather flourish etc.

Under the sericulture scheme the Government Control Silk Farm was established at Prem Nagar in the district. The farm distributes healthy mulberry trees to the silk worm rearers in the district and a good amount is earned from the production of cocoons.

Important Industries

Birla Yamaha Ltd. Lal Tappar, P.O. Resham Mazri, Dehradun, Uttaranchal.

Manufacturer: Portable Generators and Multipurpose Engines.

Indian Spices and Food Industries Ltd. Dehradun Road.

Manufacturer: Ground and Formulated Spices and Pickles.

TRADE COMMERCE AND EXPORTS

The table given below shows most important commodity manufactured in, imported into and exported from towns of the district.

Name of the towns	*Most important commodity*		
	Manufactured	*Exported*	*Imported*
1	*2*	*3*	*4*
Chakrata Cantt.	Wollen garments	Potato	Cotton cloth
Clement town	Soap	Soap	Foodgrains

Dehra Dun	Bulbs	Bulbs	Coal
Dehra Dun Cantt.	Carpets	Lime stone	Rice
Landour Cantt.	Woollen wear	Wood	Foodgrains
Rishikesh	Plaster of paris	Limestone	Potatoes
Vikasnagar	Gur	Rice	Ginger
Virbhadra	Medicines	Medicines	Sugar

The important commodities manufactured are woollen wears, bulbs, carpets, soap, walking sticks, plaster of paris, gur and medicines. These are also the important commodities which are largely exported. The important items imported are foodgrains, glass, cotton cloth, coal, potato, ginger and sugar.

TOURISM

Dehra Dun. The city, headquarters of the district is visited by a large number of tourists every year, many of them en-route to Mussorie. The climate of the city is temperate. Even during summer, it is not so warm at Dehra Dun as in the district south of it. The Forest Research Institute which is world famous for its research work in forestry and is the only institution of its kind in Asia is situated here. Besides, headquarters of the important establishments like the Oil and Natural Gas Commission; Survey of India etc., the Military Academy are also located here. The Gurudwara built by Guru Ram Raj during the reign of Aurangzeb in the Dhamanwla locality of the town is a religious place of eminence. The other places of importance is the Robber's cave, situated at a distance of about 8 kms. from Dehra Dun. The cave is a natural picnic spot surrounded by hills where water suddenly disappears from sight and goes underground only to reappear after a few yards in the form of a stream. The city has many beautiful rest houses and good hotels to provide accommodation to the tourists. For many years, it has been one of the best known educational centres in northern India. Dehra Dun is well linked by rail and road with Delhi, Bombay, Calcutta, Lucknow and Varanasi.

Mussoorie. Mussoorie, the queen of hill stations, is famous for its scenic beauty, gay social life and entertainment. The excellent climate makes it an attractive holiday resort. Thronged by holidayers, it vibrates with gaiety and merry making during the summer season. There are no steep inclines and the more adventurous can undertake enjoyable excursions to various beauty spots in the vicinity. Mussoorie affords glorious views of the mighty Himalayan peaks.

Kempty falls which are about 11 kms. from the town attract hundreds of people every day. The Bhatt falls are also famous for scenic beauty. Though the tourist here is smaller than that of Kempty yet it is a picnic spot near to the town. Yet another place of interest in the town is Depot Hill, popularly known as 'Lal Tibba'. It is the highest point in Mussoorie and beautiful Himalayan panorama is visible on all clear days from this spot. The Badrinath, Kedarnath, Bandarpoonch, Sri Kantha and Nanda Devi peaks can be seen from here. Camel's back hill also known as Gun Hill is another place of tourist interest. Camel's back hill can be reached by electric trolly. The top commands a very beautiful view both of the hills as well as the valley. On clear days, one can see even the Ganga and the Yamuna from here. Mussoorie is well connected by roads with Dehra Dun, Delhi, Roorkee and Saharanpur. There are some good hotels, recreation clubs and restaurants to cater to the needs of the tourists.

Kalsi. Kalsi, situated at a distance of 41 kms. from Dehra Dun is another place of tourist interest. The scenic beauty around Kalsi is picturesque. From the Yamuna upto Kalsi the land on the western bank of the river is formed in two successive ledges, each about 30 metres high. Near the foot of the upper ledge is the Kalsi stone containing one of Ashoka's edicts.

Lakhmandal. Lakhmandal is situated on the bank of Yamuna at a distance of 35 kms. from Chakrata and 128 kms. from Dehra Dun. To the antiquarian it provides considerable material of interest. It contains temples dedicated to Siva, the five Pandava brothers, Parasuram and Kedar. In order to burn the Pandavas, the Kauravas had built their 'Laksha Grah' (house of lac). The two remarkably well executed figures in stone of Arjuna and the other of Bhima are available in the village.

Sahasra Dhara. Sahasra Dhara, literally meaning, the 'thousand fold spring' is situated at a distance of 11 kms. from Dehra Dun. The place makes an ideal picnic spot and is of immense attraction to visitors. The water here has a fall of about 9 metres and leaves an incrustation of lime of all its touches. Particles thus accumulating over the centuries have formed a projecting ledge, and a sort of cave, from the roof of which falls a perpetual shower. There is also a sulphur spring in which visitors often take bath. Its water is said to cure skin infections and possess other medicinal properties.

Dak Pathar. It is situated amidst scenic surrounding at a distance of 45 kms. north-west of Dehra Dun on the left bank of the river Yamuna. The place has developed as an ideal picnic spot of tourist interest.

Rishikesh. It is associated with Ram. According to legend, hare he came on the advice of sage Vasistha to do penance for killing Ravana, the king of Lanka. The town is situated on the right bank of the Ganga at a distance of about 42 kms. from Dehra Dun. After the fairs at Hardwar, pilgrims, no longer deterred by the former difficulties of the journey, now visit the place in large numbers. There are scores of ancient temples and ashrams affording spiritual solace to pilgrim, the important among them being temple of Bharata Puskar temple, Shatrughan temple, Lahkhsmana temple, Geeta Bhawan and the Punjab Kshetra.

ZOO

Malsi Deer Park, Dehradun.

MUSEUMS

Botanical Survey of India, Dehradun.

Forest Research Institute and College Dehradun.

Zonal Museum, Dehradun.

Zoological Survey of India, Dehradun.

HOTELS

Hotel Madhuban, (Government approved) 3 star, Dehradun.

Access: 26 kms from Airport, 3 kms. from Railway station, 1 km. from Bus stand. Rooms: 42.

Hotel President, (Government approved) 2 star, Dehradun.

Access: 26 kms. from Airport, 3 kms. from Railway station, 1 km. from Bus stand. Rooms 18.

Hotel Relax, (Government approved) 2 star, Dehradun.

Access: 25 kms. from Airport, 1 km. from Railway station, 1/2 km from Bus stand.

Rooms: 27.

Hotel Ajanta Continental, (Government approved) Dehradun.

Access: 25 kms. from Airport, 4 kms. from Railway station, 2 kms. from Bus stand. Rooms: 29.

Hotel Great Value, Dehradun.

Access: 25 kms. from Airport, 6 kms. from Railway station, 4 kms. from Bus stand. Rooms 53.

Hotel Shahenshah, Dehradun.

Access: 25 kms. from Airport, 5 kms. from Railway station, 4 kms. from Bus stand. Rooms: 30.

Hotel Prince, Dehradun

Access: 30 kms. from Airport, 1 km. from Railway station, 1 km. from Bus stand. Rooms: 21.

Inderlok Hotels Pvt. Ltd., Dehradun.

Access: 24 kms. from Airport, 1.5 kms. from Railway station, 1 km. from Bus stand. Room 48.

Meedo's Grand, Dehradun.

Access: 25 kms. from Airport, 3 kms. from Railway station, 2 kms. from Bus stand.

Rooms: 29.

Motel Kwality, Dehradun.

Access: 25 kms. from Airport, 3 kms. from Railway station, 2 kms. from Bus stand. Rooms: 18.

FAIRS AND FESTIVALS

Important fairs and festivals organised in different parts of the district are mentioned below:

Deviji, Bissu, Jagra, Panchon, Gandhi Mela, Chandarbani, Ambika Devi, Jhanda Mela, Bawari, Jyaistha Dussehra, Mata, Bhadraj, Maru Sidh, Shivratri, Tapkeshwar Sidh, Laxman Sidh.

EDUCATION

According to 2001 Census, the poulation of the total

literates (excluding the population in the age group of 0-6 years) is 881476 persons. Of these, 506621 are males and 374855 are females. In the rural areas of the district 365554 persons (214962 males and 150592 females) are literates and in urban areas 515922 persons (291659 males and 224263 females) are literates. The rate of literacy of this population to the total population (excluding 0-6 years age group) according to 2001 Census is shown below:

1991			*2001*		
Persons	*Males*	*Females*	*Persons*	*Males*	*Females*
69.50	77.95	59.26	78.96	85.87	71.22

The ratio of 5.11 primary Schools per 10000 population is obtained in urban areas of the district ranging between the maximum of 15.93 in Mussoorie and the minimum of 0.65 in Clement town Cantt. The ratio of Middle Schools works out to 2.42 per 10000 of urban population in the district. The maximum ratio of 6.09 Middle Schools is observed in Majra and the minimum of 0.65 in Clement town Cantt. For every 10000 of urban population there are 1.45 schools of Matriculation Standard. With 5.24 schools of Matriculation Standard, Landour Cantt. presents, the highest proportion per 10000 of population. The ratio of Intermediate Colleges works out to 0.94 colleges in urban areas of the district. The maximum ratio of 5.24 colleges is observed in Landour Cantt. and the minimum of 0.46 in Dehra Dun Cantt. Thus Landour Cantt. shows the highest ratio per 10000 of population of schools of Matriculation Standard and Intermediate Colleges.

COLLEGES

DAV (CPG) College, Dehradun (Established 1961). Enrolment 12000, Teachers 122.

Dayanand Brijendra Swaroop Postgraduate College, Dehradun, (Established 1961), Enrolment 3000. Teachers 58.

Dayand Women's Training College, Dehradun, (Established 1961), Enrolment 132. Teachers 8.

Government Degree College, Dakpathar (1990).

Government PG College, Rishikesh (Established 1963), Enrolment 2000. Teachers 40.

Graphic Era Institute of Technology, Dehradun.

Indian Institute of Management and Technology, Dehradun.

Institute of Management Studies, Dehradun.

Mahadevi Kanya Pathshala (PG) Dehradun (Established 1958). Enrolment 4000, Teachers 45.

Municipal Postgraduate College, Mussoorie (Established 1963). Enrolment 700. Teachers 15.

SGRR College, Dehradun (Established 1960). Enrolment 1000. Teachers 36.

Sri Guru Ram Rai Institute of Technology and Science, Dehradun (Established 1994).

Indian Institute of Remote Sensing, Dehradun.

Defence Electronics Application, Laboratory, Dehradun.

Survey of India Research Centre, Dehradun.

ONGC Research Centre, Dehradun.

Wadia Institute of Himalayan Geology, Dehradun.

FRI Research Centre, Dehradun.

Indian Institute of Patroleum Research Centre, Dehradun.

(Above named Colleges belong to Hemwati Nandan Bahuguna Garhwal University (Etablished 1973).

MEDICAL

There are 2.84 beds per thousand of population in medical institutions in urban areas of the district. The highest ratio of 42.93 beds is observed in Landour Cantt. followed by Vikasnagar (13.22) and Mussoorie (9.19) and the minimum ratio of (0.23) beds in Dehra Dun Cantt. There are no medical institutions with bed facility in Majra town.

NEWSPAPERS

Amar Ujala, a Hindi Daily Newspaper from Dehradun. Its circulation is about 40,000.

Doon Message, A Hindi Daily Newspaper from Dehradun. The circulation is 47416.

Himachal Times, A Hindi Daily Newspaper from Dehradun. The circulation is 54,000.

Himachal Times, An English Daily Newspaper from Dehradun, the circulaton is 53790.

Nai Rashtriya Dhara, a Hindi Daily Newspaper from Dehradun, the circulation is 49133.

Pahardashi Darpan, a Hindi daily, from Dehradun, the circulation is 47416.

Shikar Sandesh, a Hindi daily from Dehradun. The circulation is 56500.

The Himachal Times, an English Daily from Dehradun. The circulation is 53790.

Chopal Ki Bate, a Hindi monthly from Dehradun, circulation is 32124.

Dev Prayag, a Hindi Biweekly from Dehradun, circulation is 46825.

Garh Atma, a Hindi Biweekly from Dehradun, circulation is 46816.

Garh Dhunia, a Hindi Biweeekly from Dehradun, circulation is 46762.

Ghad Gatha, a Hindi Biweekly from Dehradun, circulation is 46775.

Jagvaal, a Hindi weekly from Dehradun, circulation is 45600.

ADMINISTRATION

(i) Administrative Divisions:

Tehsils: Chakrata, Dehradun, Vikasnagar, Rishikesh.

Community Development Blocks: Chakrata, Kalsi, Vikas Nagar, Sahaspur, Raipur, Doiwala.

Towns with their Population, Urban Status and Literates (2001)

City/Town	*Urban Status*	*Population*			*Literates*		
		Person	*Male*	*Female*	*Person*	*Male*	*Female*
Chakrata	CB	3497	2165	1332	2619	1747	872
Clement Town	CB	19634	11470	8164	10781	6649	4132

Dehradun	M. Corp.	447808	236852	210956	343624	192672	150952
Dehradun	CB	30102	15590	14512	23770	12813	10957
Doiwala	NP	8047	4339	3708	6130	3551	2579
FRI and College	CT	5428	2861	2567	4374	2406	1968
Herbertpur	NP	9242	4866	4376	6404	3640	2764
Landour	CB	3250	1797	1453	2541	1527	1014
Mussoori	MB	26069	14721	11348	20666	12421	8245
Pratitnagar	CT	7078	3511	3567	4984	2691	2293
Raipur	CT	24887	12880	12007	20240	10926	9314
Rishikesh	MB	59671	33186	26485	44639	26689	17950
Veerbhadra	ITS	13271	6945	6326	10744	5982	4762
Vikasnagar	MB	12485	6571	5914	9471	5174	4297

(ii) Parliamentary Constituencies and Assembly Segments

No. and Name of Parliamentary Constituencies.

1. TEHRI GARHWAL; 2. GARHWAL

Assembly Constituency: 10. Chakrata (ST)

TEHSIL—CHAKRATA

Kawanu. 9. Bulhad 10. Jadi; 11. Kawanu; 12. Naraya; 13. Koruwa; 14. Sahiya; 15. Chandeo; 16. Koti; 17. Dimau; 18. Kanbua. ***Lakhamandal.*** 30. Maralho; 31. Birmau; 32. Nagau; 33. Ghanata; 34. Kawasi; 35. Mohna; 36. Barontha; 37. Khabou; 38. Manthat; 39. Lakhamandal. ***Tuni.*** 1. Tuni; 2. Anu; 3. Hanol; 4. Chilhar; 5. Chajad-Harlad; 6. Bhandrauli; 7. Mashak; 8. Kandoi. ***Forest Area.*** F 2 Kannsar Range; F 3 Rikhnad; F 4 Babbar Range; F 5 Devdhar Range; F 6 Molta Range. ***Urban Area.*** Chakrata Cantt.

Assembly Constituency: 11. Vikasnagar

TEHSIL—CHAKRATA

Kalsi. 19. Samalta; 20. Badnu; 21. Kalsi; 22. Thaina; 23. Gadog; 24. Gaskee; 25. Lakhwar; 26. Lohari; 27. Kwasa; 28. Nagthat; 29. Gangroo. ***Forest Area.*** F 1 River forest range. ***Vikasnagar.*** 1. Binhar Purav; 2. Binhar Paschim; 3. Ambari 4. Prathvipur; 5. Enfield Grant. 6. Dhakrani; 7. Dharmawala; 8. Fatehpur; 9. West Hoptown-2; 10. West Haptown-1; 12. udrapur. ***Forest Area.*** F 12 Rampur Mandi; F 2 Timli; F-1

Chohadpur. ***Urban Area.*** Herbertpur; Nagarpanchayat; Parishad; Vikasnagar; Nagarpalika Parishad.

Assembly Constituency: 12. Mussoorie

TEHSIL—DEHRAKHAS

Dehrakhas. 11. Jakhan (Part) (including village Makreti); 13. Rekhauli; 14. Johari; 15. Kyarkuli Bhatta. ***Raipur.*** 16. Chamasari; 17. Silla; 18. Sarona. ***Forest Area.*** F 5-Mussoorie; **Urban Area:** Landhaur Cantt; Mussoorie Nagarpalika Parishad.

TEHSIL—VIKASNAGAR

Jhajhra. 14. Horawala; 15. Atakfarm; 16. Rampur Bhauwala; 17. Kanswali Kothri; 18. Misras Patti; 19. Paundha; 20. Hariyawala Kalan; 21. Jhajra; 22. Central Hoptown; 23. Shankerpur; Hakumatpur; 26. Sabhawala

Vikasnagar. 11. Kedarwala; 13. Sorna; 24. Sahaspur; 25. Jassowala.

Forest Area. F-3 Malhan; F-4 Jhajra

Assembly Constituency: 13. Rishikesh

TEHSIL—DEHRADUN

Raipur. 26. Badasi Grant; 29. Dwara. ***Rishikesh.*** 1. Rishikesh; 2. Sidderwala; 3. MjriGrant; 4. Raiwala; 5. Bhogpur; 6. Gadul; 7. Sangaon; 8. Badkot Mafi; 9. Ranipokhri Grant; 10. Ramnagar Danda; 11. Bhaniyawala; 12. Sindhwalgaon; 13. Jolly Grant. **Forest Area:** F-10 Kasron; F-11 motichur; F-7 Thano; F-9 Badkot. **Urban Area:** Rishikesh Nagarpalika; Parishad.

Parliamentary Constituency: 2. GARHWAL

Assembly Constituency: 14. Dehradun Cantt.

TEHSIL—DEHRADUN

Dehrakhas (Dehradun) FRI and College Area. 1. Arcadia Grant; 2. Sewla Kalan; 10. Kaulagarh (Part) (excluding area included in Nagar Nigam Dehradun); 12. Garhi (Part) excluding area included in Nagar Nigam Dehradun). **Urban Area:** Dehradun Cantt.

TEHSIL—VIKASNAGAR

Jhajhra. 27. East Hoptown; 28. Pelio Nathuwala.

Assembly Constituency: 15. Laxman Chowk

TEHSIL—DEHRADUN

Dehrakhas. 3. Majra; 4. Bharuwala Grant; 5. Dehrakhas (excluding area included in Nagar Nigam Dehradun); 9. Kanwli. ***Raipur.*** Brahmanwla; Deharakhas; Kanvali; Majra; Niranjanpur. **Forest Area:** Forest F-6 Asarodi. **Urban Area:** Dehradun NP Ward 8; Dehradun Ward 6; Dehradun Ward 7.

Assembly Constituency: 16. Raipur

TEHSIL—DEHRADUN

Dehrakhas. 7. Adjhoiwala (excluding village Dharanpur); 8. Karanpur Khas (excluding village Bijapur Hathi Barkalan); 11. Jakhan (excluding village Makreti). ***Raipur.*** 19. Chalang; 20. Gujrada Mansingh; 21. Danda Lakhond; 22. Kandoli. ***Villages.*** Chirnowall; Dhoran Khas; Kandauni; Thani Gaon (Rajpur). **Urban Area:** Dehradun MC Ward 1; Dehradun MC Ward 13; Dehradun MC Ward 2; Dehradun MC Ward 4.

Assembly Constituency: 17. Dehradun

TEHSIL—DEHRADUN

Dehrakhas. 8. Karanpur Khas (village Bijapur Hathi Barkalan) 10. Kaulagarh 12. Garhi. ***Villages.*** Dhartawala Muafi; Garhi Uddowala; Gopiwala; Kaulagarh Maichak; Loharwala; Panditwadi; Prempur Muafi; Rangarwala; Shahpur Santor. **Urban Area:** Dehradun MC Ward 11; Dehradun MC Ward 12; Dehradun MC Ward 9; Dehradun NP Ward 10.

Assembly Constituency: 18. Doiwala

TEHSIL—DEHRADUN

Dehrakhas. 5. Dehrakhas (Part); Nayanagar, Dhoran and Nayanagar Kalaon wali; 6. Ajabpur Kalan; 7. Adhoiwala (Part)-Dharampur.

MINERALS AND ORES

Asbestos—It occurs in dolerite intrusive as slip-fibres in veinlets and as small irregular masses in the Maryville Estate.

Barytes—It is found near Rajpur.

Marble—It is found between Bhilalikhund and Nelson's point at Kulukhet.

Copper—at Kalsi (30°32':77°51').

Lead—In the valley of the Tons River about to the north of Kalsi (30°32':77°54'), Buraila (30°44':77°51'), Kuma (30°41':78°6') Konain (30°47':77°57').

Galena—at Mudhaul (30°56':77°51').

Lignite—at RAJPUR (30°24':78°09').

Limestone—at Rishikesh-Devprayag (30°09':78°36') Northern part of CHAKRATA area (30°42':77°52'), KALSI (30°32':77°51') PATHNA (30°33':77°47'), Dagura (30°37':77°57').

Glass Making Materials

Occurrences of glass sands in the older Duna gravels in the neighbourhood of DEHRA. Quartzite boulders occur at LACHMANSIDH which are crushed for yielding glass sands. Similar boulders occur on the hill west of RAJPUR (about 11 km. north of Dehra) on Angila Hill.

Gypsum—The nature and origin of certain deposits of gypsum occurring among the hills to the north of Dehradun. Nodules of gypsum occur in many places among the ferruginous clays of the Sabathu group and it forms irregular veins in limestone at SAHANSADHRA, at SALKOT, JERIPANI on the road between Rajpur and Mussoorie. It also occurs associated with limestone, dolomite and calcareous slates near MANJHARA.

Asbestos—Occurrences of asbestos in the Mary Ville Estate, Mussorie (30.6, 78.1). The mineral occurs in dolerite untrusive as slip-fibers in veinlets and as small irregular masses.

Barytes—Barytes is said to occur at Rajpur (30.4, 78.1).

Building Materials—Occurrence of marble on the spur between Bhilalikhund and Nelson's point. (and 50 ft. above the Kulukhet tool gate on the Dehradun-Mussorie motor road. Marble is also found 30 ft. above Kulukhet water works and 100 ft. below the motor road. The marble is not of sufficiently good quality for building or statutory work but is suitable for the manufacture of mosaic flooring and refining of sugar.

Copper—Occurrence of copper-ore reported from Kalsi (30.5, 77.85).

Lead—Several old Leadmines are situated in the valley of the Tons River about 25 miles to the North of Kalsi. The mines at Buraila and Maiyur were described in 1829 by Herbert, who says that they were of great extent, but had then ceased to be profitable.

At Kuma, a quartz vein occurs in slates of which 2 or 3 inches at the base are inpregnated with galena and copper pyrites.

At Kharsi, Galena in nodules occurs between beds of limestone, but it is very local in distributions. Lead-Ore occurs at Konain as at Kharsi. A galena mine is reported by him at Mudhoul.

Lignite—Deposit of lignite lies in the hills between Rajpur (30.4, 78.15) and the Jamuna.

Limestone—Large deposits of high grade limestone belonging to the Krol C Sub-stage of the upper krol lime stone occur throughout the area from Sisoli near Dehradun to Cloud end to the S.W. of Mussoorie town for a straight distance of more than 11 miles.

Large reserves of limestone of the Krol and upper Tal series occur in the Rishikesh-Devaprayag motor road cutting. The Krol limestones are too high in magnesia content to be used for cement manufacture. Limestones of the Chail series are reported to occur in the northern part of Chakrata area. Deposits of limestone belonging to the lower Jaunsars found near Kalsi, Pathna and Dagura.

Deposits of calcareous tufa are found in the Doiwala area and they occupy the high ground on the western side of the Laskar-Dehra dun railway line.

Mineral waters—Several chalebeate and sulphurous cold springs occur in the neighbour hood of Mussorie (30.45, 78.1) and Laundour (30.46, 78.1). The water is said to be beneficial in cases of debility, diseases of the liver and spleen, rheumatic and cutaneous complaints etc.

Phosphates—The discovery of a phosphatic deposit on the midlands estate at Mussoorie (30.45, 78.13). Nodules of phosphate of lime and layers of a phosphatic rock occur in a band of shale at the base of chert beds immediately overlying the Mussorie lime stones. Exposure of deposit were found at three places in a length of mile.

Sulphur—Sulphur occurs in considerable quantities in some of the galleries in the lead mines at Maiwar, on the Tons River.

Small crystals and patches of native sulphur are found associated with gypsum in dolomite to the north of Samsadhara.

Zinc—Near Kalsi, mixed ore associated with the galena, consisting principally of zinc blend with some galena, iron pyrites and quartz.

OBSERVATIONAL ORGANISATION

Surface Observatories

This district lies under Meteorological sub-division, hills of Uttar Pradesh, West (now Uttaranchal). The instrument lies in

Dehradun

Latitude : 30.3° North

Longitude : 78.03° East

Altitude : 682 m

Date of starting : 8-7-1946

Mussoorie

Latitude : 30.45° North

Longitude : 78.1° East

Altitude : 2042 m

Date of starting : 16-5-1866

Hydrometeorological Stations for Climatological Purposes

This facility is available at Chakrata, Dakpathar, and Kote. These instrument lies in

Chakrata

Latitude : 30.7° North

Longitude : 77.87° East

Altitude : 2135 m

Date of starting : 21-5-1976

Dakpathar

Latitude	:	30.5° North
Longitude	:	77.75° East
Altitude	:	396 m
Date of starting	:	22-5-1996

Koti

Latitude	:	30.6° North
Longitude	:	77.8° East
Altitude	:	1220 m
Date of starting	:	25-2-1977

Upper Air Observatories

These observatory record and report information about upper winds. This information is of vital importance, not only for casting purposes but also to pilots of air craft, who must have knowledge of the speed and direction of winds at various levels in the atmosphere. This instrument was started on first October 1958 at Dehradun.

Radiation Meteorological Station

This instrument was established on November 1969 at Dehradun.

Seismological Organisation

Seismological observatories forming the national network is located at Dehradun. Data from all these observatories are used for routine determination of epicentre of earthquakes, preparation of bulletins, special study and research.

Aeronautical Meteorological Observatories

This instrument maintain current weather watch at aerodromes or important localities along and near air routes, provide service for the use of air craft and air traffic control units. This facility is available at Dehradun.

DISASTER WEATHER EVENTS

Snowfall—On 28th December 1991, there was heavy snowfall, 12 villages remained cut-off as link road covered with snow ranging 1-2 metres, Mussoorie with snow ranging 1-2 metres, Mussoorie-Tehri, Chakrata-Dehra Dun and Chakrata-Tuni road completely closed for vehicular traffic.

From 28-30 December 1996, it was severe and several people died due to it.

Gale—On 27th June 1982, it was strong, lichi and mango crops damaged extensively, many trees uprooted, road from Mussoorie and Chakrata blocked, pipeline in city damaged, electric supply disrupted.

Hailstorm—On 31 May 1983, it was moderate type, 75 per cent of lichi crop damaged in Doon Valley.

Floods and Heavy Rains—In July 1993, it was flood, persons died, several cattle heads perished, big area of agriculture land submerged.

On 3rd July 1994, it was heavy rains and houses damaged, several persons died.

ARCHAEOLOGICAL SITES

At Jagatgram

Excavation exposed remains of three sites where the king Silavarman of the 3rd century A.D. performed *asuamedhas.* In addition to well-designed bricks in the orientation of the hawk or eagle with spread wings, bricks from the first site bore Sanskrit inscriptions in the Brahmi script of the 3rd century A.D. The other two sites produced a number of inscribed bricks.

At Jiwangarh

Small scale excavation revealed a brick platform raised over a rubble soling. It was built of re-used bricks of the earlier period datable to 1st-2nd century.

At Kalsi

Surface collection included the increased dish, bowl in plain grey ware, carinated *handi* and medium-sized vase in red ware. The collection suggest that there was a modest settlement near the Rock-edict of Asoka.

At Maya-Kund

Red ware of the Semga Kushan Assemblage.

At Rishikesh

An early historical site.

DISTRIBUTION OF *SCHEDULED CASTE* POPULATION BY SEX (1991)

	POPULATION Total	Males	Females
DEHRADUN			
	1,37,464	74,251	63,213
Agariya	106	61	45
Badhik	120	67	53
Badi	320	162	158
Baheliya	199	111	88
Baiga	116	61	55
Baiswar	64	35	29
Bajgi	5,379	2,812	2,567
Balahar	18	9	9
Balai	5	2	3
Balmiki	19,938	10,946	8,992
Bangali	173	95	78
Banmanus	4	2	2
Bansphor	129	73	56
Barwar	90	43	47
Basor	76	40	36
Bawariya	53	34	19
Beldar	21	5	16
Beriya	21	10	11
Bhantu	54	38	16
Bhuiya	193	141	52
Bhuyiar	63	42	21
Boria	177	75	102
Chamar, Dhusia, Jhusia, Jatava	59,156	30,973	28,183
Chero	201	122	79
Dabgar	41	17	24
Dhangar	325	177	148
Dhanuk	100	55	45
Dharkar	134	71	63
Dhobi	4,675	2,474	2,201
Dom	10,117	5,432	4,685
Domar	43	19	24
Dusadh	102	61	41
Ghasiya	42	23	19
Gond	2,030	1,139	891
Gual	399	254	145
Habura	2	1	1
Hari	80	43	37
Hela	14	8	6
Kalabaz	15	9	6
Kanjar	262	141	121
Kapariya	160	86	74
Karwal	118	73	45
Khairaha	33	18	15
Kharwar (excluding Benbansi)	80	34	46
Khatik	6,072	3,612	2,460
Khorot	43	24	19
Kol	2,932	1,708	1,224
Kori	6,419	3,492	2,927
Korwa	81	47	34
Lalbegi	21	14	7
Majhwar	483	261	222
Mazhabi	19	8	11
Musahar	261	140	121
Nat	129	71	58
Pankha	17	8	9
Parahiya	28	15	13
Pasi, Tarmali	6,224	3,505	2,719
Patari	58	42	16
Rawat	467	273	194
Saharya	10	7	3
Sanaurhiya	66	36	30
Sansiya	28	18	10
Shilpkar	7,691	4,303	3,388
Turaiha	59	33	26
Unclassified	908	540	368

DISTRIBUTION OF *SCHEDULED TRIBE* POPULATION BY SEX (1991)

	POPULATION		
	Total	Males	Females
	DEHRADUN		
•	84,076	44,510	39,566
Bhotia	462	282	180
Buksa	10,359	5,590	4,769
Jaunsari	71,660	37,649	34,011
Raji	42	16	26
Tharu	1,506	946	560
Unclassified	47	27	20

SKETCH MAP
OF
GARHWAL DISTRICT
TEHRI GARHWAL
RUDRAPRAYAG
HARDWAR
ALMORA
BIJNOR (UP)
Srinagar
PAURI
Paithani
Adwani
Musagali
Joshyana
Bijni
Vyasghat
Chila
Thalisain
Kandi
Banghat
Dwarikhal
Bungidhar
Pokhra
Rithakhal
Baijro
Lansdowne
Lal Dhang
Dugadda
Bironkhal
Churani
Kotdwara
Dhumakot
Badiyargaon
Kanda
Kalagarh
LEGEND
District Headquarters
Taluk Headquarters
Other Towns
Railway Line
Major Roads
Other Roads
River

GARHWAL

LOCATION AND AREA

Latitude : 29.4° North to 30.3° North

Longitude : 78.2° East to 79.2° East

Altitude : 1845 m.

The district of Garhwal is bounded by the districts Chamoli on the north-east, Bijnor on the south, Almora, Nainital and Chamoli on the east while its western boundary is formed by river Gangas as far as Rudraprayag. River Gangas divides from district Tehri-Garhwal. It lies between latitude 29°26' and 31°18' north and between longitude 78°10' and 79°10' east.

Total area of the district is 5397 sq. kms. The district headquarters is located at Pauri.

HISTORY

An array of sketchy glimpses about this district and around is available in ancient Hindu literature. We can have at best a peep into the era through Vedic, Epic and Pauranic analects without threading chronology into a history. A rough idea can be framed about this region only from the time of the Mauryan Empire. The great Mauryan king Ashoka's reign was probably associated in third century B.C. It is probable that the dominions in reach of present district were vassals under Mauryan Emperors. After the Mayura hegemony over this tract another reasonable ancient power in due course were the Kushans. The most credible time of the Empire is the second century A.D. Thereafter the history of this region is little traceable till the 7th century A.D. The stray inscriptions discovered in the neighbouring districts belonging to third, fifth and eighth centuries A.D., may extend valuable information about these centuries. In all probability the Harsha's suzerainty over this tract was of mild nature. More definite chronology of this region begins in the 8th century A.D. From then, till the close of 12th century A.D., the area was distinctly forming a part under the

Katyuri monarchs based at Joshimath in the district of Chamoli. Towards the end of 12th century A.D. the region saw the rise of paramountcy of Panwar dynasty. The period between 1451 A.D. and 1488 is credited for the change in the name of dynasty from Pal to Sah. The successive rulers of this family increasingly found it difficult to retain the country intact in face of frequent assaults imposed by Chand rulers of Kumaon Kingdom. These assaults began from the period between 1565 A.D. and 1597 A.D. These two rival dynasties of the Himalayan Alpine region scored nothing but spoil of desolation during the next two centuries of mutual conflicts. A spell of prosperity achieved by Garhwal during the rule of Mahipat Sah (1580-1630 A.D.) is briefly attested by the writings left by Farishta and a few Jesuit missions who had visited this region. Two annexation bids under the expeditions of the Mughals were thwarted but the next contest was decisive in that the ruler Prithvi Sah was forced to offer submission. The state of Garhwal still remained under grave threat from outward quarters. Hafiz Rahmat Khan subdued this dominion in 1743-44 and withdrew only on the condition of realising three lakhs of rupees. The improverished state of Garhwal was ordained to sustain looting sprees organised by Sikh, Gujar and Rajput adventurers. These numerous onslaughts brought this dynasty to the verge of bankruptcy. From the beginning of nineteenth century A.D. Garhwal principality was a mere vassal of Kathmandu. Such a rapid was the erosion of power of this state, that the Gurkha invasion of 1803 compelled this dynasty to surrender. Beginning of Gurkha rule was a turning point in history of Garhwal in the sense that this region tested the ordeal of a rule based purely on military occupation for the first time in the long chequered history. The depressed natives who were desparately gasping for a better change, got a worse substitute in the form of British occupation of the territory in 1815. The British colonialists were not a lesser evil than the archaic Gurkhas and only a long-lasted struggle ripened into political freedom of this district in 1947 A.D.

POPULATION (GENERAL, SC/ST)

Total population of the district according to 2001 Census is 696851 persons, comprising 331138 males and 365713 females. Rural population of the district is 606629 persons

(281581 males and 325048 females) and urban population is 90222 persons (49557 males and 40665 females).

The scheduled Castes and Scheduled Tribes population of the district as per 1991 Census is 92261 persons and 1502 persons respectively. The rural-urban breakup of this population is indicated below:

Rural	(i) Scheduled Castes	:	83640
	(ii) Scheduled Tribes	:	1358
Urban	(i) Scheduled Castes	:	8621
	(ii) Scheduled Tribes	:	144

The decennial growth rate of population of the district as a whole in relation to the state between the period 1981-1991 and 1991-2001 is presented below:

State/District	*Decennial growth rate of population (per cent)*	
	1981-91	*1991-2001*
Uttaranchal	24.23	19.20
Garhwal	9.05	3.87

LANGUAGES AND RELIGION

Main language spoken in the district is Hindi.

Religion-wise breakup of Population as per 1991 Census (At District Level)

Hindus: 663485, Muslims, 15495, Christians: 1639, Sikhs: 1165, Buddhists: 145, Jains: 256, Other religions and persuasions: 283, Religion not stated: 67.

GEOGRAPHY AND PHYSICAL FEATURES

The district is entirely mountainous with no level land except the pasture-land of Penai. On the banks of Alaknanda, the areas surrounding Srinagar and the Submontane tract in the southern part of the district known as Bhabar. The mountainous tract consists of a succession of steep mountain ridges separated from each other by deep glens. The central area of Garhwal is covered by Dudatoli range. The height varies between 1050 metres and 1950 metres with such an exceptions as of the supreme peak of Choprakot rising up to 2715 metres. The next high summit of Kinkwala Tibba which is located about 1.6 km. west of Pauri Town is 2595 metres. The numerous spurs in the mountain systems of central Garhwal separates the river valleys from each other. These narrow valleys at the base of the hills are generally streamless and are extensively cultivated except a few.

The *Bhaber* area lies in the south of the district. It is on the foot of the hills and almost has the characteristics akin to plain. It is about 80 kms. in length and 3.2 kms. in breadth and a large part (78 per cent) of it is shrouded with forests. The tract is well drained and cultivation can be carried on only by clearing of forests and with irrigation facilities.

A large variety of flora are found in the district depending on height and climate. Chir is found upto a height of 2000 metres. It is used in building houses and is tapped for resin and its seeds yield oil. Oak is found between 2000 to 2500 metres. There are fine clumps of *devdar* in abundance among the conifers. The wood is hard and is used for making furnitures and agricultural implements. *Ringal, mauna tilang* and *pongar* are also found in cooler and higher slopes forming Alpine pastures. However, the most extensive and noteworthy forest is in southern Bhabar area, where Sal trees form a dense canopy with trees of dry deciduous forest.

RIVERS, CANALS AND WATERWAYS

The drainage of the district is imparted by the river Ganga and its affluents. The only mighty river in this district is Alaknanda, which flows to the southwest along the border of the district and after its confluence with Bhagirathi at Devaprayag in Tehri-Garhwal forms the Ganga. River Nayer, which rises from Dudatoli mountain is chief river of the district as more than half of the area of the district is in its basin and this river is well known for carp. It drains the centre of the district and joins Ganga at Byasghat. The river Ganga flows almost to west as far as Lachman Jhula and then the direction moves to south-west along the border of the district. Ramganga flows south-east and then to east entering into Almora district. It re-enters this district near Marchula. Its chief tributary is the Mandal which drains south of Lansdowne tehsil. In the south-east part of the district Palacen and Sona rivers flow parallel to the southern outer ranges and join the Ramganga. The other rivers of the district are comparatively small streams; rising in the hills above *Bhabar* and vanish into oblivion after some length before entering the *Bhabar,* leaving *Bhabar* area nearly waterless. The Kho which rises near Dwarikhal is joined at Dogadda with Khawasan and Malar which are rivulets of minor topographical interest.

TOWNS, VILLAGES AND AMENITIES

The district at present comprises of six tehsils and 3551 villages (3205 inhabited villages and 346 uninhabited villages. The urban population of the district as percentage of total population in the census is indicated below. It also shows the sex ratio (females per 1000 males) and density (population per sq. km.) in the urban population of the district in relation to the state:

State/ District	*Urban population as percentage of total population*	*Sex ratio, (Females per 1000 males*		*Density (Population per sq. km.)*	
	2001	*1991*	*2001*	*1991*	*2001*
Uttaranchal	25.59	936	964	133	159
Garhwal	12.94	1058	1104	124	129

Amenities

Number (with percentage) of villages having one or more amenities in the district as per 1991 Census is given below:

Sl. No.	*Amenities*	*Number of inhabited villages*	*Percentage*
1.	Education	1522	47.49
2.	Medical	1104	34.45
3.	Drinking Water	3200	99.84
4.	Post and Telegraph	436	13.60
5.	Market/Hat	544	16.97
6.	Communications	713	22.25
7.	Approach by Pucca Road	376	11.73
8.	Power Supply	1809	56.44

COMMUNICATIONS

By all odds, 1330, kms. of P.W.D. roads giving a ratio of 266 kms. per 1000 square kilometres of area has put over the communictions in a desired shape. Though, Kotdwara in the district is a railway terminus but this is of only terminal importance to the district since the total length of rail tracks is only 6 kms. About 145 kms. of roads put forth through forest department and another 26 kms. by municipalities etc. have no doubt enhanced this vital means of development.

AGRICULTURE AND IRRIGATION

The cultivation possesses extremely lean potentials in the district. The topographical constraints emanting from predominance of hill and submontane terrain, make the availability of arable land scarse. The terrace cultivation on the foot of the hills and on the sloping hill sides and the primitive cultivation on the steep inclines by burning scurbs and bushes make agriculture low in productivity and not gainful activity to the persons who engage themselves. The short agricultural season and extreme climate further limits, the option of diversification of crops.

Kharif is the chief harvest accounting for 64.41 per cent of the gross cropped area of 152 thousand hectares, while rabi claims the remaining proportion of it. Coarse grain crops are raised extensively and they compete well in the extent of cultivation with paddy and wheat. Wheat occupies the most prominent position claiming the largest area of 44 thousand hectares. *Mandua,* a small millet and a coarse grain followed next with 40 thousand hectares of area under its cultivation. Paddy raised in 32 thousand hectares of area is placed in the third position, *sawan* a small millet like *mandua,* is cultivated in 24 thousand hectares. These four crops account for 88.64 per cent of the gross cropped area. The cultivation of pulses does not seem to suit the climatic conditions of the district. The most important crop that claims the largest area is raised in a total area of 897 hectares. Other crops occupy small area. The holdings in the district show up in the average size of 1.29 hectares. As high as 60 per cent of the holding families have a size less than one hectare. The units of operational holdings are by and large uneconomical being of less than two hectares, covering 78 per cent of cultivating families.

The land under the orchards of the district has swelled up to about 47 thousand hectares. Even the greater areas are likely to be covered under fruit trees and vegetables as these are of paramount value of this hilly district. In the district the production of vegetables and fruits are more profitable than the corns. A vast scope exists there for cultivation of apples and akhrot. Horticulture holds the key for the future prosperity of this district.

ANIMAL HUSBANDRY

Livestock raising is yet another valuable occupation in the sense that it supplements income and make yield that are nutritious. The strengths of livestock of somewhere near to 6.7 lakhs. The milk production is meagre, as only 30 thousand litres of milk is regularly being gained from milk cooperatives.

INDUSTRIES

No important mineral deposits are found in the district. The district may probably contain a few important minerals in the shape of metal and petro-like substance but its economic exploitation is no-where to be seen. The industrial structure of the district is not at all developed and is mainly based on utilisation of forest and other local raw materials and also the skill and craftsmanship of the local population. The small scale village industries based on woollen weaving, silk weaving and fruit preservation are getting great encouragement in the district. There are 234 small scale units functioning in the district registered with the Director of Industries. There are only 11 factories registered under Factory Act 1948.

TRADE, COMMERCE AND EXPORTS

The table given below presents most important commodities manufactured in, exported from and imported into each town of the district.

Name of the towns	*Most important commodity*		
	Manufactured	*Exported*	*Imported*
1	*2*	*3*	*4*
Bah Bazar	–	–	Cloth
Dogadda	–	Woollen cloth	Foodgrains

Kalagarh	–	–	Wheat
Kotdwara	Wooden furniture	Timber	Cloth
Lansdowne Cantt.	–	Resin	Foodgrains
Pauri	Charcoal	Apples	Wheat
Rudraprayag	–	–	Wheat
Srinagar	–	–	Wheat

The chief commodities manufactured in the district are wooden furniture and charcoal. The important commodities which are exported from the towns of the district are woollen cloth, timber, resin and apples. The commodities imported into are cloth and foodgrains.

TOURISM

Pauri Town. It is a small town located on the north slope of the Kandoliya hills. Most of the offices of the district are located here. The placce provide an un-interrupted view of the snow. It is imposed by a longridge from the south which is covered in parts with oak, deodar and pine trees, are the icy summit of Himalayas can be seen from here. Nature in naked form, bracing air currents and magnificent view of snow covered peak inspire peace and tranquility. Pauri town is well connected with all parts of Garhwal division and is also the headquarters of commissioner of Garhwal division and regional tourist officer of Garhwal region.

Kandoliya. It is hardly 2 kms. from bus station of Pauri town. Situated at a slightly higher level, it is a beautiful place covered with dense forests and offers an excellent view of the sun-set in the Himalayas.

Kinkaleshwar. This highest spot Pauri has an old temple of Lord Shiva and offers a panoramic view of peaks surmounted with snow.

Ransi Stadium. The place is only 3 kms. from the bus station of Pauri town at an altitude of 2,133 metres above sea level. It is an ideal spot for picnic.

Jwalpa Devi. The shrine of Jwalpa Devi is situated at a distance of 33 kms. from Pauri town at Pauri to Kotdwara road. Devotees from far and near visit the temple in large number.

Adyani. It is 14 kms. away from Pauri town and is connected by a motor road. Adyani provides a glimpse of the hinterland of the Garhwal district.

FAIRS AND FESTIVALS

Important fairs and festivals organised in different parts of the district are mentioned below:

Vishwat Sankranti, Shivratri, Kender-ka-Mela, Ramanavmi, Jaor Dalli, Khirsu, Khidaka-mela Dewalgarh-ka-Mela, Sabdar Khal, Jhankar, Mundneshwar, Janam Ashtmi, Baikunth Chaturdashi, Bindeshwari alias Binsar, Mansar, Makar Sankaranti, Basant Panchmi, Makar-ka-Mela, Gindi-ka-Mela, Vishwat Sankranti, Ekesh-war, Nand Khal, Vaisakhi, Kalinka, Bhaun Devi, Nausin Devi, Vaisakhi Devi, Bharoli Khal, Dabrisain, Syunsi Mela, Ladali, Kathuliya Mahadev, Dewarari Devi, Kola, Bileshwar Mahadev,s Kandiya, Melkhal, Brikand, Bhana Devi, Pand, Banjya Devi, Kunjoli, Somnath, Dhauntiyal-ka-Mela, Bandun, Malla Dhauntiyal, Sangla koti Mela, Kalika Devi, Ghandiyal, Binadhar-ka-Mela, Muchhelgaon, Devra Khal, Semal sain, Bhumi-ka-Mela, Kandai, Mahargaon-ka-Mela, Fatehpur-ka-Mela, Chauksera-ka-Mela, Sawani, Binsar, Gindi-ka-Mela, Dangla, Badri Nath, Makar Sankaranti, Sivratri.

EDUCATION

According to 2001 Census, total literates (excluding the population in the age group of 0–6 years) is 466443 persons. Of these, 255959 are males and 210484 are females. In the rural areas of the district 395935 persons (215446 males and 180689 females are literates and in urban areas 70508 persons (40713 males and 29795 females) are literates. The rate of literacy of this population to the total population, excluding 0-6 years age group according to 2001 Census is shown below:

1991			*2001*		
Persons	*Males*	*Females*	*Persons*	*Males*	*Females*
65.53	82.57	49.65	77.99	91.47	66.14

There are 6.70 Primary Schools for every 10000 of urban

population of the district. The ratio ranges between the maximum of 18.90 primary schools in Bah Bazar and the minimum of 1.87 in Kalagarh. A ratio of 2.23 Junior secondary Schools is obtained in the urban areas of the district. The highest ratio of 18.90 Junior Secondary Schools is observed in Bah Bazar against the lowest of 1.7 in Kotdwara. A ratio of 2.23 Matriculation Schools serves every 10000 of urban population of the district. The highest ratio of 18.90 Matriculation School is observed in Bah Bazar against the lowest of 0.93 in Kalagarh. There are 2.23 Intermediate Colleges for every 10000 of population in urban areas of the district. The highest ratio of 18.90 Inter Colleges is observed in Bah Bazar against the lowest of 0.93 in Kalagarh.

COLLEGES

Government Degree College, Lansdown (Established 1970). Enrolment 300, Teachers 16.

Govind Ballabh Pant Engineering College, Pauri-Garhwal (Established 1991), Enrolment 1,000.

Birla Postgraduate College, Srinagar, (Established 1961) (Constituent college).

Dr. B.G. Reddy Postgraduate College, Pauri (Established 1970) (Constituent College)

Government P.G. College, Kotdwar (Established 1971)

Government Degree College, Chaubatakhal, (Established 1979)

(Above named colleges belong to Hemvati Nandan Bahuguna Garhwal University, Established 1973).

MEDICAL

There are 6.94 beds in medical institutions for every thousand of population in the district. The highest ratio of 11.56 beds is observed in Srinagar. Pauri and Dogadda followed in that order. The lowest ratio of 3.08 beds is witnessed in Lansdowne Cantt. and there are no institutions with bed facility in Bah Bazar and Kalagarh.

ADMINISTRATION

(i) Administrative Divisions:

Tehsils: Pauri, Thailisain, Lansdowne, Kotdwara, Dhoomakot, Srinagar.

Towns with their Population, Urban Status and Literates (2001)

City/Town	Urban Status	Population			Literates		
		Person	Male	Female	Person	Male	Female
Dogadda	MB	2690	1455	1235	2106	1188	918
Kashirampur	CT	9033	4632	4401	6890	3743	3147
Kotdwara	MB	25400	13544	11856	17860	10071	7789
Lansdowne	CB	7902	5048	2854	6829	4583	2246
Pauri	MB	24742	13235	11507	19795	11099	8696
Srinagar	MB	19861	11320	8541	16502	9738	6764

(ii) Parliamentary Constituencies Along Assembly Segments (2001):

No. & Name of Parliamentary Constituencies:

2-Garhwal.

No. & Name of Assembly Segments of Garhwal Parliamentary Constituency which lies within the jurisdiction of Hardwar district.

Assembly Constituency: 28. Yamakeshwar

TEHSIL—KOTDWAR

Dugadda—82. Langur Palla-1; 83. Langur Palla-2; 84. Langur Palla-3; 85. Langur Palla-4. ***Heerakhal***—101. Udaypur Walla-1; 102. Udaypur Walla-2;103. Udaypur Walla-3; 104. Udaypur Walla-4; 105; Udaypur Walla-5 106. Udaypur Walla-6; 107. Udaypur Palla-1; 108. Udaypur Palla-2; 109. Udaypur Palla-3; 110. Udaypur Palla-4; 111. Udaypur Talla-1; 112. Udaypur Talla-2; 113. Udaypur Talla-3; 114. Talla Dhangu-1; 115. Talla Dhangu-2; 116. Talla Dhangu-3. ***Pokhal***—86. Ajmer Walla-1; 87. Ajmer Walla-2; 88. Ajmer Walla-3; 89. Ajmer Walla-4; 90. Ajmer Walla-5; 91. Ajmer Palla-1; 92. Ajmer Palla-2; 93. Ajmer Palla-3; 94. Udaypur Malla-1;95. Udaypur Malla-2; 96. Udaypur Malla-3; 97. Udaypur Malla-4; 98. Udaypur Malla-5; 99. Dabralsyun-1; 100. Dabralsyun-2. **Forest Area:** Forest Area. ***Silogi***—50. Dabralsyun-4; 51. Bichala Dhangu-1; 52. Bichala Dhangu-2; 53. Bichala Dhangu-3; 54. Malla Dhangu-1; 55. Malla Dhangu-2; 56. Malla Dhangu-3

Assembly Constituency: 29. Kotdwar

TEHSIL—KOTDWAR

Dugadda—73. Sukhron; 74. Saneh; 75. Haldukhata; 76. Motadhak; 77. Seela-1; 78. Seela-2; 79. Seela-3; 80. Seela-4; 81. Seela-5. **Forest Area:** Forest Area. **Urban Area:** Dugadda Nagar Palika; Kotdwar Nagar Palika.

Assembly Constituency: 30. Dhumakot

TEHSIL—DHUMAKOT

Dhumkot—174. Khatli Walla-1; 175. Khatli Walla-2; 176. Khatli Walla-3; 177. Khatli Walla-4; 178; Ediyakot Talla-1; 179. Ediyakot Talla-2; 180. Ediyakot Talla-3; 181. Ediyakot Talla-4. *Khirerikhal*—182. Gujudu-1; 183. Gujudu-2; 184. Gujudu-3; 185. Gujudu-4; 186. Gujudu-5; 187. Bjlot-1; 188. Bjlot-4. *Nainidanda*—189. Bungi-1; 190. Bungi-2; 191. Bungi-3; 192. Bungi-4; 193. Bungi-5; 194. Bijlot-2; 195. Bijlot-3. *Rikhnikhal*—58. Bichala Badalpur-1; 59. Bichala Badalpur-2; 60. Bichala Badalpur-3; 61. Bichala Badalpur-4; 62. Bichala Badalpur-5; 63. Bichala Badalpur-6; 64. Paino-1; 65. Paino-2; 66. Paino-3; 67. Paino-4; 69. Ediyakotmalla; 70. Ediyakotmalla-3; 71. Ediyakotmalla-4; 72. Ediyakotmalla-5. **Forest Area:** Forest Area

Assembly Constituency: 31. Lansdowne

TEHSIL—LANSDOWNE

Ekeshwar—1. D. Modarsyun-1; 2. D. Modarsyun-2; 3. D. Mondarsyun-3, 4. D. Maudarsyun-4; 5. Jitolsyun-1; 6. Jitolsyun-2; 7. U. Mondarsyun-1; 8. U. Mondarsyun-2; 9. Guradsyun-2; 10. Guradsyun-4. *Kherasain*—30. Malla Badalpur 1; 31. Malla Badalpur 2; 32. Malla Badalpur 3; 33. Malla Badalpur 4; 34. Langur Walla 2; 35. Langur Walla 3; 36. Langur Walla 4; 37. Kodiya-1; 38. Kodiya-2; 39. Kodiya-3; 40. Lansdowne—Kodiya-4; 41. Langurpalla-3; 42. Langurpalla-4; 43. Seela; 44. Talla Badalpur-1; 45. Talla Badalpur-2; 46. Talla Badalpur-3. *Silogi.* 47. Langurwalla-1; 48. Dabralsyun-2; 49. Dabralsyun-3. **Forest Area:** Forest Area. **Urban Area:** Lansdowne Cantt.

Assembly Constituency: 32. Pauri

TEHSIL—PAURI

Kot—125. Sitonsyun-1; 126. Sitonsyun-2; 127. Sitonsyun-3; 128. Sitonsyun-4; 129. Sitonsyun-5; 130. Sitonsyun-6; 131. Bangarh Syun-1; 132. Bangarh Syun-2; 133. Kandwai Syun-1

134. Kandwal Syun-3. ***Pauri***—117. Nandal Syun-1; 118. Nandal Syun-2; 119. Nandal Syun-3; 120. Gagwar Syun-1; 121. Gagwar Syun-2; 122. Idwalsyun-2; 123. Idwalsyun-3; 124. Idwalsyun-4. **Urban Area:** Pauri Nagar Palika. ***Srinagar***. 229. Katulsyun-1; 230. Katulsyun-2; 231. Katulsyun-3; 232. Rawatsyun; 233. Bangarsyun; 234. Edwalsyun-1; 235. Chlansyun-1; 236. Chlansyun-2; 237. Chlansyun-3. 238. Chlansyun-4. **Urban Area:** Srinagar Nagar Palika.

Assembly Constituency: 33. Kaljikhal

TEHSIL—LANSDOWNE

Chobttakhal. 12. Mawalsyun-1; 13. Mawalsyun-2; 14. Mawalsyun-3. 15. Mawalsyun-4.

TEHSIL—PAURI

Agroda. 155. Pedul Syun-1; 156. Pedul Syun-2; 157. Pedul Syun-3; 158. Pedul Syun-4; 159. Khat Syun-3; 160. Khat Syun-4;161. Kapolsyun-1; 162. Kapolsyun-2; 163. Kapolsyun-3; ***Mundeshwar.*** 145. Aswal syun-1; 146. Aswal syun-2; 147. Aswal syun-3; 148. Aswal syun-4; 149. Aswal syun-5; 150. East Maniyar Syun-1; 151. East Maniyar Syun-2; 152. East Maniyar Syun-3; 153. Patwal Syun-1; 154. Patwal Syun-2. ***Nahsain.*** 135. Gandwag Syun-3; 136. Gangwad Syun-4; 137. Kandwal Syun-2; 138. Kandwal Syun-4; 139. Banelsyun-1; 140. Banelsyun-2; 141. Banelsyun-3; 142. P. Maniyarsyun-1; 143. P. Maniyarsyun-2; 144. P. Maniyarsyun-3.

Assembly Constituency: 34. Bironkhal

TEHSIL—LANSDOWNE

Chobttakhal. 11. Guradsyun-1; 16. Kimgadigad-1; 17. Kimgadigad-3; 18. Ringwadsyun-1; 19. Ringwadsyun-2; 20. Pingalapakha. ***Pokhra.*** 21. Saindhar; 22. Kimgadigad-2; 23. Kolagad-1; 24. Kolagad-2; 25. Talai-1; 26. Talai-2; 27. Talai-3; 28. Talai-4; 29. Guradsyun-3. ***Rikhnikhal.*** 57. Talla Badalpur-4; 68. Ediyakotmalla-1.

TEHSIL-THALISAIN

Bironkhal. 216. Bangar Syun; 217. Dhondiyalsyun-2; 218. Sawali-1; 219. Sawali-2; 220. Sawali-3; 221. Sawali-4; 222. Sawali-5; 223. Sawali-6; 224. Khatli Palla-1; 225. Khatli Palla-

2; 226. Khatli Palla-3; 227. Khatli Palla-4; 228. Khatli Palla-5;

Assembly Constituency: 35. Thalisain

Pavaon. 164. Ghuddausyun-1; 165. Ghuddaudsyun 2 166. Ghuddaudsyun-3; 167. Ghuddaudsyun-4; 168. Ghuddaudsyun-5; 169. Bidol Syun; 170. Balikandarsyun-1; 171. Balikandarsyun-2; 172. Balikandarsyun-3; 173. Balikandarsyun-4.

TEHSIL—THALISAIN

Chakisain. 196. Kandarsyun-1; 197. Kandarsyun-2; 198. Kandarsyun-3; 199. Kandarsyun-4; 200. Kandarsyun-5; 201. haijuli-1. 202. Dhaijuli-2; 203. Dhaijuli-3; 204. Dhaijuli-4. ***Thalisain.*** 205. Choprakot-1; 206. Choprakot-2; 207. Choprakot-3; 208. Choprakot-4; 209. Chauthan-1; 210. Chauthan-2; 211. Chauthan-3; 212. Chauthan-4; 213. Maildhar; 214. Dhondiyalsyun-1; 215. Dhondiyalsyun-3

Garhwal was in Garhwal District (West)-cum-Tehri Garhwal district-cum-Bijnor district North Lok Sabha seat in 1952. the community wise break up (OBE) in Garhwal is Muslims (8 per cent), Scheduled Castes (13 per cent), Rajputs (52 per cent) and Brahmins (20 per cent). Shilpkars (13 per cent) are dominant among the Scheduled Castes. Sikhs are also present in small numbers.

MINERALS AND ORES OCCURRENCES

Building Materials

According to S.P. Nautiyal, the out crops of the Bijni quartzites at Otind (29.9, 78.6) can yield inexhaustible quantities of concrete material. The upper Krol dolomite can be used as finer grade material.

Coal

J.P. Srivastava found thin lenticles and bands of coal in the Luni Sot, Bhairon Sot and Dao Sot near Laldhang (29.8, 78.3) associated with Siwalik sandstones and shales. The bands are thin and traceable for short distance only.

Copper

Auden notes numerous occurrences of copper formerly

mined at Pakhu (30.3, 79.2) and at Dhanpur (30.2, 79.1). He states that the working are now almost unrecognisable, but that there were probably two lodes situated in chlorite-phyllites and schistose quartzites, the southern lode having a footwall of siderilic limestone. A small load of chalcopyrite and barytes occurs near milestone 46/137 on the Hardwar-Badrinath pilgrim track (near Kandi Chatti 30.1, 78.9) along a fault gone in Simla slates.

A small load of copper occurs at about half a mile to the south of village Kurli (30.2, 79.1) associated with talc-chlorite-schist. Sample yielded 0.68 per cent copper and 1.61 per cent of lead. Copper ore also occur near Gwaldam.

Lead and Silver

Barrat metions ancient leadmines at the following localities:

At Patal (30.2, 79.1) at Dhanpur (30.2, 79.1) load is over 12 ft. in width, consisting of brownish quartz thickly impregnated with galena. The yield is said to be about 6.5 per cent of metal. At Jhak (30.1, 79.4) Quartz load occurs in clay slate with pockets of galena yielding 33 per cent of lead with some silver. A small deposit of lead has been reported from about 2.5 km. to the S.S.W. of Gwar (30.2, 79.1) where the ore occurs as small pockets on the walls of burrows in dolomitic lime stone of Garhwal series. On analysis samples of the ore show 12 to 14 per cent of lead.

Lignite

Deposit of the Ignite, reported to occur on the Lansdown road between the first and eighth miles from Kotdwara (29.7, 78.6), were examined in 1906 by Cottor and Brown. They were found to be mere lenticular patches not exceeding a few inches in length.

Limestone

Lime stone belonging to the Garhwal series is exposed between the villages of Tila (30.2, 79.1) and Gwar (30.2, 79.1).

There are practically unlimited reserves of limestone low in Mgo and high in Slo_2 occurring around Bhadsi (30.1, 78.3) and other places near Lansdowne. The Blaini limestone is well exposed near Lachhman Jhula (30.1, 78.3) and Kota (30.1, 78.4).

Mica

Greenish coloured mica with cracks and heavy stains occurs in pegmatites near Badni Khal (30.1, 79.1) Kunet (30.1, 79.1) and Majholi (30.1, 79.1).

Steatite

The occurrence of a white saponaceous stone at many places in Garhwal, but no definite locality is specified. The stone is said to be turned in to cups, etc., but being rather brittle it is little used.

Copper

At Pokhri (30°21': 79°12'), Dhanpur (30°13': 79°06')

Chaliopyrite

Near milestone 46/137 on the Hardwar-Badrinath pilgrim track near Kandi Chatti (30°03':78°55'), south-west branch of the main glacier (31°02':79°16')

Baryles

Near milestone 46/137 on the Hardwar-Badrinath pilgrim track near Kandi Chatti (30°03':78°55')

Lead

At Patal in Pargana DEWAL GARH (30°11', 79°03'), Gwar (30°14':79°07')

Galena

At JHAK (30°09':79°26')

Limestone

Limestone belonging to the Garhwal series is exposed between the village of TILA (30°12':79°06') and GWAR (30°14':79°07'), BHADSI (30°06':78°21') LACHHMAN JHULA (30°07':78°25')

Gypsum—Massive irregular pockets of gypsum interbedded with dolomitic limestone of the krol series are located to the south of Garur Chatti. The most important occurrence is near KHARARI CHATTI, KHEMSAR.

Iron—Garhwal—At NAGPUR, numerous lodes of micaceous hematite occur in association with quartz. Iron occurs at Sideritie replacemenjts of limestone at DONGRA and also at POKHARI. Pits of iron ore are concentrated in the *nalla* east of the ridge named PHUT PAIRI about 5 km S.E., of BENITHAL, also at BHARNAUN, LOWAGAON, MOKH, GHAT.

OBSERVATIONAL ORGANISATION

Surface observatories

This district lies under Meteorological sub-division, Hills of Uttar Pradesh, West (Now Uttaranchal). This facility is available at Pauri. The instrument lies in,

Latitude	:	30.1° North
Longitude	:	78.8° East
Altitude	:	1845 m
Date of starting	:	9-3-1982

DISASTROUS WEATHER EVENTS

Snowfall

On 4th January, 1981, there was heavy snowfall, some people reported killed and fruits crops severally damaged.

On 29 October, 1982, it was heavy, tourist and pilgrim disrupted.

On 16 January, 1983, it was heavy and vehicular triffic disrupted.

29 May, 1986, it was heavy, 12 person killed, Badrinath and Kedarnath shrines completely cut off from rest of the country.

11-14 December, 1986, it was heavy Badrinath, Kedarnath, Tungnath and Barpuch covered under 50 to 140 cm of snow.

On 29 December 1991, it was severe and several people died due to it.

From 28-30 December, 1996, it was severe and several people died due to it.

Hailstorm

On 29 May 1981, it was heavy, Normal life disrupted and severe damage to summer fruit crops.

Thunder-storm

On 16 April 1983, it was severe, 5 labourers died and 2 injured in a land-slide along Rishikesh-Badrinath road at Dungripath.

Floods and Heavy Rains

During July (4th week), 1985, it was flash flood in river Gola and 12 persons swept away in Gola river at Kotedwar.

On 9 July 1990, it was heavy rains, 70 persons died due to landslide at Tali village.

During 3 to 20 September, 1992, there was floods in Ganga and its tributaries, crop damaged, several roads blocked due to landslides disrupting vehicular traffic.

ARCHAEOLOGICAL SITE

At Tamkhani

Red ware of Sunga-Kushan assemblage.

DISTRIBUTION OF *SCHEDULED CASTE* POPULATION BY SEX (1991)

	Total	Males	Females
GARHWAL	92,261	45,822	46,439
Agariya	312	162	150
Badhik	16	8	8
Badi	170	101	69
Baheliya	17	6	11
Baiga	108	66	42
Baiswar	86	39	47
Bajaniya	2	0	2
Bajgi	101	50	51
Balahar	5	5	0
Balai	47	25	22
Balmiki	2,453	1,407	1,046
Bangali	26	13	13
Bansphor	19	9	10
Barwar	15	11	4
Basor	11	6	5
Bawariya	6	2	4
Beldar	85	38	47
Beriya	52	39	13
Bhantu	7	4	3
Bhuiya	12	9	3
Bhuyiar	120	50	70
Boria	2	2	0
Chamar, Dhusia, Jhusia, Jatava	4,415	2,549	1,866
Chero	67	47	20
Dabgar	16	7	9
Dhangar	19	11	8
Dhanuk	24	13	11
Dharkar	25	14	11
Dhobi	309	174	135
Dom	1,921	897	1,024
Domar	1	1	0
Dusadh	5	3	2
Ghasiya	8	4	4
Gond	19	9	10
Gual	4	3	1
Habura	1	0	1
Hari	11	7	4
Hela	1	0	1
Kanjar	139	63	76
Kapariya	16	8	8
Karwal	14	8	6
Khairaha	43	18	25
Kharwar (excluding Benbansi)	1	0	1
Khatik	164	91	73
Khorot	70	31	39
Kol	812	342	470
Kori	5,151	2,531	2,620
Korwa	4	3	1
Lalbegi	3	3	0
Majhwar	2	1	1
Mazhabi	26	14	12
Musahar	14	7	7
Nat	57	27	30
Parahiya	15	5	10
Pasi, Tarmali	249	123	126
Patari	21	12	9
Rawat	148	69	79
Saharya	24	11	13
Sanaurhiya	39	19	20
Sansiya	44	25	19
Shilpkar	74,022	36,271	37,751
Turaiha	57	27	30
Unclassified	608	322	286

DISTRIBUTION OF *SCHEDULED TRIBE* POPULATION BY SEX (1991)

	POPULATION		
	Total	Males	Females
		GARHWAL	
	1,503	862	641
Bhotia	204	137	67
Buksa	1,071	593	478
Jaunsari	1	0	1
Raji	23	10	13
Tharu	203	121	82
Unclassified	1	1	0

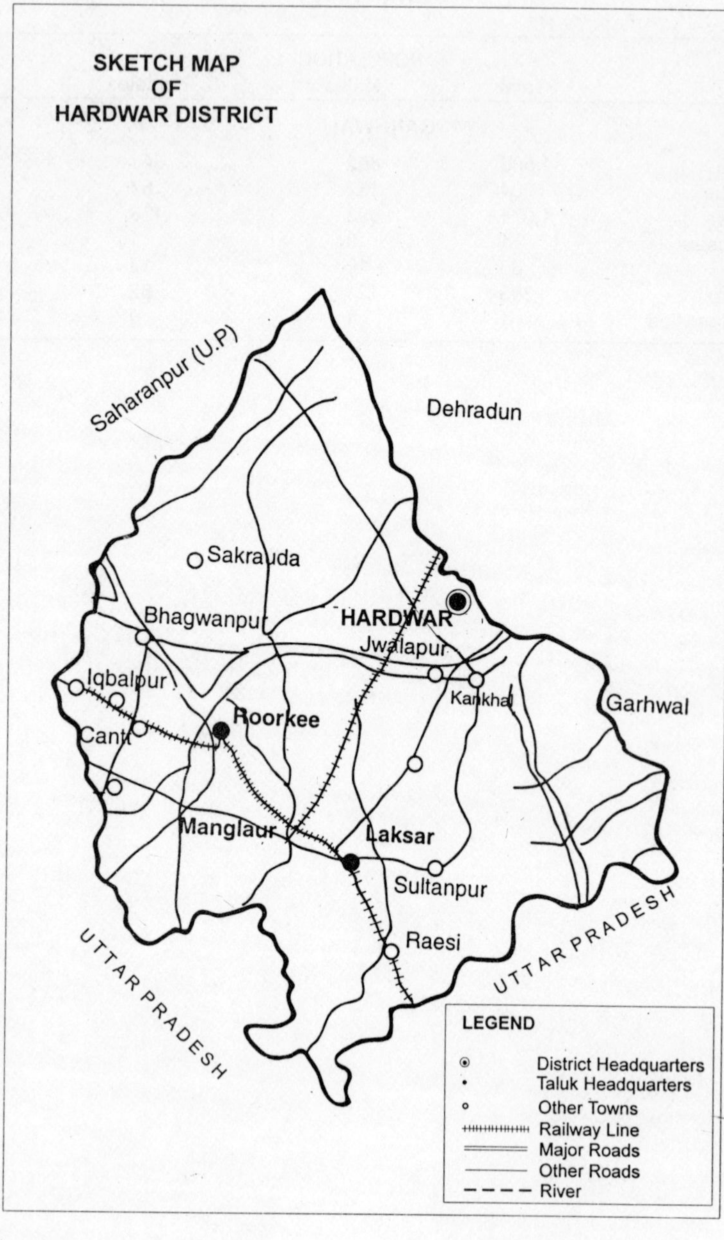
SKETCH MAP
OF
HARDWAR DISTRICT
Saharanpur (U.P)
Dehradun
Sakrauda
Bhagwanpur
HARDWAR
Jwalapur
Iqbalpur
Kankhal
Garhwal
Roorkee
Cantt
Manglaur
Laksar
Sultanpur
Raesi
UTTAR PRADESH
UTTAR PRADESH
LEGEND
District Headquarters
Taluk Headquarters
Other Towns
Railway Line
Major Roads
Other Roads
River

HARDWAR

LOCATION AND AREA

Latitude : 29.7° North to 30.1° North

Longitude : 77.9° East to 78.2° East

Altitude : 583 m

Hardwar district is spread over an area of 2360 sq. kms. and forms part of western region of Uttaranchal. It is bounded on the north by the districts of Saharanpur and Dehradun, on the east by the districts of Dehradun and Garhwal, on the south by the districts of Bijnor and Muzaffarnagar and on the west by the district of Saharanpur. The administrative headquarters is located at Hardwar town, which is a place of Hindu pilgrimage. In the age of puranas, it was named as Mayapuri. It was also known as Gangadwar and Topovan. More ancient than these names is Kapilothan, as it is said that the ancestors of Raja Bhagirath were burnt at this place by the curse of sage Kapila. For their salvation, he performed Tapa and brought Ganga from Heaven.

HISTORY

The district of Hardwar was carved out as a separate district during the decade 1981-91 due to the result bifurcation of Saharanpur district of Uttar Pradesh, alongwith the transfers of small portions of Muzaffarnagar and Bijnor districts to this newly created district. According to the said bifurcation, the only tehsil i.e. Roorkee was separated from Saharanpur district and formed a new district, being further divided into three tehsils *viz.*, Roorkee, Hardwar and Laksar. As stated above, the present district of Hardwar was a part of Saharanpur (except a few portions) its historical past is one and the same as of its parent district.

Hardwar is the principal gateway of Himalayan Tract, was probably known as Mayapur or Gangadowar and is associated with the earliest Hindu tradition and mythology. The tract was the part of ancient country of Kosala in the 6th century B.C. which became part of the Magadha empire under Nandas and then Mauryas. It came under the domination of Sungas in 184 B.C. with the fall of Mauryas and continued to be so till 72 B.C. The Kushan's domination followed next lasting till 226 A.D. It then passed to the Gupta empire which included the upper doab from 320 A.D. till at least 480 A.D. The incursions by white Huns, who could hold the country for a brief period, brought about the fall Gupta dynasty and no important power came on the scene till the rise of Harsh of Thansar who ruled many provinces of India from 606 to 647 A.D. The subsequent history "draws a blank unredeemable even by tradition till the establishment of Tomar kingdom of Delhi in the middle of 11th century replaced by Chauhans in 1151 AD.

POPULATION (GENERAL, SC/ST)

Total population of the district according to 2001 census is 1444213 persons, comprising of 773173 males and 671040 females. Rural population of the district is 998550 persons (531528 males and 467022 females) and urban population is 445663 persons (241645 males and 204018 females).

The Scheduled Castes and Scheduled Tribes population of the district as per 1991 Census are 242658 persons and 2026 persons respectively. The rural-urban breakup of this population is indicated below:

Rural	(i) Scheduled Castes	:	205386
	(ii) Scheduled Tribes	:	2004
Urban	(i) Scheduled Castes	:	37272
	(ii) Scheduled Tribes	:	22

The decennial growth rate of population of the district as a whole in relation to the state between the period 1981-1991 and 1991-2001 is presented below:

State/District	*Decennial growth rate of population (per cent)*	
	1981-91	*1991-2001*
Uttaranchal	24.23	19.20
Hardwar	28.44	26.30

LANGUAGES AND RELIGION

Hindi is the main language spoken in this district.

Religion-wise breakup of population as per 1991 Census (At District Level): Hindus: 768688, Muslims: 338146, Christians: 1990, Sikhs: 12822, Buddhists: 359, Jains: 2397, Other religions and persuasions: 17, Religion not stated: 69.

GEOGRAPHY AND PHYSICAL FEATURES

Lying immediately below the Siwalik range is known as ghar tract intersected by numerous torrents that drain rainy water into the Ganga, and its tributaries. This submontane belt, once forested, stands almost denuded with the great extension of tillage. This *ghar* consists of the series of high broken spurs. The great bulk of the district consists of plains, known as *Khadar* or low land, which comprises the broad alluvial valleys of Ganga. The Ganga Khadar varies greatly from place to place. There is considerable extent of forest and large expanses of open grass tract.

RIVERS, CANALS AND WATERWAYS

Ganga is the main river of this district. It enters the district at Hardwar. Traversing for some distance though the Siwaliks, it enters the plains and forms the eastern boundary of the district. It flows in Hardwar and for about twenty kms. south with great force through its stony bed. Thereafter it enters a sandy bed and its speed slows down. The other important river of the district is Solani.

TOWNS, VILLAGES AND AMENITIES

The district at present comprises of 3 tehsils and 6 Community Development Blocks. It has ten towns and 627 villages (503 inhabited villages and 124 uninhabited villages).

The urban population of the district as percentage of total population in the census 2001 is indicated below. It also shows the sex ratio (females per 1000 males) and density (population per sq. km.) in the urban population of the district in relation to the state:

State/ District	Urban population as percentage of total population	Sex ratio, (Females per 1000 males		Density (Population per sq. km.)	
	2001	1991	2001	1991	2001
Uttaranchal	25.59	936	964	133	159
Hardwar	30.85	846	868	485	612

Amenities

Number (with percentage) of villages having one or more amenities in the district as per 1991 Census is given below:

Sl. No.	Amenities	Number of inhabited villages	Percentage
1.	Education	367	72.96
2.	Medical	491	97.61
3.	Drinking Water	498	99.01
4.	Post and Telegraph	87	17.30
5.	Market/Hat	22	4.37
6.	Communications	175	34.79
7.	Approach by Pucca Road	406	80.72
8.	Power Supply	431	85.69

COMMUNICATIONS

The district is well connected by rail and road transports. Two broad gauge tracks pass through the district. These are Saharanpur to Moradabad connecting Roorkee and Laksar tehsil H.Qs. and another Laksar to Hardwar. No National Highway passes through the district. The State Highway no. 45 enters the district from Muzaffarnagar in southern side and goes to Rishikesh via Hardwar. In addition, there are other roads also which connect all the tehsils as well as Community Development Block headquarters.

AGRICULTURE AND IRRIGATION

Both *rabi* and *kharif* crops are sown in this district. The main *kharif* crops are paddy, maize and the main *rabi* crop is wheat, sugarcane is also extensively cultivated. The largest area is covered by wheat followed by sugarcane, paddy, maize, pulses groundnut and cotton. Production of sugarcane offer good commercial prospects. Irrigation plays an important role in increasing the agricultural production and in bringing more area under agriculture. Ganga canal passes through the district. Tubewells and canals are the main source of irrigation.

ANIMAL HUSBANDRY

Cattles, buffaloes, sheep and goats are the main livestock of this district. Efforts are being made to improve the breed of these animals. There are many veterinary dispensaries, livestock development centres and artificial insemination centres which look after the welfare of animals. The development of fishery has also gained importance. New fishery units are being setup, and several thousand were distributed.

INDUSTRIES

Industry has acquired a place of importance in the economy of the district. The establishment of a host of scientific and technical institutions as those of the prestigious Engineering University Roorkee, Training Centre for Ayurvedic System of medicines, Irrigation Research Centre etc. have induced the industrial development. The setting up of Bharat Heavy Electrical Limited and Indian Drugs and Formulations under public sector have also strengthened the industrial structure of the district. There are many sugarcane crushers producing gur and khandsari. There are also numerous small units engaged in producing medicines, iron and steel goods, construction materials, household goods, survey and drawing instruments and wood craft. The district is noted all over the country for the traditional wood carving industry and survey and drawing instruments. An industrial estate has been developed at Hardwar for all round development of industries in the district.

HANDICRAFTS

Jewellery works at Haridwar.

TRADE, COMMERCE AND EXPORT

The following table gives details on most important commodities manufactured, exported from and imported into the towns of this district. It also indicates the number of banks available in the towns:

Name of the towns	Most important commodity			
	Manufactured	Exported	Imported	Banks
1	2	3	4	5
Hardwar Urban Agglomeration:				
BHEL Ranipur	Electrical Machinery, Generator, Hydro Turbine	Electrical Machinery	Coal Steel, Oil-paints	2
Hardwar	Ayurvedic-medicines Timber, Tobacco	Ayurvedic-medicines Timber, Tobacco	Brass pots (Ganga jali), Mats, stone ware	15
Jhabrera	Bread, Khadi Cloth, Gur	Gur, Rice, Wheat	Cloth, Pulses, Spices	1
Londhaura	Boora, Gur, blankets, cloth, bricks	Blanket, cloth bricks	Wool, yarn,	1
Manglaur	Khadi, Cloth, Gur, Mustard oil	Mangoes, Rice, Gur	Yarn, Timber, Iron	3
Roorkee Urban Agglomeration:				
Roorkee	Survey and drawing Instruments, Acid, Iron goods	Survey and Drawing Instruments, Iron goods	Wood, Brass, Iron	10 10
Roorkee Cantt.	—	—	Wheat, Rice, Sugar	2

The Commodities manufactured are electrical machinery, survey and drawing instruments, ayurvedic medicines, boora, (brown sugar), gur, bread etc. The most important commodities exported are electrical machinery, ayurvedic medicines, gur, rice, blanket, and survey and drawing instruments. All the towns of this district have banking facilities.

TOURISM

Situated on the bank of Ganga which descends from the Siwalik hills, Hardwar is famous for its numerous temples, fairs and natural beauty. Following are the places of tourist interest in the district:

Har Ki Pauri. This is the most sacred bathing Ghat at Hardwar. Every 12 years the Kumbh and every 6 year Aradh Kumbh melas are held here. Arti of the Ganga performed everyday after sunset is worth-seeing.

Canal Centenary Bridge. This bridge near Har Ki Pauri commands a beautiful view of all the Ghats as well as canal.

Bhim Goda Tank. This tank is on the way to Rishikesh and is about 2.5 kms. from tourist office. It is said that while Pandavas were going to Himalayas through Hardwar Bhim made this tank with the blow of his knee.

Bhim Goda Canal Head Works. It is about half km. from the canal centenary bridge. The northern Ganga Canal diverts from this place. The area has been developed into beautiful gardens.

Sapt Rishi Ashram and Sapt Sarovar. It is situated at a distance of about 6 kms. from tourist office on the way to Rishikesh. It is said that the Ganga had split herself in seven currents at this point so that the sapt (seven) Rishis worshipping there would not be disturbed.

Sadhubela. At about 5 kms. from tourist office towards Rishikesh, it is a newly built Ashram.

Daksh Mahadev Temple and Sati Kund Kankhal. It is about 3.5 kms. from tourist office, Hardwar. The mythological story about this place is that Daksh Prajapati, father of Sati (Lord Shiva's first wife) performed Yagya at this place. Daksh Prajapati did not invite Lord Shiva and Sati felt insulted. Sati burnt herself in Yagya kund. Kankhal is one of the five sacred places around Hardwar. The five tirthas are—Ganga, Kushawart, Bilwa Tirtha, Neel Parvat and Kahkhal.

Mansa Devi Temple. 3 kms. from tourist office situated at Bilwa Parbat. To go to this temple, Uran Khatola (Ropeway) is available.

Chandi Devi. 6 kms. from Hardwar, it is situated on Neel Parbat on the other bank of the main Ganga river. One has to trek 3 kms. on the hill to reach the Chandi Devi temple. The temples of Gauri Shankar, Neeleshwar Mahadeo and Anjani Devi are at the close distance to Chandi Devi temple on the hill.

Other Temples of Hardwar. Shri Gorakhnath temple and Gupha, Bilkeswar Mahadev temple Bilkeshwar, Kal Bhairav temple, Gita Bhawan, Maya Devi temple, Vishnu Bhawan, Bhola Giri Ashram, Bhairau Nath temple of Pashupati Mahadev, Mano Kamna Siddh temple, Ganesh Ghat, Mayapur Mano Kamna Siddh-Hanuman temple, Awadhoot Mandir Jwalpur Rd., Manar Kalyan Ashram, Kankhal, Narayani Shila, Mayapur.

Solani Bridge. This bridge over the Solani river is a great feat of engineering. It is situated about half a kilometre away from Roorkee towards Hardwar. The Ganga Canal flows above the bridge and the Solani river below it. Drops of water keep on seeping down through the bridge. It is said that the bridge will survive so long as water will keep on seeping down through it. A little down the canal and the river flow at the same level after which the Ganga Canal flows below the river.

Central Building Research Institute. This Central Government Institute located in Roorkee undertakes studies in improvement of building designs and construction materials.

Roorkee University. This is one of the famous engineering institutions of India. Despite the large increase in the number of institutions in the country, this University still remains one of the foremost among them.

MUSEUM

Archaeological Museum, Haridwar.

Ayurvedic College Museum, Haridwar.

Zoological Museum, Haridwar.

HOTELS

Sagar Ganga Resorts, (Government approved), Mayapur.

Access: 1 km from Railway station, 1 km from Bus stand.

Rooms: 10

Hotel Classic Residency.

Access: 1.5 km from Railway station and 1.5 km from Bus stand.

Hotel Mid Town, Railway Road, Haridwar.

Access: 23 kms. from Airport, 1/2 km. from Railway station and 1/2 km. from Bus stand.

FAIRS AND FESTIVALS

Important fairs and festivals organised in different parts of the district are mentioned below:

Viswat Sankranti, Moltari, Bishu, Mewi, Thala, Odas Jakhandi Devta-ka-Mela, Jattar, Bhadra Kali Devi-ka-Mela, Jagra, Jatra, Thaul, Davrana, Molthat, Tansa, Tunger, Chhilora, Durwashtmi, Dewlang, Gangani, Dhantari Pujargaon, Bishtpatti Nagun, Gauri Ravantal, Barsali Garh, Gajnakhathur Thati Ramoli, Gajnakhathur Narpar, Fulali, Bhadranj, Baliraj, Kishan Mela, Bishwat Sankranti, Nautha, Naumi, Nanda Devi, Gauchar, Shivratri, Ansi, Nagnath, Madmeshwar, Makrayan, Nanda Astmi, Chifala, Mikutia Lhamsel, Jauljibi, Kartika Purnima, Tamanauli, Thal, Bikhuwat Sankranti, Kalinag, Durbashtmi, Sanai Khola, Nag fair, Berinag, Dyochla, Tania Nauli, Aathu, Deokali Tripura Devi, Nandashtmi, Kotgari, Baraun, Pandan, Maha Kali, Sanas Khola Koteshwar, Bashuki Nag, Sasauli Mool Sirakot, Panch Marh, Shera Ghat, Rameshwar, Thal Parao, Kedar Sila, Koteshwar, Patal Bhubneshwar, Lory, Chauku, Chharaudeo, Mostmanu, Thelkedar, Dhaj, Daulaikh Lechara, Chaupakhiya Bhadrika, Chandrika Ghat, Hanshaishwar, Pancheswar, Chamba Thoulu, Gajja Thoulu, Dharu Mela, Suri-ka-Mela, Bandwal Gaon, Agram Thoulu, Churiya Kheti Thoulu, Kamand Thoulu, Badsahahee Thoulu, Jamti-ka-Mela, Thattud-ka-Mela, Lalotan-ka-Mela, Khyarsi-ka-Mela, Moldhar-ka-Mela, Nagthan-ka-Mela, Takrauli-ka-mela, Srikot-ka-mela, Kali Devi, Jakh-ka-Mela, Panchbadi-ka-Mela, Surkanda, Bhind Maun-ka-Mela, Manj. Maun-ta-mela, Chhanan gaon-ka-mela, Chham, Jakhni, Kasyan, Khandogi, Aginisan, Godolia, Pankhal, Pilkhi, Kothyara, Gali, Sem Mukhan, Sri Kunjapuri Yatra, Pali Thoulu, Digoli Thoulu,

Bikhot, Baisakh Thoulu, Fateld, Nagela Devta, Mald, Dangchaura Thoulu, Thoulu, Danda Thoulu, Pauri-ka-Thaulu, Kalila Pir, Basiakha Thoulu, Hollyag, Nagendra Devta, Chandra Badni, Banjagri, Jagdajat, Chameshwar Mahadev, Basant Panchmi, Kendar-ka-Mela, Ram Naumi, Jaor Dali, Khirsu, Khudu-ka-Mela, Dewalgarh-ka-Mela, Sabdar Khal, Jhankar, Mundeshwar, Janam Ashtmi, Baikunth Chaturdashi, Bindeshwari alias Binsar, Mansar, Makar-ka-Mela, Vishwat Sankranti, Ekeshwar, Nand Khal, Vaisakhi, Kalinka Bhaun Devi, Nausin Devi, Bungi Devi, Vaisakhi Devi, Bharoli Khal, Dabrisain, Syunsi Mela, Ladali, Kathuliya Mahadev, Dewarari Devi, Kola, Bileswar Mahadev, Kandiya, Melkhal, Brikand, Bhana, Devi, Pand, Banjya Devi, Kunjoli, Somnath, Dhauntiyal-ka-Mela, Bandun, Malla Dhauntiyal, Sangla Koti Mela, Kalika Devi, Ghandiyal Bindhar-ka-Mela, Muchhelgaon, Semal Sain (Bhairob), Bhumi-ka-Mela, Kandai, Mahargaon-ka-Mela, Pharula, Fatehpur-ka-Mela, Chauksera-ka-Mela, Sawani, Binsar, Gindi-ka-Mela, Dangla, Badri Nath, Makar Sankranti.

EDUCATION

According to 2001 Census, the population of total literates (excluding the population in the age group of 0-6 years) is 1444213 persons. Of these, 773173 are males and 671040 are females. In the rural areas of the district 998550 persons (531528 males and 467022 females) are literates and in urban areas 445663 persons 241645 males and 204018 females) are litrates. The rates of literacy of this population to the total population, excluding 0-6 years age group according to 2001 Census is shown below:

1991			*2001*		
Persons	*Males*	*Females*	*Persons*	*Males*	*Females*
47.97	59.28	34.37	64.60	75.06	52.60

There are as many as 367 villages accounting for 72.96 per cent of the total number of inhabited villages in the district where educational facility of one type or other is found. Primary and Middle Schools are found in almost all towns. As regards other educational institutions, the following table gives details on various types of such institutions available in the towns of this district, inclduing the number of Public Libraries:

Name of the towns	*Educational Institutions*	*Stadia*	*Public Libraries including reading rooms*
Hardwar Urban Agglomeration:			
BHEL Ranipur	Higher Secondary/ Intermediate School (1) Secondary/Matriculation School (3), Junior Secondary and Middle School (3)	–	PL:3
Hardwar	Arts and Science College (2), Ayurvedic Medical college (1), Higher Secondary/Intermediate School (8), Secondary/Matriculation School (10), Junior Secondary and Middle School (17).	–	PL:7 RR:5
Jhabrera	Higher Secondary/ Intermediate School (1), Secondary/Matriculation School (1), Junior Secondary and Middle School (1)	–	–
Landhaura	Junior Secondary and Middle School (2)	–	–
Mánglaur	Higher Secondary/ Intermediate School (2), Secondary/Matriculation School (2), Junior Secondary and Middle School (5)	–	PL:1 RR:1
Roorkee Urban Agglomeration:			
Roorkee	Arts College (2), Science College (1), Engineering College (1), Polytechnics (1), Higher Secondary/ Intermediate School (5)	–	PL:1

COLLEGES

Kanya Gurukula Mahavidyalaya, Haridwar.
Ved & Arts College, Haridwar.

Science College, Haridwar.

Roorkee University Roorkee, Established 1949.

(Above named colleges belong to Gurukula Kangri Vishvidyalaya, Established 1900).

MEDICAL

Medical facility of one type or other is available in 491 villages which constitute 97.61 per cent of the total number of inhabited villages. The following table provides town-wise breakup of medical institutions available in the towns alongwith bed facility:

Name of The towns	*Medical institution*	*(with number of beds)*
Hardwar Urban Agglermeration		
BHEL Ranipur	Hospital (1)	150
	Dispensary (8)	–
Hardwar	Dispensary (6)	–
	Hospital (8)	246
	T.B. Cliniic (1)	50
Jhabrera	Dispensary (1)	–
	Family Planning Centre (1)	–
Landhaura	Hospital (1)	–
	Dispensary (1)	4
Manglapur	Hospital (1)	–
	Family Planning Centre (1)	–
	Dispensary (1)	12
Roorkee Urban Agglomeration:		
Roorkee	Hospital (3)	94
	Dispensary (2)	2
	Family Planning Centre (1)	2
Roorkee Cantt.	Dispensary (1)	–

NEWSPAPERS

Hawk, an English daily, published from Haridwar and its circulation is 79,000.

Badri Vishal, Hindi daily, published from Haridwar, the circulation is 51750.

Atm Satta, Hindi weekly from Haridwar.

Khojpuran Samachar, Hindi weekly from Haridwar.

ADMINISTRATION

(i) Administrative Divisions:

Tehsils: Roorkee, Hardwar, Lashkar.

Community Development Blocks: Bhagwanpur, Roorkee, Narsan, Bahadrabad, Laksar, Khanpur.

Towns with their Population, Urban Status and Literates (2001)

City/Town	*Urban Status*	*Population*			*Literates*		
		Person	*Male*	*Female*	*Person*	*Male*	*Female*
BHEL	ITS	43252	23052	20200	35092	19915	15177
Dhandera	CT	15297	7984	7313	8434	4939	3495
Hardwar	MB	175010	94650	80360	122572	70971	51601
Jhabrera	NP	9378	5007	4371	5331	3241	2090
Laksar	NP	18240	9850	8390	18324	7382	4942
Landaura	NP	16022	8659	7363	5707	3644	2063
Manglaur	MB	42782	22600	20182	15645	9674	5971
Mohanpur	CT	8700	4525	4175	5875	3399	2476
Roorkee	MB	97064	51275	45789	74248	41312	32936
Roorkee	CB	17747	12586	5161	15516	11592	3924

(ii) Parliamentary Constituencies Along Assembly Segments (1996):

No. & Name of Parliamentary Constituency: 85-Hardwar (SC).

No. & Name of Assembly Segments of Hardwar Parliamentary Constituency which lies within the jurisdiction of Hardwar district

Assembly Constituency: 19. Bhagwanpur (SC)

TEHSIL—ROORKEE

Bhagwanpur—1. Banjarewala Grant; 2. Nokara grant; 3. Dolatpurhajratpur urf Budhawashaid; 4. Fatehullapur urf Telpura; 5. Aurangjebpur; 6. Kheri Shikohpur; 7. Kheri Shikohpur J.M.; 8. Sikroda-I; 9. Sikroda-II; 10. Majahidpursatiwala; 11. Ebrahimpur Masahi; 12. Habibpur Niwada; 13. Manak Majra; 14. Jalalpur Dada; 15. Hasanpur Madanpur; 16. Chaparsherafganpur; 17. Latifpur Khubbanpur; 21. Bhagwanpur; 22. Hallumajra; 23. Dariyapur Dayalpur. ***Roorkee***—11. Gumawala; 12. Emlikheradharampur; 17. Pirankaliyar; 18.

Dhanori; 19. Dolatpur. **Forest Area.** 3. Forest Range F-1; Mohand; 4. Forest Range F-2; Dholkhand.

Assembly Constituency: 20. Iqbalpur (SC)

TEHSIL—ROORKEE

Iqbalpur—1. Delna; 2. Harjolijhoja; 3. Thausipur; 4. Mahmudpur; 5. Paniyala Chandapur; 6. Iqbalpur Kamelpur; 7. Madhopur Hajratpur; 8. Nanhera Anantpur; 9. Karondi; 10. Saliyar Shalhapur; 18. Sikandarpur Bhaswal; 19. Sirchandi; 20. Khelpur Nasrulapur; 24. Ruhalki Dayalpur; 25. Kunja Bhadarpur; 26. Chudiyala Mohanpur; 27. Bhalsawagaj; 28. Bindukarak; 29. Behedeki Saidabad; 30. Manakpur Aadampur. ***Manglor***—19. Jabrera.

Assembly Constituency: 21. Roorkee

TEHSIL—ROORKEE

Roorkee—13. Mahamadpur Panda; 14. Rampur; 15. Roorkee; 16. Malakpur Latifpur. ***Urban Area***—Jhabrera NAC; Landhura NAC; 2. Roorkee MB; 3. Roorkee Cantonment.

Assembly Constituency: 22. Landhaura (SC)

TEHSIL—ROORKEE

Manglor—5. Mundlana; 6. Harjoli Jatt; 7. Kagwali; 8. Harchand Pur; 9. Mo. Pur Jat; 10. Keda Jatt; 14. Nakibpur urf Ghosipura. ***Roorkee***—20. Baderirajputan; 21. Bhounri; 22. Margobpurdidaheri; 23. Danderi Khawajgipur; 24. Belda; 24. Rajpur Mustafabad urf Gadharona; 25. Landhora; 25. Todakalyanpur; 26. Sikarpur; 27. Bijholi; 28. Dandhera; 29. Jorasi

Assembly Constituency: 23. Manglor (SC)

TEHSIL—ROORKEE

Manglor—1. Libbarheri; 2. Manglaur; 3. Bhagwanpur; Chandanpur; 4. Banhera Tanda; 11. Kalyanpur urf Narsan; Kalan; 12. Nagalasalaru; 13. Tikola Kalan; 15. Lakhnota; 16. Jhabrerikalan; 17. Sherpur Khelmau; 18. Kotwalalampur; 20. Lathardevahun; 21. Thitkikawadpur; 22. Kurdi; 23. Udalheri.

Assembly Constituency: 24. Laksar

TEHSIL—LAKSAR

Khanpur—1. Gordhanpur; 2. Raghunathpur urf Baiawali;

3. Abdipur; 4. Ebrahimpur; 5. Gidhawali; 6. Jogawala; 7. Tugalpur; 8. Prahladpur; 9. Madabela; 10. Lalchandwala; 18. Dabkikalan; 19. Akodaorangjeb Pur; 20. Dahadekidhanamajahidpur; 21. Natwala Saidabad; 22. Raisi. ***Laksar***—1. Athelbujurg; 2. Maharajpur Kalan; 3. Ismaielpur; 4. Khadanja Kutubpur; 9. Akodamukarmatpur; 11. Laksar; 12. Sidhadu; 13. Ladpur Kalan; 14. Dosani.

Assembly Constituency: 25. Hardwar

TEHSIL—HARDWAR

Urban Area: Hardwar NP.

Assembly Constituency: 26. Bahadrabad

Jwalapur—1. Sekhupur urf Kankhal; 2. Ahmadpur Karach 3. Jwalapur; 4. Bhadrabad; 5. Bodahedimohiudeenpur; 6. Atmalpur Bongla; 7. Rohalki Kishanpur; 8. Mirpur Mawajpur; 9. Salempur Mahdod 1; 10. Salempur Mahdod 2; 11. Aannekihetampur; 12. Aurangabad; 13. Garh; 14. Shivdaspur urf Teliwala; 15. Kotamuradnagar; 16. Sohalpur Sikroda; 17. Daluwala; 18. Shadevpur Shawajpur; 19. Mukarpur; 20. Alawalpur; 21. Ahamadpur Grant; 22. Dadupur Govindpur. **Forest Area:** Forest Area; **Urban Area:** BHEL Ranipur NAC; Jwalapur University (NAC).

Assembly Constituency: 27. Laldhang (SC)

TEHSIL—HARDWAR

Ferupur Ramkhera. 23. Bahadarpur Jatt; 24. Nasirpur Khurd; 25. Hardevpurshadev urf Ranimajra; 26. Padartha urf Dhanpura; 27. Ferupur Ramkhera; 28. Jamalpur Kalan; 29. Katarpur Alipur; 30. B. Pur S. Pur Bhattipur; 31. Mohamadpur Kunhari; 32. B. Pur A. Pur urf Ibrahimpur; 33. B. Pur A. Pur urf Ikkad 34. Nasirpur Kalan; 35. Bhogpur I; 36. Bhogpur II; 37. Kangdi; 38. Rasulpur Mithi Beri; 39. Laldhang; 40. Gandhi Khatta; **Forest Area:** Forest Range F 3; Hardwar.

TEHSIL—LAKSAR

Laksar. 5. Dargahapur; 6. Khanpur; 7. Bukkanpur; 8. Sultanpur Aadampur; 10. Rampur Raighati; 15. Niranjanpur; 16. Bhikkampurjitpur; 17. Bakkarpur. ***Raipur.*** 23. Badripur; 24. Doodhli; 25. Nakraunda; 27. MakhamGrant-I; 28. MarkhamGrant-II; 30. Raipur; 31. Mianwala; 32. Nathuwa Wala. ***Villages.*** Chakshahnagar; Shahnagar. **Forest Area:** F 8

Lachhiwala; ***Raipur.*** Clement town Cantt. ***Urban Area.*** Dehradun NP Ward 5; Doiwala; Nagarpanchayat Parishad

Hardwar was in Dehradun Lok Sabha seat from 1957 to 1971. The community wise break up (OBE) in Hardwar is Muslims (26 per cent), Scheduled Castes (28 per cent), Gujjars (6 per cent) and Sainis/Malis, Kahars, Brahmins, Rajputs and Vaishyas around (4 per cent) each. Jats are also present in small numbers. Chamars (24 per cent) are most numerous among the Scheduled Castes.

MINERALS AND ORES

Qurtz: Pebbles and cobbles of quartzite derived from conglomerates occur in large quantities at Motichur (30.1, 78.2).

OBSERVATIONAL ORGANISATION

Surface Observatories

The district of Hardwar lies under meterological sub-division, Plains of Uttar Pradesh, West (Now Uttaranchal). This instrument facility is available at two places in Roorkee.

The instrument lies in

Latitude : 29.85° North
Longitude : 77.9° East
Altitude : 274 m
Date of starting : 1-1-1863

Latitude : 29.85° North
Longitude : 77.9° East
Altitude : 261 m
Date of starting : 1954

Agricultural Meteorological Station

This facility is availahle at Roorkee. The instrument lies in

Latitude : 29.91° North
Longitude : 78.1° East
Altitude : 275 m
Date of starting : 29-10-1968

Hydrometeorological Stations for Climatological Purposes

This facility is available at Hardwar. The instrument lies in

Latitude	:	29.95° North
Longitude	:	78.16° East
Altitude	:	583 m
Date of starting	:	11-4-1976

DISASTROUS WEATHER EVENTS

Snowfall

From 28-30 December, 1996, it was severe and several person died due to it.

Floods and Heavy Rains

In July 1993, there was flood in the Ganges and its tributaries, several persons died cattleheads perished, agricultural land submerged.

DISTRIBUTION OF *SCHEDULED CASTE* POPULATION BY SEX (1991)

	POPULATION		
	Total	Males	Females
HARDWAR			
All Scheduled Castes	2,42,658	1,31,652	1,11,006
Agariya	112	66	46
Badhik	16	9	7
Badi	86	53	33
Baheliya	41	14	27
Baiswar	4	3	1
Bajaniya	6	2	4
Bajgi	1	1	0
Balahar	91	50	41
Balai	26	13	13
Balmiki	19,880	10,619	9,261
Bangali	372	180	192
Bansphor	22	18	4
Barwar	47	41	6
Basor	3	1	2
Bawariya	18	14	4
Beldar	36	16	20
Beriya	1	1	0
Bhantu	44	30	14
Bhuiya	77	40	37
Bhuyiar	433	259	174
Boria	38	27	11
Chamar, Dhusia, Jhusia, Jatava	2,11,898	1,14,833	97,065
Chero	202	111	91
Dabgar	48	33	15
Dhangar	105	58	47
Dhanuk	15	7	8
Dharkar	164	94	70
Dhobi	2,519	1,389	1,130
Dom	26	19	7
Domar	10	6	4
Dusadh	286	159	127
Gharami	26	17	9
Ghasiya	18	13	5
Gond	33	20	13
Gual	31	25	6
Habura	1	1	0
Hari	24	14	10
Hela	1	1	0
Kalabaz	21	18	3
Kanjar	479	285	194
Kapariya	3	3	0
Karwal	20	14	6
Khairaha	1	0	1
Kharwar (excluding Benbansi)	4	0	4
Khatik	1,281	747	534
Khorot	8	5	3
Kol	46	23	23
Kori	1,480	882	598
Korwa	23	10	13
Lalbegi	9	9	0
Majhwar	36	7	29
Mazhabi	59	34	25
Musahar	11	7	4
Nat	23	10	13
Pankha	3	2	1
Parahiya	4	3	1
Pasi, Tarmali	746	439	307
Patari	31	13	18
Rawat	94	59	35
Sanaurhiya	3	2	1
Sansiya	550	303	247
Shilpkar	98	68	30
Turaiha	9	5	4
Unclassified	855	447	408

DISTRIBUTION OF *SCHEDULED TRIBE* POPULATION BY SEX (1991)

	POPULATION		
	Total	Males	Females
	HARDWAR		
	2,026	1,128	898
Buksa	671	368	303
Jaunsari	3	1	2
Raji	1	1	0
Tharu	1,349	756	593
Unclassified	2	2	0

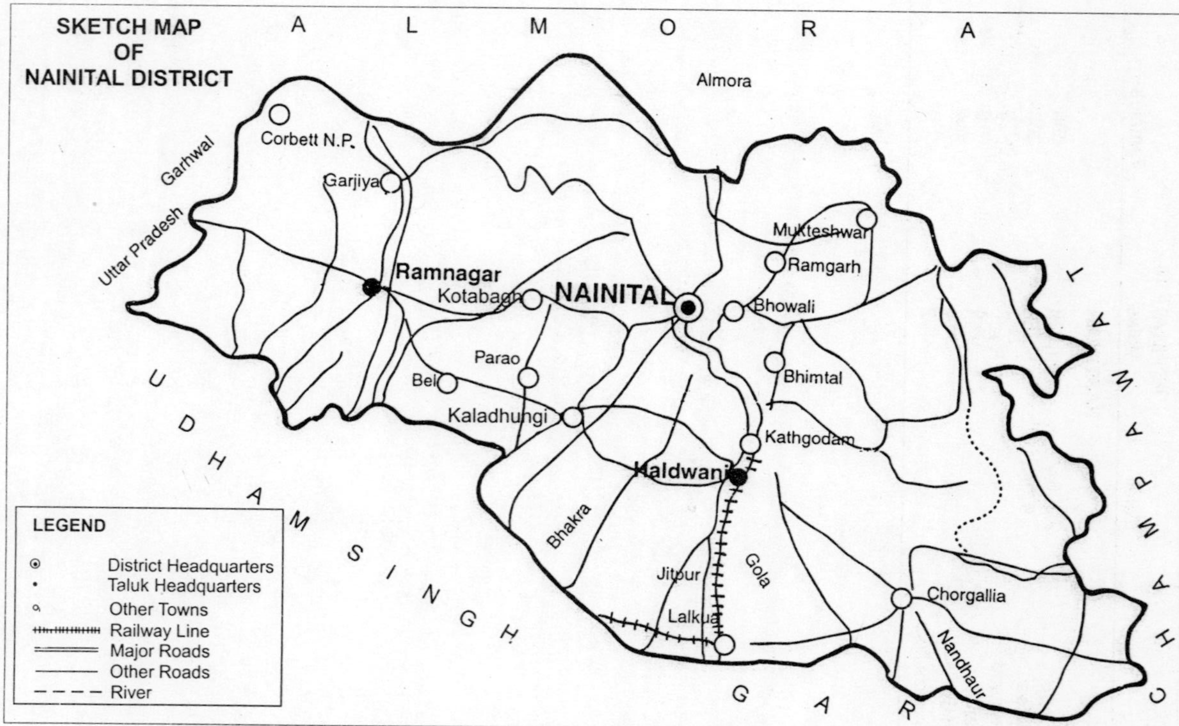
SKETCH MAP
OF
NAINITAL DISTRICT
A L M O R A
Almora
Corbett N.P.
Garjiya
Garhwal
Uttar Pradesh
Ramnagar
Kotabagh
NAINITAL
Mukteshwar
Ramgarh
Bhowali
Bhimtal
Parao
Bel
Kaladhungi
Kathgodam
Haldwani
Bhakra
Jitpur
Gola
Lalkua
Chorgallia
Nandhaur
T A W A P M A H C
U D H A M S I N G H
G A R
LEGEND
District Headquarters
Taluk Headquarters
Other Towns
Railway Line
Major Roads
Other Roads
River

NAINITAL

LOCATION AND AREA

Latitude : 28.8° North to 29.6° North

Longitude : 78.85° East to 80.1° East

Altitude : 1953 m.

The district of Nainital comprises of hills and is bounded on the north by Almora on the west by district Garhwal, Bijnor and on the south by Uddham Singh Nagar, on the east by Champawat district. It is irregular in shape and occupies the southern and south-eastern portion of the Kumaon division. This district has a total area of 3853 sq. km.

The district headquarters is located at Nainital.

HISTORY

Consisting of widely varying topographical features—the hill strips and the *Bhabhar* and highly heterogenous demographic and racial characteristics, this land of Nainital at the southern rim of Himalayas was never in entirely under a single ruler except for a brief interval of time. The history of the district in its tortuous course is the saga of relentless struggles among the various tribes for domination. It is believed that the earliest settlers in this hilly and sub-montane area belonged to the hill tribes—Asuras, Rikeshas and Nagas. Kiratas, Kulindas and Khasas came next subjugating the earlier settlers and holding the area under their sway. The later part of the history of these tracts is dominated by the account of strifes for domination among the various ethnic groups, mainly Khasiyas, Katyuris and Chands. Khasiya rebellion was a constant nightmare for the Chanda rulers especially to Bina Chand. Khasiyas potential for prompting strife forced the new rulers in defensive. Trilokchand built a fort at Bhim Tal, Kirat Chand gave a staggering blow to the Katyuris in 1488, and his period of apogee was marked with the possession of the entire district. Khawas Khan, in 1541 inflicted worst destruction of royal territories in the reign of Manik Chand. Balo Kalyan Chand exterminated enemies from the fort of Khagmara, the present day Almora and Bhabhar by Hussain Khan Tukriya. Badauni corroborates above fact. Kalyan Chand swept Rudrapur and Kashipur.

Gurkha invasion led by Amar Singh Thapa in 1795, paved the way, for their suzerainty over hilly tracts and *bhabhar* areas of the district. At that time the district was an attraction to the British and an imminent war ensued between them in 1818. After the war, the district went into a popular revolt in 1857 which was quelled by the Britishers by notorious killing of mutineers at Phansigadera. On 15th October 1981, the district was carved out. On 29th September 1995, the district of Nainital was bifurcated.

POPULATION (GENERAL, SC/ST)

Total population of the district according to 2001 census is 762912 persons comprising 400336 males and 362576 females. Rural population of the district is 493126 persons (456642 males and 236484 females) and urban population is 269786 persons (143694 males and 126092 females).

The decennial growth rate of population of the district as a whole in relation to the state between the pe..od 1981-1991 and 1991-2001 is presented below:

State/District	*Decennial growth rate of population (per cent)*	
	1981-91	*1991-2001*
Uttaranchal	24.23	19.20
Nainital	30.01	32.88

LANGUAGES AND RELIGION

Main languages spoken in the district are Hindi, Bengali, Punjabi and Urdu.

Main religions of the district are Hindus, Muslims, Christians, Sikhs, Buddhist and Jains.

GEOGRAPHICAL AND PHYSICAL FEATURES

The district is divided into two main regions (i) Hilly region and (ii) Bhabhar region.

The tehsil Nainital mostly comprises the hilly region of the district. The height of the hills ranges from 1800' to 8000' from the sea level. The general elevation of the outer Himalayas in this region is about 6500' 'from the sea level, while the tallest summits attain heights of over 8000'. The chief mountain range is the Gagar. This region is covered with forests. Snowfall on the hill tops is a common occurrence during the winter.

The Bhabar region along the foot of the hills is a stretch of a narrow belt of the country, only eight to twenty four kilometres in breadth. It is called Bhabar because of being a water-less belt of forest. The tehsil of Haldwani comprises the waterless belt of forest land. It's elevation from the sea level is between 1200' and 1800'. Although extremely hot in summer, the climate of this region becomes cool and pleasant during winter.

The hill sides have a very thin covering of alluvial top soil. The best irrigated lands are known as *Talaon* and the uplands when not artificially irrigated as *Uparaon.* The tracts having imperfect irrigation are designated as *Panchar.* The Bhabar consists of a new deposit of alluvium over a mass of boulders and gravel.

In the forests below the hills and those clothing the outer spurs, the most common and at the same time the most valuable trees are the *sal* and *shisham.* Next to these, come *khair,* is *deodar, dhauri, haldu,* and *sain.* These are found in places up to a height of 3000 feet. There are four species of *dhak* found in the district, *viz.,* the *banj, kharsu, tilonj* and *nirai.* The *banj* found in all parts of the upper hills is the commonest. Flourishing at high elevations, *kharsu,* found in Nainital and several other places in great abundance. The *niarj* occurs near Nainital and a few other places, the *chir* is found throughout the Kumaon division from 2500 feet upwards. Other trees of the district are of little importance. Bamboos form the most important portion of the minor forest produce of all forest divisions. The fruit trees of the district fall into two main classes (i) the wild fruit trees and (ii) the cultivated ones. Among the former are, walnut, pomegranate, wild pear, apple, cherry and *jamun.* The latter are numerous, the most common being mango and then come apple, pear, cherry, citron, lime, orange, guava, peaches, apricot and plum.

RIVERS, CANALS AND WATERWAYS

Except the Kosi, none of the rivers in this district has its origin in the snowy heights of the Himalayas. The Kosi alone rises in the north of the district in the hilly country of Almora. All other rivers spring from the lower ranges of hills well within Nainital itself or Garhwal. The hilly country, and specially the Chhakhata pargana contains several lakes of great size and beauty, the chief among them being Nainital, Bhim Tal, Malwa Tal, Sat Tal, Naukutchiya Tal and Khurpa Tal. There are a number of smaller lakes also such as Sukha Tal, Sariya Tal, Khuriya Tal etc. These lakes form one of the most remarkable and beautiful features of the lower Himalayas in Kumaon.

TOWNS, VILLAGES AND AMENITIES

The district at present comprises of 4 tehsils and 8 towns.

The urban population of the district as percentage of total population in the census years 2001 is indicated below. It also shows the sex ratio (females per 1000 males) and density (population per sq. km.) in the urban population of the district in relation to the State:

State/ District	*Urban population as percentage of total population*	*Sex ratio, (females per 1000 males)*		*Density (Population per sq. km.)*	
	2001	*1991*	*2001*	*1991*	*2001*
Uttaranchal	25.59	936	964	133	159
Nainital	35.36	881	906	149	198

Amenities

Number of villages having one or more amenities in the district are Education, Medical, Drinking water, Post and telegraph, Market and Hat, Communications, Approach by Pucca Road and Power supply.

COMMUNICATIONS

The Bhabhar areas is served by metregauge railway tracks,

i.e. (i) Moradabad-Kashipur-Ramnagar and (ii) Bareilly-Kichha-Haldwani-cum-Kathgodam. As regards road communications, state Highways and other district roads inter-connect the tehsil headquarters, Community Development Block headquarter and important towns with each other. No national highway passes through the district. The hilly tracts lack communications infrastructure in the district.

AGRICULTURE AND IRRIGATION

Agriculture has a commanding role in economy. Important harvests are *kharif* and *rabi*. *Zaid* has negligible area in the district. The most important crop is wheat that is cropped in the largest area which constitutes 46 per cent cf the total area under foodgrains and 34 per cent of total cropped area. The second important crop is paddy. Maize, *madua,* barley, sawan and jowar, bajra are other main foodgrains in that order. Masoor, gram and urad are the main pulse crops which hardly occupy a place of importance. Sugarcane and potato are cash crops of the district. More land is accruing to cultivation of potato after every year.

Modern methods of farming in vogue in *Bhabar* regions are on the forefront for their use of improved seeds, fertilizers, pesticides, insecticides and modern implements. University of Agriculture at Pantnagar in the district is a renouned institution for researches in agriculture, that started Green Revolution. *Tarai-Bhabhar* region is fastly becoming nucleous of this revolution in the state. University is rendering pioneering services by holding an annual agricultural fair and by extending help in farming. The processing problem is to secure hilly areas for horticulture uses since the production of *madua* and *jhnugarb* (small millets) are uneconomical. In Haldwani a soyabeen processing plant is being set up so that the farmers could take up the cultivation of this crop for better economic returns and nutrition. Small holdings are a hurdle in production. The places of terrace cultivation in hills are peculiar for these.

The irrigation network include government canal, tubewells and pumping sets in the non-hilly tracts. The hilly tracts are served by tanks (hauz) and channels (gul). There is a canal head at Kathgodam at Gaula river which irrigates the major part of *Bhabhar* areas. •

ANIMAL HUSBANDRY

Animal husbandry is an important source of income for the rural people. Cows, buffaloes, sheep are main livestock of the district. The production of milk per milch animal is very low. All most every household spin and weave the wool of their indigenous sheep. Many veterinary institutions are functioning in the district.

INDUSTRIES

So far as economical mineral deposits are concerned the districts is practically barren. With the exception of building stones and roofing slates and soradic pockets of gypsum, no profitable mineral deposits are known. Pockets and lentils of gypsum are found in the upper Krol and lime stone about three km north of Dhapla in the Nihal valley. Minor deposits of alum have been reported from near Kharina in the Kosi valley.

Industries of the district are basically agro-based. Extensive cultivation of sugarcane in *Bhabhar* prompted many sugar mills to come up. There is a H.M.T. unit at Ranibagh established at the cost of Rs. 45 crores and producing about one lakh of watches annually. Other worth mentioning units are Milk Dairy at Lal Kuan, Soyabeen Plant at Haldwani, Teletronics Ltd. at Bhimtal, Parvat Plastics at Kathgodam and a mushroom unit at Bhowali. These units have been incorporated by various government agencies i.e., Hill development Corporation, Kumaon Mandal Vikas Nigam and U.P. State Agro Industries Corporation Ltd. Industrial Sheds are being developed at Bhimtal and Haldwani.

In a hilly district like Naini Tal industrial progress should not take place in isolation to ecological hazards due to ruthless exploitation of local resources and thereby creating environmental pollution. It will mar the prospect of tourism industry in the district. Industries, such as electronics, optics, precision instruments etc. are proper for the district and government is seriously considering that the district should be judicious to industrial development. For the above reason, the top priority is being accorded to khadi, village and cottage industries. Development of woollen industry is entrusted with the Directorate of Handicrafts and Handlooms. Forest, fruit and vegetable based industries are being promoted. These have immense potential in this district. Fruit processing plants, packing cases, paper pulp units, furnitures, saw mills, terpen-tines and matches are being manufactured profitably and these are the industries earmarked for future expansion. Oil mills, cane crushing units and rice mills are other small industries that are being accorded top priority.

Important Industry, 1996

Belwal Spinning Mills Ltd. Ramnagar.

Manufacturer: Industrial and sewing threads of different counts.

TRADE, COMMERCE AND EXPORT

The chief commodities manufactured in towns are sugar, television, fruit juice, cable wire, lime, milk products and candles. The most important commodities exported are television, fruits, rice, stone, timber, paddy and candles. The most important commodities imported are television parts, rice, cement, bricks, cloth and wood.

The following table presents most important commodities manufactured in, exported from and imported into the towns of the district. It also indicates the number of banks in the towns.

Name of the towns	*Most important commodity*			
	Manufacturea	*Exported*	*Imported*	*Banks*
1	*2*	*3*	*4*	*5*
Bhimtal	Television	Television	Television parts	1
Bhowali	Fruit juice	Fruits	Rice	2
Haldwani-cum-Kathgodam	Cable wire	Stone	Cement	12
Kaladhungi	Lime	Mangoes	Bricks	2
Lal Kuan	Milk products	Wood	Bricks	2
Nainital	Candles	Candles	Rice	9
Nainital Cantt.	—	Fruits	Wood	2
Ramnagar	Sugar	Timber	Cloth	5

TOURISM

Nainital is a jewel among tourist places in the state. Lower ranges of outer Himalayas and a good chunk of *Bhabhar* comprise the district. As the name of the district imply, it has been attracting tourist for sheer beauty and serene environs of the lakes. Brisk climate of hill stations of the district is quite in contrast with the ennervating heat and humdrum landscape of the gangetic plains. Tourists rush to Nainital to have solace from heat and dust and rejuvenate in clean and fresh air. It is an apt saying that the district is a retreat for all seasons of the year, it is a refuge from scorching heat of the summers, enchantment in the autumn a sport paradise in the winters and an angler's delight in the spring.

The captivating beauty of the famous lake is greatly attributed by nearly emarald peaks that seems like enchanting willows. City is bestowed with richly coloured villas and bungalows and ponies, rickshaw and sail boats. In the stillness of darkness reflections of city light in the lake water presents a unique phenomenon, a many splendoured rendezvous.

Naina peak (height 2611 metres) offers the visitor to have a glorious view of show tipped crests of the world's highest mountain chain, the Himalayas, the glacial wall dividing India from Tibet and China. The peak has star attraction to tourists for that reason. The lake of city could also be glanced from the peak. To have a view of breath-taking beauty of sub-urban lakes, *Laria-Kanta* (height 2481 metres) is most suitable peak. Snowly peaks of Himalayas are dreams for a nature lover. These could be gazed from Snow View (height 2270 metres), that is, obviously an easily accessible mountain top. Encircled by terraced fields of slopy hill sides, Khurpa Tal's magnificent view could be had from *Lands End* (height 2118 metres). Hanumangarhi is a beautiful spot to have an ecstatic view of sun set. The place is of religious importance. Anglers may have amusing time at *Khurpa Tal* atop, 1635 metres. *State Observatory* and *Dorothy Seat* are the other tourist places of the district. The latter is a memorial to an English lady. For those who enjoy quite and Olympian calm. *Kilbury* is an ideal holiday resort. *Bhowali,* rich in hill fruits is a popular health resort. *Bhimtal,* 22.5 km. away from city of Nainital, is famous lake for boating and an islet in the centre of the lake is always full with picnickers. *Naukuchia Tal* is another heaven for anglers. It is 26 kms. away from town of Nainital. The lake harbours birds of remote countries. Nature is supreme at alluring *Sat Tal. Jeolikot* is favourite place of butterfly-catchers. It is a health resort. There is also a bee-keeping centre at this place. Ramgarh and Mukteshwar are other stations of tourist interest.

ZOO

Pandit Gobind Ballabh Pant, High Altitude Zoo, Nainital.

HOTELS

Vikram Village Inn (Government Approved) 4 star.

Near A.T.I. Mallital, Nainital.

Access: 72 kms. from Airport, 35 kms. from Railway station, 2 kms. from Bus stand.

Rooms: 37.

Beveldere Palace, Awagarh Estate (Government Approved) Heritage.

Access: 78 kms. from Airport, 32 kms. from Railway station, 1/2 kms. from Bus stand.

Rooms: 22.

Fairhavens Hotel (Government Approved) Heritage, Nainital.

Access: 55 kms. from Airport, 35 kms. from Railway station, 1.5 kms. from Bus stand.

Rooms: 32.

Royal Hotel (Government Approved) Heritage, Nainital.

Access: 70 kms. from Airport, 1 km. from Bus stand.

Rooms: 49.

Hotel Arif Castle (Government Approved) 3 star. Mullital, Nanital.

Access: 55 kms. from Airport, 40 kms. from Railway station, 2 kms. from Bus stand.

Rooms: 66.

Shervani Hill Top Inn (Government Approved) 3 star. Mellital, Nainital.

Access: 70 kms. from Airport, 35 kms. from Railway station, from Bus stand.

Rooms: 21.

Hotel Silverton, Sher-Ka-Danda, Nainital.

Access: 34 kms. from Railway station, 1/2 km. from Talital. Rooms: 25.

The Claridges Corbett Hideway, Ramnagar, Nainital.

Access: 13 kms. from Railway station, 11 kms. from Bus stand. Rooms 28

The Manu Maharani, Luxury, Grassmere Estate, Nainital.

Access: 62 kms. from Air port, 30 kms. from Railway station, 1/2 km. from Bus stand.

The Palace Resorts, Mallital, Nainital. Rooms: 95

Tiger Tops Corbett Lodge (Government approved) 3 star, Ramnagar.

Access: 30 kms. from Airport, 8 kms. from Railway station, 8 kms. from Bus stand. Rooms: 24

Hotel Metropole (Government approved) 2 star, Mallital, Nainital.

Access: 78 kms. from Airport, 32 kms. from Railway station, 1 km. from Bus stand. Rooms: 50.

Mountain Trail: (Government approved) 2 star, Mukteshwar, Nainital.

Access: 100 kms. from Airport, 60 kms. from Railway station. Rooms: 10.

Swiss Hotel: (Government approved) 2 star, Nainital.

Access; 70 kms. from Airport, 40 kms. from Railway station, 1 km. from Bus stand.

Corbett River Side Resort: (Government approved), Dhikuli, Nainital.

Access: 90 kms. from Airport, 10 kms. from Railway station, 10 kms. from Bus stand.

Rooms: 18.

Hotel Pratap Regency: (Government approved), Nainital.

Access: 72 kms. from Airport, 36 kms. from Railway station. Rooms: 36.

Lakeside Inn, (Government approved) Nainital.

Access: 76 kms. from Airport, 34 kms. from Railway station, 500 metres from bus stand.

Rooms: 20.

Claridges Naini Retreat (A unit of Leisure Hotels Ltd.) (Government approved) Mallital, Nainital.

Access: 36 kms. from Railway station, 4 kms. from Bus stand. Rooms: 32.

Grand Hotel: Nainital.

Access: 36 kms. from Railway station, 1 km from Bus stand. Rooms: 31.

Hotel Classic, The Mall, Nainital.

Access: 1 km. from Bus stand. Room 25.

Hotel Everest, Nainital.

Access: 60 kms. from Airport, 32 kms. from Railway station, 1/2 km. from Bus stand.

Hotel Radha Continental Mallital, Nainital.

Access: 70 kms. from Airport, 35 kms. from Railway station, 1.5 kms. from Bus stand. Rooms: 33.

FAIRS AND FESTIVALS

Important fairs and festivals organised in different parts of the district are mentioned below:

Janam Astmi, Chitrasila, Sita Bani, Shivratri, Bal Sundary Devi, Zahar Aulia, Chamunda Devi, Gudashi, Ganga Baba, Naumi Mela, Buddha Babu, Kartika Purnima, Moteshwar, Muharram, Poornagiri, Attaria, Uldhan, Bale Miyan, Chellum, Janam Ashtmi, Sarwarpir, Ghat Fair, Sisla, Jharhi Mahadeo, Bhimeshwar, Nanda Ashtmi, Kailash.

EDUCATION

According to 2001 Census, the population of total literates (excluding the population in the age group of 0-6 years) of undivided district of Nainital district is 520133 persons. Of these, 299751 are males and 220382 are females. In the rural areas of the district 326637 persons (190859 males and

135778 females) are literates and in urban areas 193496 persons (108892 males and 84604 females) are literates. The rate of literacy of this population to the total population, excluding 0-6 years age group according to 2001 Census is shown below:

1991			2001		
Persons	*Males*	*Females*	*Persons*	*Males*	*Females*
68.36	80.42	54.51	79.60	87.39	70.98

The following table provides information on various types of educational institutions available in the towns of the district, including the number of stadia and Public Libraries:

Name of the towns	*Educational Institutions*	*Stadia*	*Public Libraries including reading rooms*
Bhimtal	Higher Secondary/ Intermediate School (1), Secondary/Matriculation School (1), Junior Secondary and Middle Schools (2), Primary Schools (4)	–	–
Bhowali	Higher Secondary/ Intermediate Schools (2), Junior Secondary and Middle School (1), Primary School (1)	–	–
Haldwani-cum-Kathgodam	Arts College (1), Higher Secondary/Intermediate Schools (3), Secondary/ Matriculation Schools (6), Junior Secondary and Middle Schools (12), Primary Schools (45)	–	–
Kaldhungi	Higher Secondary/ Intermediate School (1), Secondary/Matriculation		

	School (1), Primary School (1)	—	—
Lal Kuan	Junior Secondary and Middle School (1), Primary Schools (2)	—	—
Nainital	Arts, Science and Commerce College (1), Polytechnics (1), Higher Secondary/Intermediate School (6), Secondary/ Matriculation Schools (4), Primary Schools (32)	—	PL:1
Nainital Cantt.	Higher Secondary/Intermediate School (1), Junior Secondary and Middle School (1), Primary School (1)	—	—
Ramnagar	Arts and Commerce College (1), Higher Secondary/Intermediate Schools (2) Secondary/ Matriculation School (1), Junior Secondary and Middle Schools (3), Primary Schools (9)		

COLLEGES

DSB Campus College, Nainital, (Established 1951) (Constituent College). Enrolment 3685, Teachers 135.

Birla Institute of Applied Sciences, Bhimtal, (Established 1989).

Government Girls Degree College, Haldwani, (Established 1996). Enrolment 115.

Government Postgraduate College, Ramanagar (Established 1975). Enrolment 1854, Teachers 25.

Motiram Baburam Government Postgraduate College, Haldwani, Nainital (Established 1960). Enrolment 8160. Teachers 66.

R.H. Government Postgraduate College, Kashipur, (Established 1969). Enrolment 3691, Teachers 40.

(Above named Colleges belong to Kumaun University, Established 1973).

MEDICAL

The following table furnishes information on types of medical facilities available in the towns of this district alongwith facilities available therein:

Name of the Towns	*Medical institutions (alongwith bed facilities)*	
Bhimtal	Hospital (1)	–
	Primary Health Centre (1)	8
Bhowali	Hospital (1)	–
	Dispensary (1)	4
	T.B. Clinic (1)	378
Haldwani-	Hospital (4)	265
cum-Kathgodam	Dispensary (2)	–
	T.B. Clinic	–
Kaladhungi	Hospital (1)	–
	Dispensary (2)	–
	T.B. Clinic (1)	–
Lalkuan	Dispensary (2)	1
Nainital	Hospitals (6)	220
	Family Planning Centre (1)	–
	Dispensary (1)	–
	Others (2)	–
Nainital Cantt.	Hospital (1)	–
Ramnagar	Hospital (3)	24
	Dispensary (1)	–

Newspapers. Uttar Ujala (Hindi).

Rajdhani Samikaran, a Hindi fortnightly, Nainital.

Nagrik Adhikaron Ko Samarpit, a Hindi Fortnightly, Nainital.

ADMINISTRATION

(i) Administrative Divisions

Tehsils: Nainital, Kosiha Kutsauli, Dhari, Haldwani.

Towns with their Population, Urban Status and Literatures (2001)

City/Town	Urban Status	Population			Literates		
		Person	Male	Female	Person	Male	Female
Bhimtal	NP	5875	3178	2697	4587	2563	2024
Bhowali	MB	5302	2846	2456	4248	2348	1900
Haldwani-cum-Kathgodam	MB	129140	68826	60314	88903	49948	38955
Kaladungi	NP	6126	3218	2908	3790	2240	1550
Lalkuan	NP	6524	3567	2957	4552	2728	1824
Nainital	MB	38559	20951	17608	31366	17929	13437
Nainital	CB	1281	667	614	1052	576	476
Ramnagar	MB	47099	24656	22443	31073	17486	13587

(ii) Parliamentary Constituency along assembly segments (2001):

No. & Name of Parliamentary Constituency:

4-NAINITAL

No. & Name of Assembly Segments of Nainital Parliamentary Constituency which lies within the Jurisdiction of Nainital district.

Assembly Constituency: 52. Mukteshwar (SC)

TEHSIL—DHARI

Paharpani—43. Chaubhensi; 44. Sundarkhal; 52. East Agar.

TEHSIL—KUTOLI

Betalghat—11. Talla Koshiyan; 12. Betalghat; 13. Malli Sethi; 14. Joshikhola; 15. Malli Palli; 16. Malla Koshiyan; 17. Uchakot. ***Pyura***—1. Simalkhan; 2. Padli; 3. Bargal; 4. Majhera; 5. Dhaniyakot; 6. Beduli; 7. Suyalbari; 8. Talli Kutoli; 9. Pyura; 10. Mona. **Forest Area:** Forest Area

TEHSIL—NAINITAL

Bagar—34. Syat; 35. Tallakota; 36. Saurh. ***Bhimtal***—26.

Chanfi. ***Ramgarh***—18. Gahna; 19. Nathuwakhan; 20. Satbunga; 21. Ramgarh; 22. Devdaro; 23. Malli Kutoli.

Assembly Constituency: 53. Dhari

TEHSIL—DHARI

Chaugad—45. Chaugad; 46. Gauniyarod; 47. Gargari; 48. Bhadrakot; 49. Wisjyula; 50. Chyudigarh; 51. Padampur; 54. Pinraon; 55. Babiyar. ***Paharpani***—38. Naai; 39. Patliya; 40. Dholigaon; 41. Talla Kanda; 42. Malliraoi; 53. Sarana. **Forest Area:** Forest Area

TEHSIL—HALDWANI

Haldwani—73. Dewalchaur. ***Bhimtal***—29. Rausil. ***Kathgodam***--61. Kisanpur; 62. Khera; 64. Jagatpur; 65. Lachampur; 76. Chorgaliya; 77. Lakhanmandi. ***Lalkua***—56. Lalkua; 57. Motahaldu; 58. Jaipur Bisa; 59. Hathikhal; 60. Arjunpur; 70. Chandnichauk; 75. Anandpur; **Forest area and Urban Area:** Lalkuan.

Assembly Constituency: 54. Haldwani

TEHSIL—HALDWANI

Haldwani. 63. Haldwani Khas; 66. Lamachaur; 67. Fatehpur; 68. Bhagwanpur; 69. Kamluwaganja; 71. Lohariyashal; 74. Kusumkhera; ***Kathgodam.*** 72. Damuwadhunga; **Forest Area:** Forest Area; **Urban Area:** Haldwani MB.

Assembly Constituency: 55. Nainital

TEHSIL—HALDWANI

Kaladhungi. 95. Patliya; 96. Kaladungi; 97. Guljarpur; 98. Rampur. **Forest Area:** Forest Area; **Urban Area:** Kaladhungi NAC.

TEHSIL—NAINITAL

Bagar. 30. Choupara; 31. Khurpatal; 32. Mangoli; 33. Bagar. ***Bhimtal.*** 24. Bhawali; 25. West Chhakhata; 27. Pandegaon; 28. East Chhakhata. **Forest Area:** Forest Area. **Urban Area:** Bhawali MB; Bhimtal (NAC); Nainital Cantt; Nainital MB.

Assembly Constituency: 56. Ramnagar (SC)

TEHSIL—HALDWANI

Bailparaw. 99. Awalakot; 100. Bandarjuda; 101. Nauda; 102. Bailparaw; 103. Gaibuakhas; 104. Nathunagar; 105. Hansrampur. ***Chilkiya.*** 78. Patkot; 82. Shivlalpur; 83. Chilkiya; 84. Baljuri 90. Bukshar; 91. Thari; 92. Chhoi; 93. Khushalpur.

Kaladhungi. 94. Kamola. ***Ramnagar.*** 79. Ramnagar; 80. Shwalde; 81. Maldhanchaur; 85. Basae; 86. Kahiya; 87. Motipur; 88. Pirumdara; 89. Choupara. **Forest Area:** Forest Area. **Urban Area:** Ramnagar MB.

TEHSIL—NAINITAL

Bagar—37. Amgarhi.

MINERALS AND ORES OCCURRENCE

Copper

Occurrence of malachite patches at Thoca Dalna Dhar, Jhutia (29.43, 79.55), Tama Khani (29.45, 79.55) Khairana (29.5, 79.5) and near Dabani (29.4, 79.37), Incrustations of malachite and disseminations of chalcopyrite and pyrite in the acid and basic rocks near Dhaka Khet (29.35, 79.5) Dahra (29.3, 79.56) and Sirwa Tak (29.3, 79.6).

Lignite

Occurrences of narrow beds of lignite have been reported from Deochauri (29.4, 79.4) and Nihal Nadi (29.35, 71.41).

Limestone

Limestone deposits low in magnesia content from near Jaurasi (29.5, 79.5) and Bardhau Talla (29.53°, 79.41°). A band of limestone runs from near Lusgiani (29.46, 79.58) upto Sat Bunga (29.45, 79.61). Similar narrow bands also occur near Nai (29.4, 79.75).

Several deposits of calcareous tufa occurs in the Chunakhan (29.31, 79.25) area and are included between 29.28 to 29.31 North and 79.23° to 79.3° East.

Near Nainital there are two calcareous tufa deposits, on lying near Saulia (29.36, 79.45) on the right bank of Khurpatal Nala and the other of Adhaura (29.4, 79.4) on the northern side of the Tegara nala.

There are two large outcrops of Krol limestone near Nainital which are worked at places for lime burning. They are very high in magnesia and so, unsuitable for cement manufacture.

Mica

Occurrence of mica in pegmatites near Mukteswar (29.46°, 79.65°) and Paharpani (29.43°, 79.65).

Ochre

Yellow Ochere occurs near Baital Ghat (29.55, 79.35) and is used locally as a pigment.

Malachite

Malachite at thock Dalna Dhar, Jhutia (29°26': 79°33'), Tama Khani (29°27': 79°33') Khairana (29°30': 79°29') Dabani (29°24': 79°22')

Chalcopyrite and Pyrite

In the basic and acid rocks near Dhaka (29°21': 79°29'), Dhara (29°18':79°34') and Sirwa Tak (29°18': 79°37').

Lignite

At DEOCHAURI (29°23':79°23'), NIHAL nadi (29°21':71°25')

Limestone

At JAURASI (29°31':79°31'), BARDHAU TALLA (29°32':79°25'), LUSGIANI (29°28':79°35') upto SAT BUNGA (29°27':79°37') CHUNAKHAN (29°19':79°15') Near SAULIA (29°22':79°27') and near ADHAURA (29°24':79°24')

Gypsum—The occurrence of large deposits of gypsum on the Nihal stream between KALADHUNGI and Nainital. The most important masses are situated about a mile to the north of DHAPILA.

Iron—At DHANIAKOT, RAMGARH, KOSILA River, BIJAPUR, DECAURI, JHAM, LOHA BHABAR near Kaladhungi, LUSGIAN, Sat Bunga, Khurpa Tal, Old working of iron are found at CHAUKHUTA PARWARA, DALAR.

OBSERVATIONAL ORGANISATION

Surface Observatories

The district of Nainital lies under Meterological sub-division, hills of Uttranchal. This facility is available at three places in the district, the places are, Mukteswar (Kumaun), Nainital. These instruments lies in

Mukteswar (Kumaun)

Latitude	: 29.46° North
Longitude	: 79.65° East

Altitude : 2311 m

Date of starting : 1-3-1897

Nainital

Latitude : 29.4° North

Longitude : 79.46° East

Altitude : 1953 m

Date of starting : 20-7-1952

Hydrometeorological stations for climatological purposes

This facility is available at Banbasa, the instrument lies in

Latitude : 28.8° North

Longitude : 80.15° East

Altitude : 213 m

Date of starting : 28-3-1976

Aeronautical Meteorological Observatories

This observatories maintain current weather at aerodrome or important locations along and near air routes, provide services for the use of air craft and air traffic control units. This facility is available at Pantnagar.

DISASTROUS WEATHER EVENTS

Snowfall

From 28-30 December, 1996, it was severe and several people die due to it.**Floods and Heavy Rains**—On 29th June 1984, it was heavy rains, 6 persons and large number of cattleheads perished in a landslide. On 30th July 1984, it was heavy rains, 8 persons killed in Puran village on Nainital road.

Floods and Heavy Rains

On 29th June 1984, it was heavy rains, 6 persons and large number of cattleheads perished in a landslide. On 30th July 1984, it was heavy rains, 8 persons killed in Puran village on Nainital road.

During 2nd and 3rd week of 1985, there was flood in the river and its tributary, several people killed and injured.

On 14 August 1995, it was heavy rains, large number of houses washed away, due to it persons died and injured.

Hailstorm

During 16-19 October, 1986, it was heavy, 50-60 per cent paddy crop damaged in Mukteshwar.

DISTRIBUTION OF *SCHEDULED CASTE* POPULATION BY SEX (1991)

	POPULATION		
	Total	Males	Females
NAINITAL	2,43,314	1,30,402	1,12,912
Agariya	175	96	79
Badhik	95	58	37
Badi	128	71	57
Baheliya	395	216	179
Baiga	1,027	565	462
Baiswar	25	15	10
Bajaniya	11	5	6
Bajgi	8	3	5
Balahar	12	7	5
Balai	40	21	19
Balmiki	17,826	9,433	8,393
Bangali	6,318	3,235	3,083
Banmanus	20	4	16
Bansphor	266	156	110
Barwar	78	53	25
Basor	18	6	12
Bawariya	10	3	7
Beldar	102	46	56
Beriya	15	8	7
Bhantu	83	39	44
Bhuiya	290	167	123
Bhuyiar	127	71	56
Boria	17	14	3
Chamar, Dhusia, Jhusia, Jatava	73,884	41,164	32,720
Chero	175	115	60
Dabgar	45	19	26
Dhangar	91	49	42
Dhanuk	272	159	113
Dharkar	93	60	33
Dhobi	4,330	2,299	2,031
Dom	460	258	202
Domar	22	20	2
Dusadh	530	280	250
Ghasiya	103	58	45
Gond	2,874	1,596	1,278
Gual	198	118	80
Habura	755	340	415
Hari	40	21	19
Hela	9	7	2
Kalabaz	145	78	67
Kanjar	1,201	627	574
Kapariya	41	18	23
Karwal	57	40	17
Khairaha	54	26	28
Kharwar (excluding Benbansi)	202	130	72
Khatik	941	470	471
Khorot	15	9	6
Kol	114	64	50
Kori	9,446	5,079	4,367
Korwa	63	43	20
Lalbegi	21	12	9
Majhwar	207	132	75
Mazhabi	2,848	1,567	1,281
Musahar	183	131	52
Nat	444	236	208
Pankha	33	18	15
Parahiya	37	23	14
Pasi, Tarmali	1,267	767	500
Patari	34	16	18
Rawat	669	349	320
Saharya	109	39	70
Sanaurhiya	36	21	15
Sansiya	182	99	83
Shilpkar	1,12,525	58,711	53,814
Turaiha	401	210	191
Unclassified	1,072	632	440

DISTRIBUTION OF *SCHEDULED TRIBE* POPULATION BY SEX (1991)

	POPULATION		
	Total	Males	Females
	NAINITAL		
	90,020	46,313	43,707
Bhotia	1,220	714	506
Buksa	20,180	10,119	10,061
Jaunsari	56	35	21
Raji	59	33	26
Tharu	67,422	34,829	32,593
Unclassified	1,083	583	500

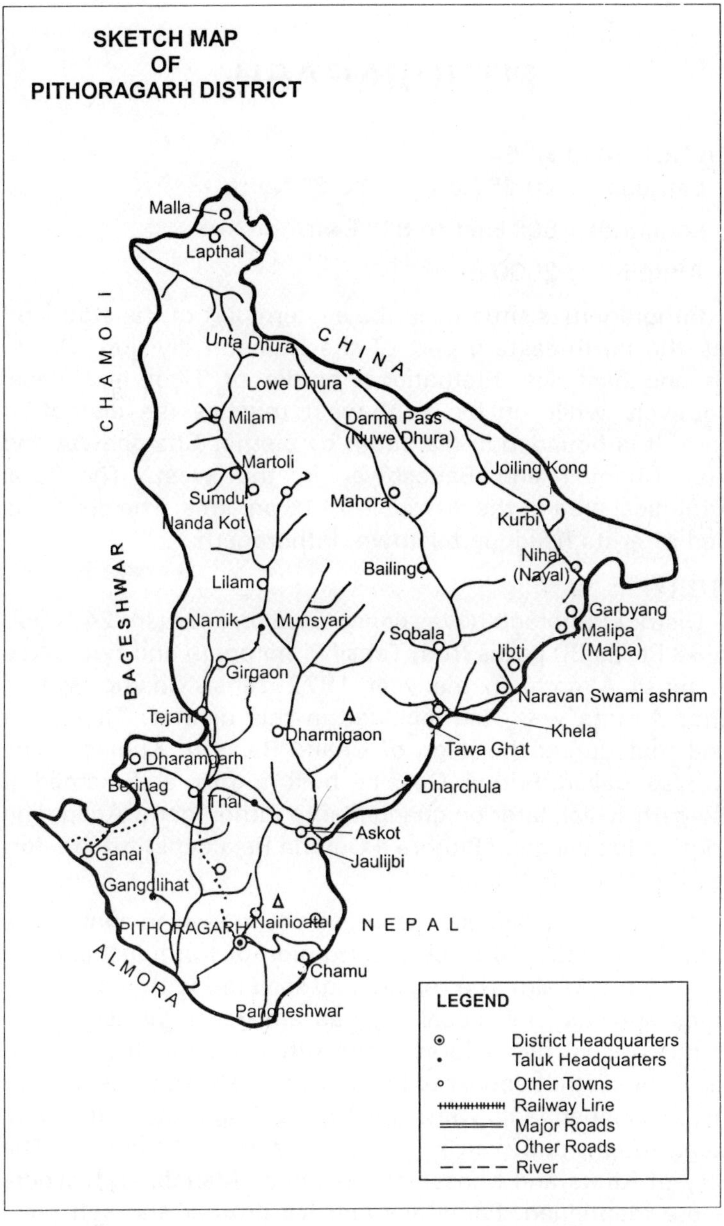
SKETCH MAP
OF
PITHORAGARH DISTRICT
CHINA
CHAMOLI
BAGESHWAR
ALMORA
NEPAL
Malla
Lapthal
Unta Dhura
Lowe Dhura
Milam
Darma Pass
(Nuwe Dhura)
Martoli
Sumdu
Nanda Kot
Mahora
Joiling Kong
Kurbi
Nihal
(Nayal)
Bailing
Lilam
Namik
Munsyari
Sobala
Garbyang
Malipa
(Malpa)
Jibti
Girgaon
Narayan Swami ashram
Tejam
Dharmigaon
Khela
Tawa Ghat
Dharamgarh
Berinag
Thal
Dharchula
Askot
Jaulijbi
Ganai
Gangolihat
PITHORAGARH
Nainioatal
Chamu
Pancheshwar
LEGEND
District Headquarters
Taluk Headquarters
Other Towns
Railway Line
Major Roads
Other Roads
River

PITHORAGARH

LOCATION AND AREA

Latitude : 29.4° North to 30.8° North

Longitude : 80° East to 81° East.

Altitude : 2500 m

Pithoragarh is situated in the eastern part of the state and forms the north-eastern part of the Kumaon division. On its north and east lies international border of Tibet and Nepal respectively while on its south-west touches the district of Almora. It is bounded in the south by district Champawat and district Chamoli and Bageshwar in the west. The total geographical area of the district is 7118 sq. kms. The district is named after its headquarter town, Pithoragarh.

HISTORY

District Pithoragarh was constituted on February 24, 1960 with 32 Pattis-30 pattis from Tehsil Pithoragarh and two pattis from tehsil Almora. In the year 1972 Tehsil Champawat of District Almora was also included in this district. There is a legend that during the reign of Chand Rajas of Kumaon, one Piru, also called Prithvi Gosain, built a fort and named it Prithvigarh which later on changed into Pithoragarh. According to another local legend Pithora a Gurkha Raja constituted a fort called the place, Pithoragarh.

Kumaon, the popular name of the region in which the district lies is believed to be a corruption of Kurmanchala, the name of a mountain. The region is associated with many tales of gods and demons. Local legends are generally associated with mountains, rivers forests and other sites in the district. Parts of the district appear to have been inhabited since ancient times. Early inhabitants were, the Asuras, Nagas etc., who were perhaps fought and won by Kirats, Khasas and Kuninds. The history of Kirats and Khasas are as old as Mahabharat, where they are mentioned. Parvataka and his brother and son were probably the hill chiefs of the Kumaon-Garhwal Himalayas about 325 B.C. About the last quarter of the first century A.D. the region was included in the empire of Kushans under Kanishka. During the 11th and 12th centuries the area covered by the present district of Pithoragarh appears to have been divided among the Katyuri chiefs of Askot, Sira, Shor, Gangoli, Baijnath, the Khasa, Thakurs of Danpur and Darma and Chands of Champawat, all of whom were probably subordinate to the maharajas of Doti.

Tohar Chand (1261-1275 A.D.) was the first Chand Raja to start the Chand Dynasty on the entire Kumaon region. The Chand Dynasty continued its domination over Kumaon until 1790 when Gurkhas invaded Kumaon. In 1816 the Gurkhas lost Kumaon, including the region covered by the present district of Pithoragarh to East India Company. The whole of Kumaon including Pithoragarh participated in the freedom movement. Pithoragarh attained independence alongwith other parts of the country on August 15, 1947 and was formed as an independent district in the year 1960.

POPULATION (2001)

Total population of the district according to 2001 Census is 662149 persons, comprising 227592 males and 234557 females. Rural population of the district is 406025 persons (197517 males and 208508 females) and urban population is 56124 persons (30075 males and 26049 females).

The decennial growth rate of population of the district as a whole in relation to the state between the period 1981-1991 and 1991-2001 is presented below:

State/District	*Decennial growth rate of population (per cent)*	
	1981-91	*1991-2001*
Uttaranchal	24.23	19.20
Pithoragarh	14.11	10.92

LANGUAGES AND RELIGION

Main language spoken in the district is Hindi.

Main religion of the district are Hindus, Muslims, Christians, Sikhs, Buddhists and Jains.

GEOGRAPHY AND PHYSICAL FEATURES

Lying in the upper Himalayas, Pithoragarh contains within itself varying geographic environments. Situated at the altitude between 2000 to 20000 feet above the sea level, it sprawls in the rugged terrain of the mystic Himalayas. According to geological formations of the district, it may be divided into four broad belts, viz., (1) the inner most Siwalik hills ranges (2) the lesser and middle Himalayas (3) the inner Himalayas and (4) the thin belt bordering the Tibetan Himalayas, roughly tending east-south east. The bigger part of the district lies under perpetual snow and a considerable area is rocky and barren. Cultivation is, therefore, limited to the river valleys and gently sloping hills.

Taking into consideration the difference in the altitudes and the climatic conditions the flora of the district can be divided into four divisions (1) the Sal forests (2) Chir forests (3) oak forests and (4) coniferous forests. The northern part of the district where there are mountains, is rock and covered with perpetual snow. The forests are, therefore confined in the southern parts of the district. Roughly an area of 330288 hectares is covered with forests which includes 79338.93 hectares reserve forest.

In the sal forests, the chief tree sal is found upto a height of about 1220 m. The sal logs are mainly used for building purposes. Other associated trees in these forests are haldu sain, Kharik and tun Kharik. The mango and pipal trees are also frequently found in those forests. Chir trees are found upto the altitude of about 1800 m. The chir wood is used for building purposes and is exported in the shape of sleepers. Resin is also extracted from the trees. Different varieties of oak are found in different altitude zone between the altitude of 3250 m. and 4000 m. the dominant species, are the conifers. The main species are chil, thaner, ragha and surain.

RIVERS, CANALS AND WATERWAYS

The important rivers that flow through the district are Saryu, Ramganga, Gawri, Kali, Dhauli and Kuti. In addition there are many other streams and small rivers.

TOWNS, VILLAGES AND AMENITIES

The district, at present comprises of four tehsils and four towns. The urban population of the district as percentage of total population in the census years 2001 is indicated below. It also shows the sex ratio (female per 1000 males) and density (population per sq. km.) in the urban population of the district in relation to the State:

State/ District	*Urban population as percentage of total population*	*Sex ratio, (Females per 1000 persons*		*Density (Population per sq. km.)*	
	2001	*1991*	*2001*	*1991*	*2001*
Uttaranchal	25.59	936	964	133	159
Pithoragarh	12.14	992	1031	59	65

Amenities

Villages having one or more amenities in the district are Education, Medical, Drinking Water, Post and Telegraph, Market and Hat, Communications, Approach by Pucca road and Power Supply.

COMMUNICATIONS

District Pithoragarh is not served by railways and communications depend solely on roads and pathways. The district is served by a total length of 846 kms. of roads managed under P.W.D. which gives a ratio of 95.53 kms. per thousand square kms. Other roads cover a distance of 280 kms. Out of which 13 kms. are managed by Zila Parishad and 267 kms. by D.G.B.R. National Highway does not pass through this district. State Highway No. 29 passes through the district which connects with National Highway No. 24 at Bareilly.

AGRICULTURE AND IRRIGATION

The economy of the district pivots around agriculture. Throughout the greater part of the district there are two harvests, Kharif and Rabi. But due to cooler climate the crops require a longer period to ripe than the plains.

The chief kharif crops are paddy, jhangora, maize, mandua, pulses and tomatoes. The rabi crops include wheat, barley, mesur, peas, linseed and mustard. Ginger and pepper are also grown in the district. Sugarcane is grown in the southern valleys.

Horticulture is another field that can boost up the economy of the district. Forestry too place a dominant role in the economy of the district. Resin is extracted from pine trees and provides employment for 8 months in a year. Pine tar is obtained from the highly resinous stump wood of rejected or fallen pine trees.

District Pithoragarh is totally hill area. There are many streams and rivers in the district. But the species of fish that are found in cold region are dwindling. Due to the encouragement by the authorities the interest of the people in fisheries is growing. Irrigation tanks are also being used for fisheries.

ANIMAL HUSBANDRY

Animal husbandry is an important source of income for the rural people. Most of them spin and weave the wool of their indigenous sheep. Out of the total livestock cows account for major portion followed by sheep and goats and buffaloes. Out of the total cows and buffaloes, milching varieties include crossbreed cows Indians cows and buffaloes.

INDUSTRIES

A number of minerals are found in the district. Copper ore is found to occur as disseminations in crystalline dolomites. Several scattered deposits of magnesite are found in the area around Pithoragarh. Very little work has been done on these deposits. Other promising deposits occur at several scattered locations. Several small deposits of soapstone occur in association with magnesite. The soapstone found in this district is of first rate quality of commercial and cosmetic industries. As per stray surveys arsenic, sulpher, kynite, limestone and graphite deposits occur in the district. State quarries exist throughout the district and it is utilised locally for building purposes.

There has been hardly any industrial development in the district. There are only four factories registered under Factory Act, 1948 giving employment to 435 persons and produce goods worth Rs. 232 lakhs annually. Small industries units registered under Directorate of Industries numbers 141 and employes 592 persons. Wool spinning and weaving are old cottage industries. Another old time handicraft of this district is baskets and matting manufactured out of ringal. Furniture is produced out of pine. 303 cottage industry units employ 998 persons in the district.

TRADE, COMMERCE AND EXPORT

Carpets and timber are manufactured in the towns of Dharchulla and Pithoragarh. Potatoes and carpets are the commodities largely exported from the towns of the district. The commodities imported mainly are wheat, rice, rubber and sugar.

The following table give most important commodities manufactured, imported and exported from the towns of the district.

Name of the towns	*Most important commodity*		
	Manufactured	*Exported*	*Imported*
1	*2*	*3*	*4*
Dharchula	Carpets	Carpets	Rice
Didihat	—	—	Wheat
Pithoragarh	Timber	—	Sugar

TOURISM

For tourist promotion, Kumaon Mandal Vikas Nigam is running tourist lodges at Pithoragarh, and Chow-kori. Following places are important for tourism.

Askot. The name is derive from "Assikot" meaning eighty forts. The village is surrounded by hills and ridges. It is also surrounded by forests of pine, shisham, sal, khair and oak.

Berinag. The place is named after the temple of Berinag (a local deity). At a small distance from this place, at Guraun there is a high waterfall. Berinag is also a market place 102 kms. from Pithoragarh situated amidst tea gardens, Berinag offers an enchanting view of a wide range of Himalayas.

Didihat. Near the place, remains of a fort Sherakot are found. Sherakot is placed on the top of a hill. So it presents a beautiful scene of Himalayas. Near to the place there is Narain Nagar which is an attractive locality.

Munsiari. Munsiari is tehsil headquarter. It is very pleasant in the summers. From the town are visible the five peaks of mountains which have been named after five Pandavas as they are supposed to have fallen there doing their last Journey. It is a famous manufacturing centre of thulmas (large rugs).

Pithoragarh. Pithoragarh is a small town which gives its name to the district. It lies in the centre of western side of the shor valley and resembles Kashmir. From high spots in town, many peaks are clearly visible. Other noteworthy spots in and around Pithoragarh include Hanuman Garhi, Ulka Devi temple, Radha Krishna Temple, Raigufa and Bhatkote.

Other important places in the district are Punyagiri, Chandak, Thal Kedar, Dhwaj, Gangolihat, Shyamala Tal, Sukhidang, Retha Sahib among others. Pithoragarh being a border district, entry to certain areas is prohibited.

FAIRS AND FESTIVALS

Important fairs and festivals organised in different parts of the district are mentioned below:

Nanda Ashtmi, Shivratri, Chifala, Milkutia, Lahamsel, Jauljibi, Kartika Purnima, Tamanauli, Maha Kali, Kotgari, Thal, Bikhuwat Sankranti, Rameshwar, Kalinag, Durbashtmi, Sanai Khola, Nag fair, Berinag, Dyhochla, Dyochla, Tania Nauli, Atathu, Deokali, Tripura Devi, Baraun, Rameshwar, Pandan, Sonar Khola, Koteshwar, Bashuki Nag, Dasauli Mool, Sirakot, Panch Marh, Shera Ghat Rameshwar, Thal Parao, Kedar Sila Deity, Patal Bhubneshwar, Lory, Chauka, Chharaudeo, Mostmanu, Thelke-dar, Dhaj, Daulaikh, Lechara, Chaupakhiya, Bhadrika, Chandrika Ghat, Hanshaishwar, Pancheswar.

EDUCATION

According to 2001 Census, the population of total literates (excluding the population in the age group of 0–6 years) is 299798 persons. Of these, 172696 are males and 127102 are females. In the rural areas of the district 255338 persons (147677 males and 107661 females) are literates and in urban areas 44460 'persons (25019 males and 19441 females) are literates. The rate of literacy of this population to the total population, (excluding 0-6 years age group) according to 2001 Census is:

1991			2001		
Persons	*Males*	*Females*	*Persons*	*Males*	*Females*
61.38	80.31	42.41	76.48	90.57	63.14

A ratio of 8.51 Primary Schools per 10000 of population is obtained in the urban areas of the district. The maximum ratio of 19.44 schools is observed in Dharchula town. The lowest ratio of 4.89 is observed in Didihat. There are 2.96 Junior Secondary/Middle Schools per 10000 of population in urban areas of the district. Every 10000 of urban population in the district is served by 1.85 schools of Matriculation Standard. There are 2.96 Inter Colleges per 10000 of urban population in urban areas of the district.

COLLEGES

Government Degree College Baluwakot, Dharchula. (Established 1996), Enrolment 72.

Government Degree College, Berinag (Established 1975). Enrolment 447, Teachers 18

Government P.G. College, Pithoragarh (1963), Enrolment 4117, Teachers 62.

Government Degree College, Narayannagar, Didihat (Established 1983), Enrolment 120 Teachers 6.

(Above named colleges belong to Kumaun University. Established 1973).

MEDICAL

The maximum ratio of 9.17 beds per thousand of population is observed in Pithoragarh town.There is no medical institution with bed facility in Dharchula town. The urban areas of district is served by 6.74 beds per thousand of population.

ADMINISTRATION

(i) Administrative Division:

Tehsils: Munsiari, Dharchula, Didihat, Pithoragarh.

Towns with their Population, Urban Status and Literates (2001)

City/Town	Urban Status	Population			Literates		
		Person	Male	Female	Person	Male	Female
Dharchula	NP	6424	3,490	2934	4815	2789	2026
Dharchula	CT	3738	1897	1841	2394	1402	992
Didihat	NP	4805	2634	2171	3819	2201	1618
Ranikhet	CB	41157	22054	19103	33432	18627	14805

(ii) Parliamentary Constituencies and Assembly Segments:

No. and Name of Parliamentary Constituency

3-ALMORA

No. and Name of Assembly Segments of Almora Parliamentary Constituency which lies within the Jurisdiction of Pithoragarh District.

Assembly Constituency: 66. Pithoragarh

TEHSIL—PITHORAGARH

Gurana. 26. Igyar; 27. Tharkot; 28. Gogna; 29. Puran; 30. Chamali; 31. Siling; 32. Patharkani; 33. Badabe; 34. Salla. ***Munakote.*** 18. Kotli; 19. Naghar; 20. Badari; 21. Madshon; 22. Kwiter. ***Pithoragarh.*** 1. Maharkhash; 2. Dhanaura; 3. Paun; 4. Sukauli;; 5. Baste; 6. Sintoli; 7. Digtoli; 8. Chandak. ***Satsiling***—12. Nainisaini. **Urban Area:** Pithoragarh (MC)

Assembly Constituency: 67. Gangolihat (SC)

TEHSIL—DIDIHAT

Berinag—42. Khitoli; 43. Tripuradevi; 44. Rajagar; 45. Chourmanya; 46. Dungripant; 47. Bhuwaneshwar. ***Ganai***—12. Khirmande; 13. Nainoli; 14. Simlata; 15. Chauhana; 16. Chack; 17. Ganai; 18. Gawadi; 19. Devrari Pant; 20. Bankote. ***Gangolihat***—1. Chauypata; 2. Boyal; 3. Balatari; 4. Dasaithal; 5. Chodiyar; 6. Ku-Upreti; 7. Chahaj; 8. Chamdungra; 9. Bokta; 10. Bungli; 11. Chourpal.

Assembly Constituency: 68. Knalichhina

TEHSIL—DIDIHAT

Askote—29. Kuta; 30. Askote; 31. Bagrihat; 32. Garkha; 33. Singali; 34. Ogla; 35. Hachila; 36. Jourasi; 37. Narayan nagar.

Kanalichhina—20. Pipli; 21. Barmou; 22. Charandev; 23. Khwankot; 24. Gobarsa; 25. Kanalichhina; 26. Siroli; 27. Bisonakhan; 28. Devalthal.

Muwani—11. Bungachina; 16. Modi

TEHSIL—PITHORAGARH

Munakote—17. Munakote; 23. Gaurihat; 24. Majirkanda; 25. Dauli.

Satsiling—9. Jibi; 10. Bisabajer; 11. Totanaula; 13. Kharkdoli; 14. Marhmanle; 15. Banda; 16. Satgal.

Assembly Constituency: 69. Didihat

Berinag—38. Berinag; 39. Chokori; 40. Kalasil; 41. Garthir. *Didihat*—1. Didihat; 2. Sandev; 3. Adichora; 4. Pamtori; 5. Bhatar; 6. Bhainsyuri; 7. Borabunga; 8. Chobati; 9. Devbisona 10. Dunakote. *Muwani*—12. Algada; 13. Chamu; 14. Muwani; 15. Bomdoli; 17. Satyalgaon; 18. Chitagalgaon; 19. Chopda. *Thal*—48. Thal; 49. Bhatigaon; 50. Kotgari; 51. Amthal; 52. Sildaun; 53. Sangoud; 54. Pankhu; 55. Kalati; 56. Lohathal; 57. Uprada Pathak.

TEHSIL—MUNSIARI

Nachni—11. Tejam; 12. Dor; 13. Quiti; 14. Nachni; 15. Bhainskote; 16. Rigoniya; 17. Bansbagar; 18. Latkote; 19. Selmali.

Assembly Constituency: 70. Dharchula

Dharchula—1. Lumti; 2. Baram; 3. Jauljibi; 4. Baluwakote; 5. Dharchula; 6. Ranthi. *Khela*—7. Jumma; 8. Khet; 9. New; 10. Dugtu; 11. Sosa; 12. Sirkha; 13. Gunji.

TEHSIL—MUNSIARI

Munsiari (Jauhar)—1. Tiksen; 2. Sewila; 3. Darkote; 4. Lilam; 5. Kanalka; 6. Farwekote; 7. Madkote; 8. Basantkote; 9. Mawani Dawani.

Nachni—10. Girgaon; 20. Samkote.

OBSERVATIONAL ORGANISATION

Surface Observatories

This district lies under Meteorological sub-division, Hills

of Uttar Pradesh, West (Now Uttaranchal). This facility is available at Askote, Dharchula and Mansyari. These instrument lies in

Askote

Latitude	:	29.76° North
Longitude	:	80.33° East
Altitude	:	1468 m
Date of starting	:	16-3-1959

Dharchula

Latitude	:	29.85° North
Longitude	:	80.53° East
Altitude	:	817 m
Date of starting	:	20-3-1959

Mansiyari

Latitude	:	30.11° North
Longitude	:	80.53° East
Altitude	:	3414 m
Date of starting	:	3-4-1959

Hydromeoteorological Stations for Climatological Purposes

This facility is available at Rameshwar and Tijim, the instrument lies in

Rameshwar

Latitude	:	29.5° North
Longitude	:	80.1° East
Altituude	:	555 m
Date of starting	:	20-11-1981

Tijim

Latitude	:	30.1° North
Longitude	:	80.56° East
Altitude	:	1847 m
Date of starting	:	28-11-1956

Seismological Observatories

Data from this observatory is used for routine determination of epicentre of earth quakes preparation of bulletins etc. This facility is available at Pithoragarh.

DISASTROUS WEATHER EVENTS

Snowfall

From 28-30 December, 1996, it was severe and several person died due to it.

Floods and Heavy Rains

During 9–24 September, 1983, it was heavy rain and due to it 16 people died in a massive landslide.

DISTRIBUTION OF *SCHEDULED CASTE* POPULATION BY SEX (1991)

	POPULATION Total	Males	Females
PITHORAGARH			
	1,15,832	59,210	56,622
Agariya	7	4	3
Badhik	1	0	1
Badi	65	35	30
Baheliya	33	10	23
Baiga	33	22	11
Baiswar	4	4	0
Bajaniya	18	9	9
Bajgi	121	49	72
Balai	4	2	2
Balmiki	1,026	605	421
Bangali	10	8	2
Barwar	4	0	4
Basor	6	5	1
Bhantu	1	1	0
Bhuiya	10	6	4
Bhuyiar	5	4	1
Chamar, Dhusia, Jhusia, Jatava	2,235	1,197	1,038
Chero	28	14	14
Dabgar	17	11	6
Dhanuk	2	2	0
Dhobi	87	69	18
Dom	217	119	98
Domar	11	7	4
Ghasiya	3	0	3
Gond	58	31	27
Gual	5	3	2
Hela	5	4	1
Kalabaz	2	0	2
Kanjar	2	2	0
Khairaha	5	5	0
Khatik	34	31	3
Kol	17	12	5
Kori	71	48	23
Korwa	7	3	4
Lalbegi	5	3	2
Majhwar	3	0	3
Mazhabi	11	8	3
Musahar	7	5	2
Nat	9	1	8
Pasi, Tarmali	45	39	6
Patari	4	0	4
Rawat	12	6	6
Saharya	18	9	9
Sanaurhiya	15	8	7
Sansiya	25	14	11
Shilpkar	1,11,323	56,689	54,634
Turaiha	19	11	8
Unclassified	182	95	87

DISTRIBUTION OF *SCHEDULED TRIBE* POPULATION BY SEX DISTRICTWISE (1991)

	POPULATION		
	Total	Males	Females
	PITHORAGARH		
	18,313	9,181	9,132
Bhotia	17,657	8,827	8,830
Buksa	12	7	5
Jaunsari	6	1	5
Raji	620	335	285
Tharu	18	11	7

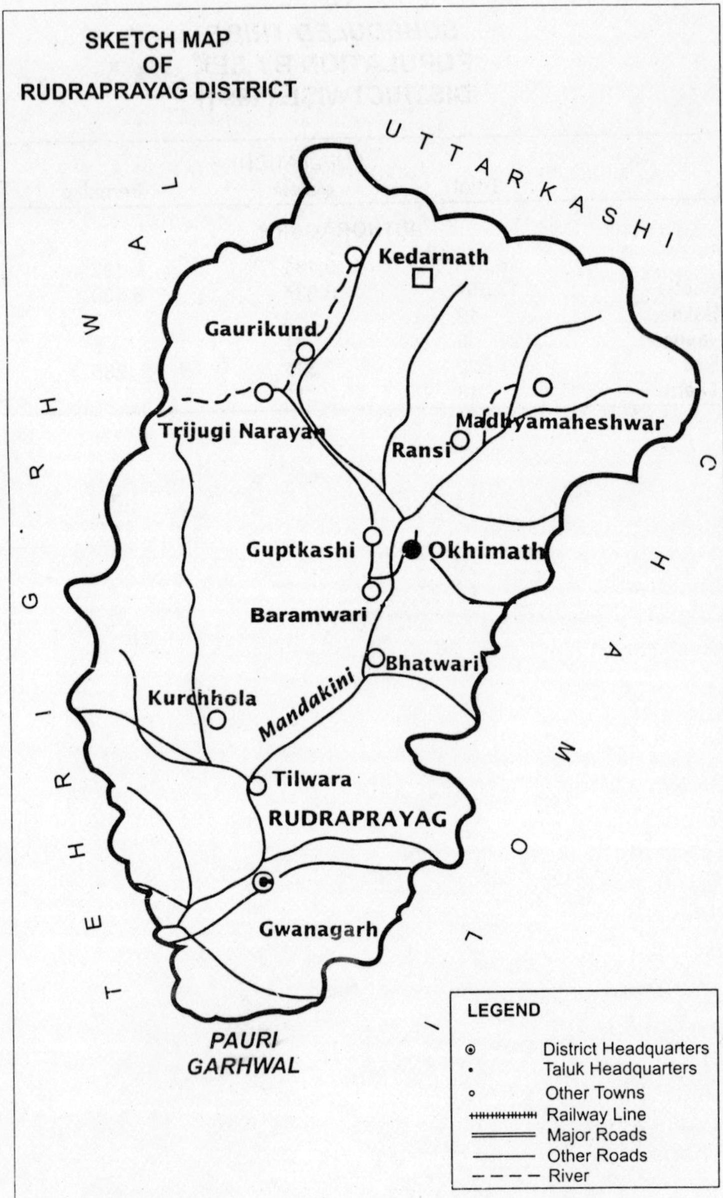

SKETCH MAP
OF
RUDRAPRAYAG DISTRICT
UTTARKASHI
CHAMOLI
TEHRI GARHWAL
PAURI GARHWAL
Kedarnath
Gaurikund
Trijugi Narayan
Madhyamaheshwar
Ransi
Guptkashi
Okhimath
Baramwari
Bhatwari
Kurchhola
Mandakini
Tilwara
RUDRAPRAYAG
Gwanagarh
LEGEND
District Headquarters
Taluk Headquarters
Other Towns
Railway Line
Major Roads
Other Roads
River

RUDRAPRAYAG

LOCATION AND AREA

Latitude : 30.2° North to 30.7° North

Longitude : 79° East to 79.4° East.

Rudraprayag is one of the districts in Uttaranchal which lies in awesome crests of the Himalayas. It is bounded on the north by Tehri Garhwal and Uttarkashi districts, on the north-east and east by Chamoli district, on the south by Garhwal and on the west by Tehri Garhwal district. The district headquarters is located at Rudraprayag town, and the district is spread over in an area of approximately 1895 sq. km.

HISTORY

The district of Rudraprayag has been carved out as a separate district vide State Government Notification No. 2867/1-323/97-R-5 dated 18th September, 1997. In pursuance of the said notification, Rudraprayag and Ukhimath tehsils of Chamoli district, Jakholi sub-tehsil (C.D. Block) of Tehri Garhwal district and Vachansyunpatati area of Srinagar tehsil of Garhwal district were detached from their respective districts and merged together to form the present new district.

The area comprising present district was one of the spiritual centres of Hinduism. This land of 'Kedar-Kshetra' was of grave importance to Devas and Brahma who took the solemn pledge to create the world, to Siva who resided in 'Panch-Kedar' to Manu and Narad, to Kuber and Ravana, to Pandu, to Pandavas who disposed their destinies here during their last sojourn in this district.

Between 8th and 10th century, this region was ruled over by Katyuri dynasty and it was succeeded by the 'Pal' dynasty of Garhwal, which was changed to 'Sah' during the 15th century. During this reign, the blood stained history of conflict with Chand dynasty of Kumaon was a ghastly tragedy. In 1804, Amar Singh Thapa, the Gurkha took over the suzerainty of this area and assumed the governorship. With the annexation of Garhwal in British territory, it was split up into eastern and western Garhwal, the former retained by the British government. In 1839, Kumaon was divided into the district of Garhwal. In 1947, like the rest of the country, this part of erstwhile Garhwal district was also liberated from British rule.

POPULATION (GENERAL, SC/ST)

Total population of the district according to 2001 census is 227461 persons, comprising of 107425 males and 120036 females. Rural population of the district is 224740 persons (105539 males and 109201 females) and urban population is 2721 persons (1886 males and 835 females)

Total population of this district as per 1991 census is 240035 persons. Of these, rural population is 219401 persons and urban population is 20634 persons.

The decennial growth rate of population of the district as a whole in relation to the state between the period 1981-1991 and 1991-2001 is presented below:

State/District	*Decennial growth rate of population (per cent)*	
	1981-91	*1991-2001*
Uttaranchal	24.23	19.20
Rudraprayag	17.51	18.44

LANGUAGES AND RELIGIONS

The dialect spoken by the people of this district is known as Garhwali. Hindi language is used for inter-group communications. English and Urdu are also spoken, but mostly in urban areas.

Main religion of the district are Hindus, Muslims, Christians, Sikhs, Buddhists.

GEOGRAPHY AND PHYSICAL FEATURES

The district is entirely mountainous, stretches across the snow free valleys to the sky scraping peaks with perpetual snow and glaciers. The terrain consists of ridges of Nanda Devi range and Badrinath range and leaves only the narrow valleys such as on the banks of Alaknanada. The adjacent ridges of the valleys are the homes of dense forests. The areas surrounding Srinagar is known as Bhabar and almost has the characteristics akin to plain. The nature is at its best in expressing its flora and fauna in the district. The serrated snowy peaks and high ridges are interpersed with a variety of vegetation, amidst which the streams, brooks and rivers provide ideal habitat for an amazing variety of wild life. The forests consist of Himalayan subtropical pine between the heights of 910 mts. and 1825 mts., moist temperate sesal forest between the altitude 1210 mts and 2150 mts. Banj Oak forests between the height of 1825 mts., and 2450 mts. at places the limit of Banj Oak forests ascend upto 2600 mts., Oak scrub forest also occur in the localities of Banj Oak forests, and so on.

RIVERS, CANALS AND WATERWAYS

Alaknanda alongwith its tributary Mandakini is the main river of this district. The other rivers are Kaliganga, Mandaniganga and Markandaganga.

TOWNS, VILLAGES AND AMENITIES

The district is at present comprised of two tehsils and two towns. The urban population of the district as percentage of total population in the census year 2001 is indicated below. It also shows the sex ratio (females per 1000 males) and density (population per sq. km.) in the urban population of the district in relation to the state:

State/ District	*Urban population as percentage of total population*	*Sex ratio, (Females per 1000 persons*		*Density (Population per sq. km.)*	
	2001	*1991*	*2001*	*1991*	*2001*
Uttaranchal	25.59	936	964	133	159
Rudraprayag	1.19	1094	1117	106	120

Amenities

Number of villages having one or more amenities in the district are Education, Medical, Drinking Water, Post and Telegraph, Market and Hat, Communications, Approach by Pucca Road and Power Supply.

COMMUNICATIONS

The district suffers from weak infrastructure because of its rugged terrain. The rail links are not at all available in the district and therefore, the communication is solely dependent on roads and pathways. In remote areas transportation is done through pack animals like horses, ponies, she-goats, etc.

AGRICULTURE AND IRRIGATION

The terraces made on slopping hill sides are the main fields of cultivation. The steep hills do not land themselves to terracing and are used for shifting cultivation. Generally, the holdings are small. The average land holding is below one hectare. Paddy, small millets and potato are the main kharif crops and wheat and barley the main rabi crops. The improved methods of cultivation are not much in vogue. Irrigation network includes governmental canals, metalled and non-metalled gulls (chennels), pumping sets in addition to hauz (a sort of tank). The low fertility of soil, short-cropping season, low temperature, high-altitude, soil erosion and small holdings mar the prospect of agriculture.

ANIMAL HUSBANDRY

Animal husbandry is an important source of supplementing the income of people of this district, particularly in rural areas. Cattle, goats and sheep are the main livestock. The quality of livestock is poor and the milk yield per milch animal is very low. Measures are being taken to improve the breed of the livestock. Forestry and horticulture employ a sizeable number of people but are not well developed sector of the economy. Production of silk cocoon is almost 717 kg. annually.

INDUSTRIES

The economy of the district pivots on agriculture. Animal husbandry including sheep rearing, orchard raising and village industries mainly wool spinning and weaving play an important role in sustaining the population of the district. There are no major industries in the district except one medium scale concern in Augustmuni in public sector. Wool and woollen goods occupy prominent place in the district. Namdas, tweeds and blankets are the main products up to the height of 1525 metres. Basket-making, mat-weaving and wood-craft are the other important cottage industries. Forest and horticulture based industries have much avenues in the district. Transportation and marketing facilities are to be created to develop these industries.

TRADE

The Table given below provides information on most important commodities manufactured, exported from and imported in the towns of this district. It also indicates the number of banks available in these towns:

Name of the town	*Most important commodities* *Manufactured*	*Exported*	*Imported*	*Banks*
Rudraprayag	–	–	Wheat, sugar, cloth	1
Kedarnath	–	–	Rice, flour, sugar	–

TOURISM

Situated in the Himalayan terrain, the district is blessed with some of the most beauteous spots and a host of religious places which offer attraction to the tourists both for pleasure as well as for religious visits. A brief account of some of the very important places of tourists interest in the district is given below:

Kedarnath: The temple lies at an elevation of 11,753 feet (3581 metres) above the level of the sea. It is one of the twelve Jyotirlingas of Lord Siva. From the time immemorial pilgrims from all the parts of India have travelled through these mountains to visit this great shrine. The legend asserts that after the great Mahabharata war, the Pandavas brothers erected this sacred temple to atone for their acts of violence and misdeed. This temple is situated in the valley of the Mandakini river. Karnataka family of Zingayat Saira Brahmins are the successive head priest of the temple for centuries. The temple of Kedarnath remains open from May to October and during winter, the temple establishment retires to Ukhimath. The other important seeing place is in the south of Kedar temple on a lofty mountains is Bhairao Ji Ka Mandir. *Kedar* is the local name of Lord Siva.

The other worth seeing sacred places are Sonprayag which is the confluence of the rivers Son Ganga and Mandakini and is in the pathway to Trijuginarayan which is almost three kilometres away from Sonprayag, Gauri Kund where the temples of Parvati Ji and Krishna Ji are located and there is a hot water spring. Ukhimath famous for the temples of Usha, Shiva, Parvati, Anirudha and Mandhata and is the most important Shiva Pith after Kedarnath, is the residence of Rawal Priests and also it is an important halting place on way to Kedarnath. Besides, above places the other sacred places in the district and in the adjoining district of Chamoli are Badrinath, Hemkund Saheb, Karanaprayag, Nandprayag, Joshimath, Pandukeshwar, Tungnath, Rudranath, Kalpnath, August-muni, Kalimath and Guptakashi. The places of religious importance of adjoining district of Chamoli are referred to in this para because, while taking a religious visit to Kedarnath-Badrinath, the people/ tourists generally wish to see these places as well.

FAIRS AND FESTIVAL

Important fairs and festival organised in different parts of the district are mentioned below:

Kishan Mela, Bishwat Sankranti, Nautha, Naumi, Nanda Devi, Gaucher, Shivratri, Ansi shivratri, Nagnath, Bikhot, Madmeshwear, Makrayan.

EDUCATION

According to 2001 Census, total literates (excluding the population in the age group of 0-6 years) is 142481 persons. Of these 80715 are males and 61766 are females. In the rural areas of the district 140489 persons (79289 males and 61200 females) are literates and in urban areas 1992 persons (1426 males and 546 females are literates. The rate of literacy of this population to the total population, excluding 0-6 years age group according to 2001 Census is 74.23 persons, of these 90.73 are male and 59.98 female.

Information on educational institutions, stadia and public libraries (including reading rooms) available in the towns of this district is provided in the table given below:

Name of the town	*Educational institutions*	*Stadia*	*Public libraries including reading rooms*
Rudraprayag	Higher Secondary/ Intermediate Schools	—	—

(2), Secondary/Matriculation Schools (2), Junior Secondary and Middle Schools (2), Primary Schools (2)

COLLEGES

Birla Postgraduate College, Augustmuni (Established 1974), Enrolment 450, Teachers 14, (Affiliated College)

College Development Council Srinagar (1995), Constituent College *(Hemvati Nandan Bahuguna Garhwal University, Established 1973).*

MEDICAL

The following table gives information on medical institutions (alongwith beds facility) available in the towns of this district.

Name of the town	*Medical institutions (alongwith beds facility)*	
Rudraprayag	Dispensaries (2)	: 12
Kedarnath	Hospital (1)	: —

ADMINISTRATION

(i) Administrative Divisions:

Tehsil: Rudraprayag, Ukhimath, Jakholi.

Towns with their Population, Urban Status and Literates (2001)

City/Town	*Urban Status*	*Population*			*Literates*		
		Person	*Male*	*Female*	*Person*	*Male*	*Female*
Kedarnath	NP	2242	1418	842	1691	1129	562
Rudra Prayag	NP	479	468	11	301	297	4

(ii) Parliamentary Constituency and Assembly Segments

No. and Name of Parliamentary Constituency. 2-GARHWAL

No. and Name of Assembly Segments of Garhwal Parliamentary Constituency which lies within the Jurisdiction of Rudra Prayag District.

Assembly Constituency: 36. Rudraprayag

TEHSIL—RUDRAPRAYAG

Barma—29. Tuneta; 30. Kot; 31. Khaliyan; 32. Pounthi; 33. Panjna; 34. Taila; 35. Kumri; 36. Bastabarma; 37. Thatibarma; 38. Futgarh; 39. Syunra. **Bhardar**—18. Budhana; 19. Bajeera; 20. Jakholi; 21. Barseer; 22. Tyunkhar; 23. Jakhal; 24. Kanda; 25. Saunda; 26. Saunra Khal; 27. Jawari; 28. Synri. **Rudraprayag**—7. Rudraprayag; 8. Chopra; 10. Nagrasu; 11. Punar; 12. Tilani; 13. Ratura; 14. Kherakhal; 15. Margaon; 16. Kandai; 17. Pipali. **Bhardar**—Forest Range. **Barma**—Rudraprayag NAC.

Assembly Constituency: 37. Kedarnath

TEHSIL—RUDRAPRAYAG

Choptajkhani—1. Chopta; 2. Ghimtoli; 3. Augastmuni; 4. MaiKoti; 5. Jaggi Kandai; 6. Saterakhal. ***Rudraprayag***—9. Sari. ***Guptkashi***—1. Fata; 2. Guptakashi; 3. Lamgaundi; 4. Bheeri; 5. Chandrapuri; 6. Pathalidhar. ***Ukhimath***—7. Kalimath; 8. Ukhimath; 9. Daira; 10. Parkandi; 11. Bhatwarisunar; 12. Barab; 13. Ganeshnagar. **Forest Area:** Forest Range.

OBSERVATIONAL ORGANISATION

Hydrometeorological Stations for Climatological Purposes:

This facility is available at Gourikund. This instrument is for the study of Rainfall snow Hydrology and Glaciology of Himalayas. These places lies in:

Gaurikund

Altitude	:	2000 m
Date of Starting	:	5-11-1985

DISASTER WEATHER EVENTS

Snowfall

From 28-30 December, 1996, it was severe and several person died due to it.

Heavy Rains

October 4th week 1985
17-18 July 1984
9 July 1990
18 August 1991
3 July, 1999

Hailstorms

20 May 1986, moderate.

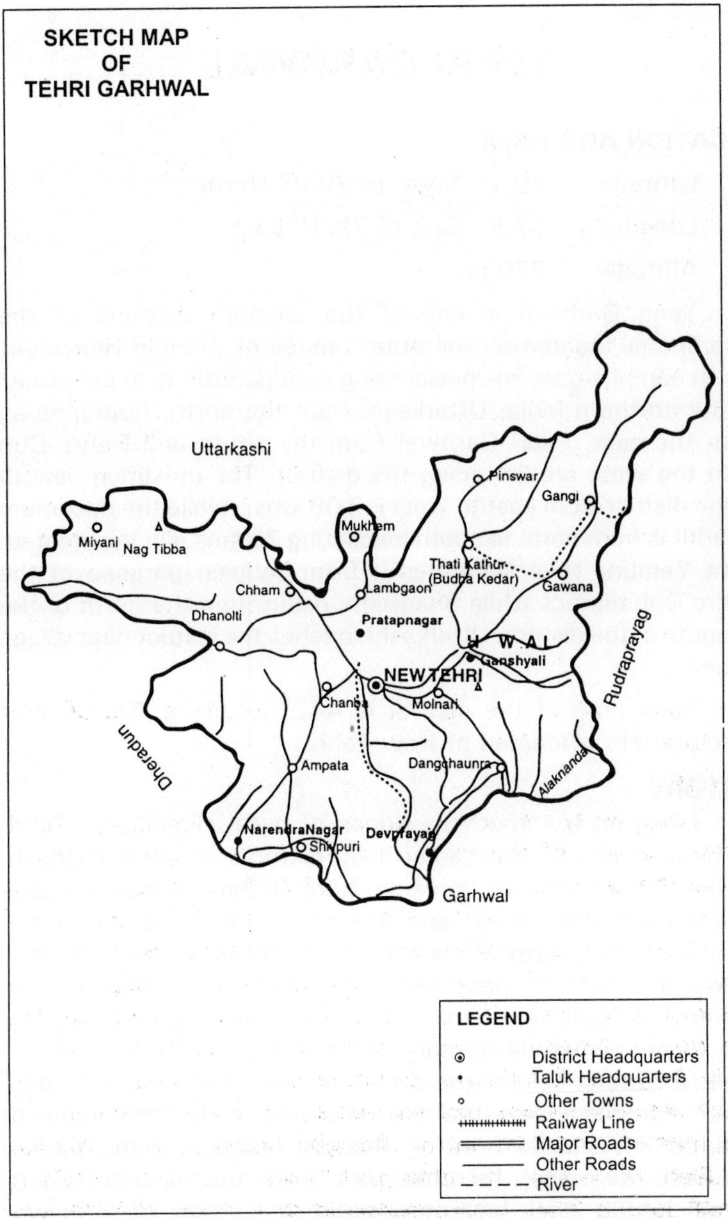
SKETCH MAP
OF
TEHRI GARHWAL
Uttarkashi
Miyani
Nag Tibba
Mukhem
Pinswar
Gangi
Thati Kathur
(Budha Kedar)
Gawana
Chham
Lambgaon
Dhanolti
Pratapnagar
Ganshyali
NEW TEHRI
Chanba
Molnari
Rudraprayag
Dheradun
Ampata
Dangchaunra
Alaknanda
NarendraNagar
Shivpuri
Devprayag
Garhwal
LEGEND
District Headquarters
Taluk Headquarters
Other Towns
Railway Line
Major Roads
Other Roads
River

TEHRI GARHWAL

LOCATION AND AREA

Latitude : 30.1° North to 30.9° North

Longitude : 77.9° East to 79.1° East

Altitude : 770 m.

Tehri Garhwal is one of the western districts of the Uttaranchal located on the outer ranges of the mid Himalayas which comprise low line peaks rising contiguously with the planes of the northern India. Uttarkashi from the north, Rudraprayag from the east, Pauri Garhwal from the south and Dehra Dun from the west are bounding the district. The maximum length of the district from east to west is 109 kms., while the maximum breadth is from north to south measuring 70 kms. On the western front Yamuna river separates it from Jaunsar pargana of the Dehra Dun district while Bhagirathi rising from the north of the Gangotri in the district. Uttarkashi touches the district near village Nagon.

Total area of the district is 4421 sq. kms. The district headquarters is located at New Tehri.

HISTORY

Lying on the southern slopes of outer Himalayas, Tehri-Garhwal is one of the sacred hilly districts of Uttar Pradesh. Before the creation of universe, Lord Brahma is said to have meditated on this sacred land. Muni-ki-Reti and Tapoban of the district are the places of penance for the ancient *Rishis*. Its hilly terrain and lack of easy communications have helped it to preserve its culture almost intact. Tehri and Garhwal are the two words combined for naming the district as Tehri-Garhwal. While the prefix Tehri is the corrupted form of the word '*Trihari*' which signifies a place that washes away all the three types of sins, namely sins born out of thought (*Mansa*), word (*Vacha*) and deed (*Karmana*), the other part 'Garh' means country fort. In fact during olden days possession of number of forts was considered as a significant measuring rod of the prosperity and power of their rulers. Prior to 888, the whole of the Garhwal-region was divided into small *garhs* ruled by separate independent kings known as Rana, Rai or Thakur. It is said that the prince Kanakpal who hailed from Malwa visited Badrinath Ji (presently in Chamoli district) where he met the then mightiest king Bhanu Pratap. King Bhanu Pratap was impressed with the prince and got his only daughter married to him and also handed over his kingdom. Gradually Kanakpal and his descendents extended their empire by conquering all the *garhs.* Thus up to 1803 i.e. for 915 years the whole of the Garhwal region remained under their control.

During 1794-95 Garhwal was under the grip of severe famine and again in 1883, the country was terribly shaken by an earthquake. Gorkhas had by then started invading this territory and heralded their influence over the region. The people of the region being already affected by natural calamities were in the deplorable condition and therefore could not resist Gorkhas invasion. On the other hand whose several attempts for capturing the fort Langoor Garhi had earlier failed, were now in powerful position. In 1803, therefore, they again invaded Garhwal region when king Pradumn Sah was the ruler. King Pradumn Sah was killed in the battle in Dehra Dun but his only son (Sudrashan Sah was minor at that time) was clearly saved by the trusted courtiers. With the victory of Gorkhas in this battle their dominion was established in Garhwal region. Later on their kingdom extended up to Kangra and they ruled over this region continuously for 12 years before they were thrown away from Kangra by Maharaja Ranjit Singh. On the other hand Sudarshan Sah would manage help from East India Company and got his kingdom freed from Gorkha rulers. The East India Company merged Kumaon, Dehra Dun and East Garhwal in the British Empire and the West Garhwal was given to Sudarshan Sah which was then known as Tehri *Riyasat.*

King Sudarshan Sah established his capital at Tehri town and afterwards his successors Pratap Sah, Kirti Sah and Narendra Sah established their capitals at Pratap Nagar, Kirti Nagar and Narendra Nagar respectively. Their dynasty ruled over this region from 1815 to 1949. During the Quit India Movement people of this region actively participated for the independence of the country. Ultimately when the country was declared independent in 1947, the inhabitants of Tehri *Riyasat,* started their movement for getting themselves freed from the clutches of *Maharaja*. Due to the movement, the situation became out of his control and was difficult for him to rule over the region. Consequently the 60th king of *Pawar Vansh,* Manvendra Sah accepted the sovereignty of Indian Government. Thus in 1949 Tehri Riyasat was merged in Uttar Pradesh and was given the status of a new district. Being a scattered region it posed numerous problems for expediting development. Resultantly on 24th February, 1960 the UP Government separated its' one tehsil which was given status of a separate district named as Uttarkashi.

POPULATION (GENERAL, SC/ST)

Total population of the district according to 2001 Census is 604608 persons, comprising 294842 males and 309766 females. Rural population of the district is 546133 persons (259078 males and 287055 females) and urban population is 58475 persons (35764 males and 22711 females).

The Scheduled Castes and Scheduled Tribes population of the district as per 1991 Census is 82384 persons and 615 persons respectively. The rural-urban breakup of this population is indicated below:

Rural	(i) Scheduled Castes	:	79013
	(ii) Scheduled Tribes	:	548
Urban	(i) Scheduled Castes	:	3371
	(ii) Scheduled Tribes	:	67

The decennial growth rate of population of the district as a whole in relation to the state between the period 1981-1991 and 1991-2001 are presented below:

State/District	*Decennial growth rate of population (per cent)*	
	1981-91	*1991-2001*
Uttaranchal	24.23	19.20
Tehri Garhwal	16.59	16.15

LANGUAGES AND RELIGION

Main language spoken in the district is Hindi.

Hindus: 574330, Muslims: 4818, Christians: 285, Sikhs: 412, Buddhists: 70, Jains: 139, Other religions and persuasions: 66, Religion not stated: 33.

GEOGRAPHY AND PHYSICAL FEATURES

A major portion of the district is having hilly tract. The plain area is more fertile than the plateau area.

Bulk of the area of the district is under forest which occupy a place of importance not only in the ecology but also in the economy of the district. These forests are rich in vegetations. Wood of commercial value is produced. These forests are also famous for production of herbs and plants of medicinal value. There has been a denudation of forests in the past, resulting in impoverishment of forest wealth. Under five year plans efforts have been made to plant trees under afforestation programme. Availability of soft wood has given rise to the manufacturing of wooden toys in the area.

RIVERS, CANALS AND WATERWAYS

Bhagirathi, Bhilangana, Balganga, Mandakini and Alaknanda are the main rivers that flow in the territory of the district. Bhagirathi from Uttarkashi district and Alaknanda from Chamoli district enter into the district and meet at Devaprayag from where onwards, the Bhagirathi flows towards the plains through Rishikesh and Haridwar and acquires the name Ganga. Alak-nanda rising from Badrinath meets Mandakini originating from Kedarnath at Rudraprayag. There are many other rivers rivulets and streams that drain the area. Situated in hilly terrain, the area of the district is largely slopy.

TOWNS, VILLAGES AND AMENITIES

The district at present comprises of 5 tehsils and 6 towns.

The urban population of the district as percentage of total population in the census 2001 is indicated below. It also shows the sex ratio (females per 1000 males) and density (population per sq. km.) in the urban population of the district in relation to the State:

State/ District	*Urban population as percentage of total population*	*Sex ratio, Females per 1000 males*		*Density (Population per sq. km.)*	
	2001	*1991*	*2001*	*1991*	*2001*
Uttaranchal	25.59	936	964	133	159
Tehri Garhwal	9.67	1048	1051	128	148

Amenities

Number (with percentage) of villages having one or more amenities in the district as per 1991 census is given below:

Sl. No.	*Amenities*	*Number of inhabited villages*	*Percentage*
1.	Education	1069	54.57
2.	Medical	396	20.21
3.	Drinking Water	1959	100.00
4.	Post and Telegraph	285	14.55
5.	Market/Hat	183	9.34
6.	Communications	425	21.63
7.	Approach by Pucca Road	229	11.89
8.	Power Supply	1169	59.67

COMMUNICATIONS

Rail links are not at all available in the district while the total length of pucca roads in the district runs to 1029 kms. Besides, Zila Parishad's kachcha road traverses a total length 217 kms. Being a hilly district covered with dense forests the net-work of road links is not only unsystematic but insufficient also. The only National Highway is from Risnikesh to Kirtinagar which runs parallel to Ganga river and reaches Devprayag after crossing the Bhagirathi. On an average, a thousand sq. km. of area is served by 232.75 kms. of road. Private buses largely ply on these roads. Pathways and tracks play an important role in providing, communication in the difficult terrain. Pack animals which can negotiate sharp bends and take easily to spiralling roads, tracks and pathways continue to be important means of transport.

AGRICULTURE AND IRRIGATION

Most of the people earn their livelihood through agriculture. This is so inspite of the adverse circumstances that the surface of the land is plateau and slopy. Moreover variations in the climate and altitude in the district too plays a prominent role for the determination of land to be put to different uses. 13 per cent of the total area was used for agriculture purposes but the proportion of population dependent on agriculture during the same year was 92 per cent. However, with the launching of various development plans, there is a rising trend in the area under main crops. Wheat and paddy are the two main crops being grown in the district. Millets (*sawan & mandua*) occupy the prominent position claiming as much as 52490 hectares of the gross area of 131719 hectares under foodgrains followed by wheat (48161 hectares and paddy (23783 hectares).

There are four tehsils in the district and the climate of all the three is almost similar. The upper portion is largely covered with dense forest while valleys are used for agricultural purposes. Most of the agricultural holdings are scattered and uneconomical. Due to small size of holding, farmers are not in a position to make use of modern tools and implements and with the result there are hardly five per cent farmer who can produce to meet their requirements for the whole year. Among commercial crops potato is mostly grown and gives good yield.

ANIMAL HUSBANDRY

Animal husbandry plays an important role in an overwhelming rural economy of the district by supplementing the income of the farmers as well as by providing draught power for agricultural operations. Bovine population including buffaloes account for over two-thirds of the total population of live-stock. While there were 23990 milch cows, there were 38028 milch buffaloes. The goats numbered 100833 heads against 33732 heads of sheep. The quality of live-stock is very poor in the area and the average milk yield per she-buffalo is estimated to be merely 2.2 litres per day against 1.11 litres per milch cow. The production of mutton is estimated to be 15 tonnes while the production of wool is of the order of 29 tonnes per annum. Efforts are under way for improving the quality of live-stock especially milch animals and sheep. As many as 14 veterinary hospitals, 10 artificial insemination centres and sub-centres, two sheep breeding farms and 8 sheep and wool propagation centres are functioning in the district.

INDUSTRIES

As it is a characteristic of hill districts, this district too suffers from weak infrastructure and almost insignificant industrial development. There are only four factories registered under Factory Act. Cottage, village and smali scale industries engage 156 persons in 104 units. Manufacturing of wooden toys and weaving of woollen garments, rugs and carpets, lime, footwear and battery plates are some of the village and small scale industries. Training centres have been opened by the Government for imparting training in manufacturing of wooden toys, weaving and hosiery besides providing credit and market facilities and making available the raw material.

TRADE, COMMERCE AND EXPORT

It can be observed that there are hardly any manufacturing activities in the towns of the district. Only woollen shawls and soaps have been reported to have been manufactured. The important commodities of import are foodgrains.

The following table gives most important commodity manufactured, imported and exported from towns.

Name of the towns	*Most important commodity*		
	Manufactured	*Exported*	*Imported*
1	*2*	*3*	*4*
Devaprayag	—	—	Foodgrains
Kirtinagar	—	—	Wheat
Muni-ki-Reti	Soap	Soap	Foodgrains
Narendranagar	—	—	Wheat
Tehri	Woollen shawls	Mangoes	Foodgrains

TOURISM

The district formed part of Kedar Khand which is a

celebrated centre of Vedic culture since ancient days. It is said that hymns of the *Vedas* have been collected and compiled in this region. The district, thus had been matrix of religious and cultural learning. Following its ancient pursuit, the district has made considerable advance in the field of education.

Tourism possesses great potential for development in the district. Situated in the Himalayan terrain, the area is blessed with some of the most beauteous spots and a host of religious places offer great attraction for tourists. Efforts are under way to develop infra-structure for tourism.

The detailed description of some of the important places of interest is given below:

Tehri. Known as Ganesh Prayag, it is situated at the height of 700 m. at the meeting point of Bhagirathi and Bhilangana. At the time of Maharaja Sudarshan Sah, it was capital of his kingdom. Apart from university and a number of educational institutions, there are temples of Badrinathji and Kedarnathji. It is said that Swami Ram Tirth had lived in a cave near Tehri on the bank of Bhilangana river for quite some time. A monument has been constructed at Simlasue in his memory.

Pratapnagar. This is one of the most fascinating places located barely 15 kms. away from Tehri at an altitude of 2011 m. It is surrounded by dense forests of bamboo and bushes. The hills of Badrinath, Kedarnath, Gangotri and Yamunotri covered with white snow present a beautiful spectacle and can be seen vividly from this place. It is now easily approachable through a motorable road.

Devaprayag. Famous for its Ragunath Ji temple, this place lies on a rock at the confluence of Bhagirathi and Alaknanda. Dev Sharma, a *Tapasvi* is said to have got it constructed at this place in ancient days.

Kirtinagar. It was named after Raja Kirti Sah, this place lies on Tehri-Srinagar road. A number of government offices are situated here.

Narendranagar. It was a small village earlier named as Odathali but presently it is the district headquarters and is located on Rishikesh-Tehri road at an altitude of 1150 m from the sea level and it has been named after Raja Narendra Sah. From this place during the night, the Ganga river filled with glittering stars looks most fascinating. The climate of this place is, very healthy.

Muni-ki-Reti. This place is adjacent to town Rishikesh situated on the bank of Ganga river. Swami Shivanand Ashram and Kailash Ashram are the famous religious temples located here.

Besides, Thati Kathur, Kukhem, Kanaktal, Sirkanda. Kaungapuri and Chandrabadni are other important religious places in the district.

FAIRS AND FESTIVALS

Important fairs and festivals organised in different parts of the district are mentioned below:

Chamba Thoulu, Gajja Tholou, Dharu Mela, Suri-ka-Mela, Bandwal Gaon, Agram Thoulu, Churiya Kheti Thoulu, Kamand Thoulu, Badshahee Thoulu Jamti-ka-Mela, Thattud-ka-Mela, Lalotan-ka-Mela, Khyarsi-ka-Mela, Moldhar-ka-Mela, Naghthan-ka-Mela, Takrauli-ka-Mela, Srikot-ka-Mela, Kali Devi, Jakh-ka-Mela, Panch-badi-ka-Mela, Surkanda, Bhind Maun-ka-Mela, Manj Maun-ka Mela, Chhanangaon-ka-Mela, Jakhni, Kasyan, Khandogi, Aginisan, Godolia, Pankhal, Pilkhi, Kothyara, Gali, Sem Mukhan, Sri Kunjapuri Yatra, Pali Thoulu, Digoli Thoulu, Bikhot, Baisakh Thoula, Fateld, Negela Devta, Mald, Dangchaura Thoulu, Danda Thoulu, Pauri-ka-Thoulu, Kaila Pir, Baisakha Thoulu Hollyag, Nagendra Devta, Chandra Badni, Banjagri, , Jagdajat, Chameshwar Mahadev, Basant Panchmi.

EDUCATION

According to 2001 census, total literates (excluding the population in the age group of 0–6 years) is 340878 persons. Of these, 209806 are males and 131072 are females. In the rural areas of the district 295987 persons (180582 males and 115405 females) are literates and in urban areas 44891 persons (29224 males and 15667 females) are literates. The rate of literacy of this population to the total population, excluding 0–6 years age group according to 2001 census is shown below:

1991			*2001*		
Persons	*Males*	*Females*	*Persons*	*Males*	*Females*
48.46	72.09	26.31	67.04	85.62	49.76

There are 5.84 Primary Schools in urban areas of the district per ten thousand of population. The maximum ratio of 13.59 Primary Schools is observed in Kirtinagar and the minimum of 3.27 in Tehri. A ratio of 3.41 Junior Secondary/Middle Schools is obtained per ten thousand of population in urban areas of the district. The largest ratio of 13.59 schools is observed in Kirtinagar against the minimum of 2.45 in Tehri. There are 3.41 schools of Matriculation Standard per ten thousand of urban population of the district. The maximum ratio of 13.59 schools of Matriculation Standard is observed in Kirtinagar followed by 5.88 in Devaprayag while the minimum ratio of 2.45 is observed in Tehri. Kirtinagar and Muni-ki-Reti do not have any Inter College. The ratio of Inter Colleges works out to 2.43 per ten thousand of urban population in the district. The maximum ratio of 5.88 Inter Colleges is observed in Devaprayag while the minimum of 2.45 in Tehri. As a matter of fact there is one Inter College in each of the three towns which gives a ratio more than unity because of small population size and the variation between towns is attributable to the variation in population size.

COLLEGES

Swami Ramtirth P.G. College, Tehri (1970). Enrolment 2100, Teachers 57 (Constituent College).

Government Degree College, Chamba (1979).

Omakaranand Mahavidhyalaya, Deopriyag, Enrolment 80, Teachers 3.

(Above named colleges belong to Hemwati Nandan Bahuguna, Garhwal University. Established 1973.)

MEDICAL

There are 4.09 beds per thousand of population in medical institutions of the urban areas of the district. The maximum ratio of 10.01 beds per thousand of population is obtained in Narendranagar followed by 5.88 beds in Devaprayag against the minimum of 1.77 beds in Muni-ki-Reti.

ADMINISTRATION

(i) Administrative Divisions:

Tehsils: Ghansali Pratap Nagar, Tehri, Narendra Nagar, Devaprayag.

Towns with their Population, Urban Status and Literates (2001)

City/Town	Urban Status	Population			Literates		
		Person	Male	Female	Person	Male	Female
Chamba	NP	6579	3908	2671	5032	3205	1827
Dhaluwala	CT	11206	6153	5053	8512	5121	3391
Kirtinagar	NP	1040	597	443	790	480	310
Muni Ki Rati	NP	7879	4983	2896	5751	3931	1820
Narendra Nagar	MB	4796	2844	1952	3909	2455	1454
Tehri	MB	25425	16493	8932	19780	13423	6357

(ii) Parliamentary Constituencies along Assembly Segments:

No. and Name of Parliamentary Constituency

1- TEHRI GARHWAL

No. and Name of Assembly Segments of Tehri Garhwal Parliamentary Constituency which lies within the Jurisdiction of Tehri Garhwal district.

Assembly Constituency: 4. Tehri Garhwal.

TEHSIL—GHANSALI

Jakhnidhar. 1. Nandgaon; 2. Gadoliya; 3. Jakhnidhar; 4. Nawakot; 5. Khandogi; 6. Anjanisain; 7. Garakot; 41. Paurikhal; 42. Gaumukh; 43. Rauddhar; 44. Jagdhar

TEHSIL—TEHRI

Chamba. 18. Dibnu; 19. Gyansu; 20. Ranichauri; 25. Nail; 26. Tangala; 27.Devtadhar; 28. Kanatal; 29. Nagrajadhar; 30. chamba; 31. Chopriyali. ***Udaipur.*** 15. Pali; 16. Sirain; 17. Padiyargaon. **Forest Area:** Forest area Chamba KC. **Urban Area:** N.P. Tehri.

Assembly Constituency: 5. Pratapnagar

TEHSIL—GHANSALI

Chamiyala. 36. Baheri. ***Dangi.*** 8. Mandar; 9. Devtadhar; 10. Chandreshwarsain.

TEHSIL—PRATAPNAGAR

Lambgaon. 9. Silari; 10. Godari; 11. Lambgaon; 12.

Kotalgaon; 13. Pujargaon; 14. Paniyala; 15. Khetpali; 16. Burkot; 17. Kandiyalgaon; 18. Garwangaon; 19. Deengaon; 20. Mukthem.

Pratapnagar. 1. Okhala; 2. Chherapdhar; 3. Raulakot; 4. Kothaga; 5. Pratapnagar; 6. Manjaf; 7. Siwalgaon; 8. Pilanidhar; 21. Madananegi; 22. Kathuli; 23. Siloli;24. Kauchounri. **Forest Area:** Forest Area (Lambgaon KC).

Assembly Constituency: 6. Ghansali

TEHSIL—GHANSALI

Chamiyala. 24. Thatikathur; 25. Pinswar; 26. Binayakhal; 27. Dalgaon; 28. Kapholgaon; 29. Amarsar; 30. Bhatgaon; 31. Gongarh; 32. Aargarh; 33. Tungana; 34. Chamiyala; 35. Kontibangaon; 37. Gangi; 38. Ghuttu; 39. Dhopardhar; 40. Devath. ***Dangi.*** 11. Paukhal; 12. Pilkhi; 13. Thela; 14. Holta; 15. Muyalgaon; 16. Dangi; 17. Maigadhar; 18. Akhori; 19. Dhaunikhal; 20. Pakh; 21. Kathur-Hindaw; 22. Chanji; 23. Pangriyana. ***Forest Area.*** Forest Area

Assembly Constituency: 7. Deoprayag

TEHSIL—DEOPRAYAG

Chandarbadni. 6. Toli; 7. Palethi; 8. Gosil; 16. Chandarbadni; 17. Devalkandi; 18. Hinsriyakhal; 19. Patakhal; 20. Bagadwaldhar; 21. Kunri; 23. Nandi; 24. Karakot. ***Deoprayag.*** 4. Lalathpatoun; 5. Lalurikhal; 9. Birakot; 10. Hindolakhal; 11. Amani; 12. Mahar; 13. Bhatkot; 15. Dansara. ***Kirtinagar.*** 22. Jakhi; 25. Thatidagar; 26. Dhundsir; 27. Sirsed; 28. Silkahal; 29. Palidangchaura; 30. Badon; 31. Maletha; 32. Kilkileshwar; 33. Sendri; 34. Badiyargarh; 35. Ghandiyaldhar 36. Chiledi; 37. Ringoli. **Urban Area:** N.P. Deoprayag

Assembly Constituency: 8. Narendranagar

TEHSIL—DEOPRAYAG

Deoprayag. 1. Kurn; 2. Baunth; 3. Bachelikhal; 14. Bharpur. **Forest Area:** Forest Area (Devprayag KC).

TEHSIL—NARENDRA NAGAR

Chaka. 5. Odada; 8. Bhainsyarow; 9. Ampata; 13. Maroragad; 14. Shrikot; 15. Ranakot; 16. Palkot; 17. Chaka;

18. Kweeli; 19. Pokhri; 20. Bamangaon. ***Narendra Nagar.*** 1. Narendranagar; 2. Aagrakhal; 3. Dyuli; 4. Tapovan; 6. Fakot; 7. Kumali; 10. Jamola; 11. Kakhur; 12. Pajegaon; 21. Nai; 22. Maindath. **Forest Area:** Forest Area (KC Narendranagar). **Urban Area:** Munikireti N.P., Narendra Nagar N.P.

Chamba. 21. Nakot; 22. Kothi; 23. Naicholi; 24. Gaja; 32. Nagni

Assembly Constituency: 9. Dhanolti

TEHSIL—TEHRI

Dhanolti. 1. Mathiyangaon; 2. Lwarkha; 3. Bhutsi; 4. Satyoun; 5. Gawana; 6. Aginda; 7. Than; 8. Dhanolti; 9. Bharamsari; 10. Thatyur; 11. Ontan; 12. Sunaon. ***Nainbag.*** 13. Kyari; 14. Tuneta; 15. Kempti; 16. Bhatoli; 17. Takama; 18. Bel; 19. Kharson; 20. Nainbag; 21. Rampurnegiyana; 22. Basangaon; 23. Biror; 24. Munogi. ***Udaipur.*** 1. Katkhet; 2. Laluri; 3. Bayargaon; 4. Maindkhal 5. Lawani; 6. Kandarkhal; 7. Chham; 8. Bangiyal; 9. Kailar; 10. Kamand; 11. Thauldhar; 12. Bhaldiyana; 13. Kandikhal; 14. Kafalpani

MINERALS AND ORES

Galena—at Pindki (30°55':78°25').

Limestone—at GUINOTA (30°45':78°15'), BARAHAT (30°15':78°27'), SATENGAL (30°22':78°13')

Copper—Copper belt from Bagroi (30°18': 78°44') for a distance of about 60 km.

Chalcopyrite—near Lhelta (30°36':78°48')

Malachite—near Lathwar (30°32': 77°58'), Dasumudu (31°9': 79°85')

Gypsum—Economically workable gypsum is found as replacement pockets in the Krol dolomite limestone at SERA and in the Nirgad and DHAUL SOT *nalas* to the north of LACHMANJHULA. The gypsum deposits of DHAULSOT and Nir Gad areas near GUGTHANI village occur very much interelated with red shales and limestones.

Iron—Occurrences of iron-ore as sideritie replacements in limestone are reported from BIRETI and along the JALKON *nadi* N.N.W. of BHELUNDA. Veins of limonite in brecciated granite are seen in the MANA GAD near the snout of the MANA GLACIER.

Arsenic—A small vein of arsenopyrite has been recorded near Maku (30.5, 79.1). The occurrence appears to be very small. The sample on assaying yielded 0.67 ozs. of silver per long ton.

Building Materials. Excellent roofing slates are said to be found along the valley of the Aglar River (30.5, 78.1) to the North of Mussorie.

Copper—A copper belt has been traced from Bagori (30.5, 78.4) to Kaproli (30.3, 78.7) for a distance of about 65 kms. Occurrence of pebbles of chalcopyrite near Lehta (30.6, 78.8) associated with galena. Traces of malachite occur in Nagthat quartzite below Lathwar (30.5, 77.9) and the Garhwal quartzites near Terri Gangotri Pilgrim track.

Limestone—Occurrence of lime stone has been reported (30.3, 78.3) which contains a few bands of high grade limestone intercalated among highly silicious dolomitic limestones of the Krol series. Other occurrences of limestone are reported from Guinota (30.7, 78.2), Barahat (30.7, 78.4), Satengal (30.4, 78.2).

Pyrites—A small deposit of pyrites occurs near Sergid (30.4, 79.2).

OBSERVATIONAL ORGANISATIONS

Surface observatories

This district lies under Meteorological sub-division, Hills of Uttar Pradesh, West (now Uttaranchal). This instrument lies at Mukhim and at Tehri.

Mukhim

Latitude	:	30.6° North
Longitude	:	78.5° East
Altitude	:	1981 m
Date of starting	:	10-12-1955

Tehri

Latitude : 30.4° North

Longitude : 78.5° East

Altitude : 770 m

Date of Startling : 1-12-1955

Hydrometeorological Stations for Climatological Purposes

This facility is available at Dharasu and Ghuttu. The instrument lies in:

Dharasu

Latitude : 30.6° North

Longitude : 78.3° East

Altitude : 792 m

Date of Starting : 20-12-1955

Ghuttu

Latitude : 30.5° North

Longitude : 78.8° East

Altitude : 1524 m

Date of starting : 20-12-1955

DISASTROUS WEATHER EVENTS

Snowfall—From 28-30 December 1996, it was severe and several person died due to it.

Hailstorm—On 20th May 1986, it was moderate, wheat and other fruit crops damaged.

Floods and Heavy Rains—During 17-18 July, 1986, it was severe, 14 persons died in the villages of Devprayag tehsil and hundred of cattle washed away.

On 18 August 1991, it was heavy rains, 5 cattle heads perished 3 houses completely damaged. On 3rd July 1994, it was heavy rains, several housed damaged, several persons died.

DISTRIBUTION OF *SCHEDULED CASTE* POPULATION BY SEX (1991)

	POPULATION		
	Total	Males	Females
TEHRI GARHWAL	82,384	41,590	40,794
Agariya	273	138	135
Badhik	13	7	6
Badi	441	211	230
Baheliya	25	15	10
Baiga	267	77	190
Baiswar	260	96	164
Bajaniya	12	5	7
Bajgi	8,053	4,010	4,043
Balahar	108	50	58
Balai	43	18	25
Balmiki	1,275	737	538
Bangali	57	28	29
Banmanus	72	35	37
Bansphor	16	6	10
Barwar	16	12	4
Basor	121	62	59
Bawariya	3	2	1
Beldar	6	6	0
Beriya	21	15	6
Bhantu	40	17	23
Bhuiya	13	6	7
Bhuyiar	7	4	3
Chamar, Dhusia, Jhusia, Jatava	7,970	4,104	3,866
Chero	140	74	66
Dabgar	8	6	2
Dhangar	8	8	0
Dhanuk	76	51	25
Dharkar	57	36	21
Dhobi	337	201	136
Dom	6,856	3,601	3,255
Domar	47	17	30
Ghasiya	19	12	7
Gond	22	13	9
Gual	121	56	65
Habura	6	5	1
Hari	152	74	78
Hela	24	17	7
Kalabaz	4	3	1
Kanjar	10	7	3
Kapariya	1	1	0
Karwal	15	9	6
Khairaha	21	7	14
Kharwar (excluding Benbansi)	3	3	0
Khatik	85	47	38
Khorot	11	5	6
Kol	1,259	609	650
Kori	6,519	3,202	3,317
Korwa	8	3	5
Lalbegi	29	17	12
Majhwar	109	59	50
Mazhabi	11	6	5
Musahar	31	18	13
Nat	31	18	13
Pankha	4	1	3
Parahiya	94	52	42
Pasi, Tarmali	318	166	152
Patari	20	14	6
Rawat	192	114	78
Saharya	62	26	36
Sanaurhiya	112	56	56
Sansiya	187	106	81
Shilpkar	46,173	23,156	23,017
Turaiha	51	24	27
Unclassified	39	29	10

DISTRIBUTION OF *SCHEDULED TRIBE* POPULATION BY SEX (1991)

	POPULATION		
	Total	Males	Females
	TEHRI GARHWAL		
	615	266	349
Bhotia	283	152	131
Buksa	18	16	2
Jaunsari	292	83	209
Tharu	18	11	7
Unclassified	4	4	0

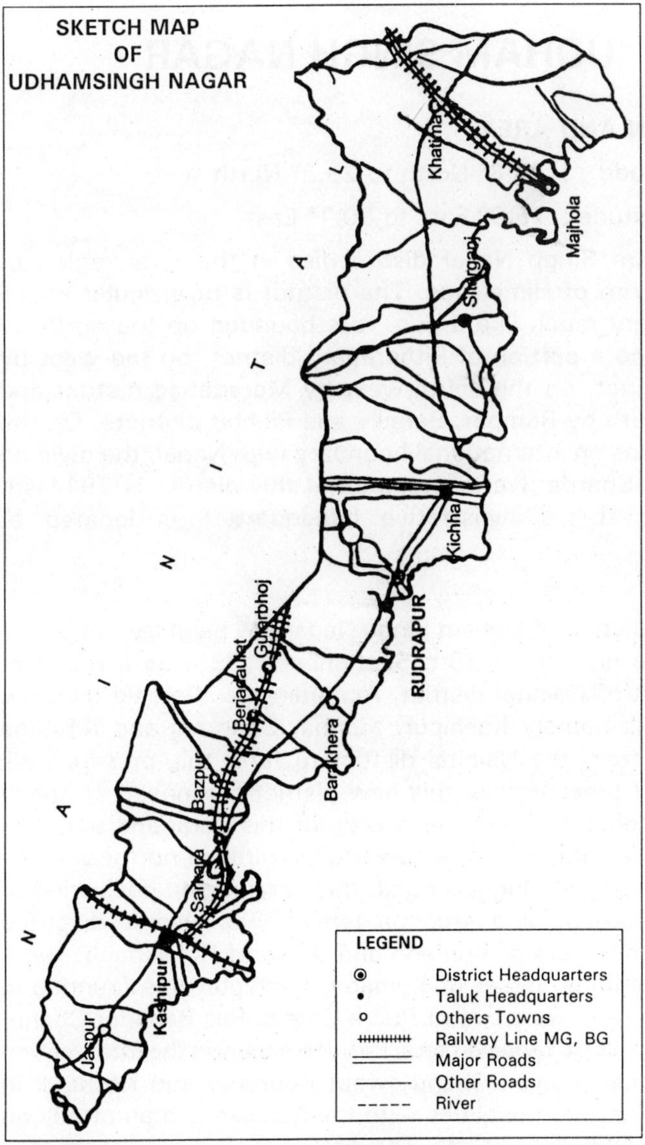

SKETCH MAP
OF
UDHAMSINGH NAGAR
N A I N I T A L
Khatima
Majhola
Sitarganj
Kichha
RUDRAPUR
Gularbhoj
Barakhera
Bazpur
Kashipur
Jaspur
LEGEND
District Headquarters
Taluk Headquarters
Others Towns
Railway Line MG, BG
Major Roads
Other Roads
River

UDHAM SINGH NAGAR

LOCATION AND AREA

Latitude : 28.8° North to 29.2° North

Longitude : 78.9° East to 80.1° East

Udham Singh Nagar district lies in the tarai region of Southern rim of Himalayas. The district is of irregular shape looking very much like a gun. It is bounded on the north by Nainital and a portion of Pithoragarh district, on the west by Bijnor district, on the south-west by Moradabad district and on the south by Rampur, Bareilly and Pilibhit districts. On the east it forms an international boundary with Nepal, the dividing line being Sharda river. Total area of this district is 2911 sq. kms. and the administrative headquarters is located at Rudrapur.

HISTORY

The district of Udham Singh Nagar has been carved out as a separate district on 29th September, 1995, as a result of bifurcation of Nainital district. According to the said division, four tehsils namely Kashipur, Kichha, Sitarganj and Khatima detached from the Nainital district to form this present new district. At present also, this new district comprised ot above said four tehsils. The earlier history of this Tarai and the plain tracts is associted with the powerful empires of northern India. During the period Mughals ruled, this Tarai region consisting of Kichha, Sitarganj and Khatima tehsils was always disputed between the rulers of Kumaon and those of Rohilkhand. *Ain-i-Akbari* mentions Sarkar of Kumaon, Kashipur was founded in 1639 by a representative of Rudra Chand. Baz Bahadur Chand, who died in 1698 regained tarai through securing the intervention of Shahjahan. Kalyan Chand swept Rudrapur and Kashipur in 1730 after a long hostilities with the Rohillas and an attack on him by the Nawab of Avadh. The district of Nainital was created on 15th October, 1981.

POPULATION (2001)

The population of the district according to 2001 census is 1234548 persons comprising 6490220 males and 585528 females. Rural population of the district is 831407 persons (434162 males and 397245 females) and urban population is 403141 persons (214858 males and 188283 females).

The decennial growth rate of population of the district as a whole in relation to the state between the period 1981-1991 and 1991-2001 is presented below:

State/District	*Decennial growth rate of population (per cent)*	
	1981-91	*1991-2001*
Uttaranchal	24.23	19.20
Uddham Singh Nagar	44.46	27.79

LANGUAGES AND RELIGION

Main language spoken in the district is Hindi. Main religion of the district are Hindus, Muslims, Christians, Sikhs, Buddhists, and Jains.

GEOGRAPHY AND PHYSICAL FEATURES

The general appearance of the tract is that of a plain gently sloping towards the south-east. Topographically, the region is akin to the plains, having good forests and jungles or savennahs of grass and reed. There are damp and marshy tracts also due to heavy rainfall averaging annually from 1371.6 ms. to 1625.6 ms. This region has the most fertile land. In the upper portion of the Tarai, the soil is a light sandy loam. Further south, however, the soil contains more alum and less silika and lower down a stiff clay is found which occurs everywhere in the depressions. The western Tarai has a soil which is a fairly dark consistent loam but towards the east the soil is light and friable. The best irrigated lands are known as Talaon and when not artificially irrigated as Uparaon. The land, with imperfect irrigation facility are called as Panchar. The zoology is very varied and deserves some attention. The wide range of climate and elevations furnishes a list comprising most of the animals of the plains as well as those of the hill tracts of this state. The wild elephants are still to be found in considerable number between the Sharda and the Ganga. The tiger is found here and there, from the Tarai upto the highest points of the district. In the Tarai, the tiger attains a very large size, i.e. of over ten feet in length. The other mammals found in abundance are snow leopard, Himalayan black bear, sambhar, wild hill goat etc.

RIVERS, CANALS AND WATERWAYS

To the east of this district, there is the river Sharda indeed, but it merely touches the eastern fringe of Pargana Bilehri. On western portion of the district, the river Kosi passes through it from north to south direction. Other rivers are Phika, Gola, Deoha and Kalauna.

TOWNS, VILLAGES AND AMENITIES

The district at present comprises of three tehsils, 7 Community Development Blocks and 17 towns. It has 845 villages.

The urban population of the district as percentage of total population in the census year 2001 is indicated below. It also shows the sex ratio (females per thousand males) and density (population per sq. kms.) in the urban population of the district in relation to the state.

State/ District	*Urban population as percentage of total population*	*Sex ratio, females per 1000 males*		*Density (Population per sq. km.)*	
	2001	*1991*	*2001*	*1991*	*2001*
Uttaranchal	25.59	936	964	133	159
Udham Singh Nagar	32.65	881	906	149	198

COMMUNICATIONS

The district is served by three metre gauge railway lines i.e. (i) Moradabad-Kashipur-Ramnagar, (ii) Bareilly-Kichha-Haldwani cum Kathgodam, and (iii) Pilibhit-Khatima-Tanakpur. There is another metre gauge tract between Kashipur-Sultanpur-Bazpur-Lalkuan. As regards road communication, the State Highway No. 12 passes through the district from west to east direction which interlinked most of the tehsils, Community

Development Blocks headquarters apart from the important towns. Another State Highway No. 41 run through Kashipur interconnecting Thakurdwara (Moradabad) from south-west to northern direction. These indicate that the district is well served by both rail and road transports.

AGRICULTURE AND IRRIGATION

Cultivation is the main occupation in this district. The most important crop is wheat followed by paddy. Maize, Madua, Barley, Sawan and Jowar-bajra are other main foodgrains in that order. Masoor, gram and urad are the pulse crops of the district but these are grown in the small area. Sugarcane and potato are cash crops of the district. In the district, more than 80 per cent land of the total area is cultivable of which 66.75 per cent, 73.19 per cent, 34.79 per cent and 27.31 per cent are irrigated in Kashipur, Kichha, Sitarganj and Khatima tehsils respectively. The irrigation network of the district include canal and tube wells. The canal system of the district consists of a big canal head at Ban Basa at Sharda river which irrigates a large area of Tarai tract. The reservoirs at Dhaura in Kichha, Begul and Nanak-Sagar in Sitarganj, and Tumaria in Kashipur strengthen the canal system in the district.

ANIMAL HUSBANDRY

The livestock population of the district consists of cattle, buffaloes and sheep. There are many veterinary hospitals, veterinary dispensaries, artificial insemination centres etc. which look after the welfare of animal wealth.

INDUSTRIES

Industries of the district are basically agro-based. Extensive cultivation of sugarcane in the district prompted many sugar mills to come-up. Bazpur, Kashipur, and Kichha sugar mills are using sugarcane produced in the district. The crushing capacity of Bazpur mill that was about 1600 tonnes a day is raised to 3000 tonnes. The distillery capacity of Bazpur mill has also been raised from 25000 litres to 50000 litres. Kichha mill is equipped with the crushing capacity of 3000 tonnes a day. Two new sugar mills are also started at Sitarganj and Gadarpur. U.P. Textile Corporation has setup cotton spinning mills at Kashipur and Jashpur. Kashipur spinning mill is of 25000 spindles. A unit of Hindustan Paper Corporation has been etablished at Kashipur with the cost of Rs. 255 crores. Kashipur is fastly emerging as an industrial centre. Other worth mentioning unit in the district is Solvent Extraction at Kashipur.

Important Industries:

Daulat Electronics Ltd. 7th K.M. Stone, Moradabad-Kashipur Road.

Production of video housing and video magnetic tape/ cassettes. The company has collaboration with M/s. Magnetic Chemical Ltd. Hong Kong.

Ester Industries Ltd. P.O. Charubeta, Pilibhit Road, Khatima.

Manufacturer: Bottle grade chips, PBT yarn and audio grade film.

India Glycols Ltd. A-1, Industrial Area, Bazpur Road.

Manufacturer: Ethylene, glycol, ethylene oxide, di-ethylene glycol and heavy glycol.

Khaitan Hostombne Spinels Ltd. (Formerly known as Khaitan Refractories Ltd.) Tanakpur.

Manufacturer: Dead burnt magnesite pear and ramming mass.

Polyplex Corporation Ltd. Lohia Head Road, Khatima.

Manufacturer: Polyster film and lacquered film.

Prakash Pipes & Industries Ltd. 5th K.M. Stone, Kashipur-Moradabad Road, Gangapur.

Manufacturer: Rigid PVC pipes, profiles, fittings and moulded fittings, 14" TV picture tubes, magnetic tapes for video cassettes, blank video cassettes, glass shell and electron gun for 14" TV picture tubes.

Shriram Honda Power Equipment Ltd. (Vill. & P.O.) Bhigwara, (via) Kichha.

Manufacturer: Portable generating sets.

TRADE, COMMERCE AND EXPORT

The following table presents most important commodities manufactured in, exported from and imported into the towns of the district. It also indicate the number of Banks available in the respective towns.

Name of the towns	Most important commodity			Banks
	Manufactured	*Exported*	*Imported*	
1	*2*	*3*	*4*	*5*
Bazpur	Sugar	Sugar	Salt, Edible oil, soap	5
Gadarpur	Rice, Sugar	Rice, Wheat, Sugarcane	Soap Medicines, Edible oil	3
Jaspur	Gur Rice	Wood, Gur, Rice	Spices, Soap, Pulses	2
Kashipur	Printed quilt, Sugar Starw Board	Sugar Foodgrains, Handloom cloth	Leather Medicines, Yarn	7
Khatima	Rice, Flour	Rice, Wheat, Wood	Cloth Soap, Sugar	3
Kichha	Sugar	Paddy Oil seeds, Sugar	Fish, Vegetables, Fruits	4
Rudrapur	S.P. Solvent Oil, Tractor trollies, Agricultural Implements	Rice, Tractor trollies, S.P. Solvent oil	Iron, Cloth Fertilizers	8
Sitarganj	—	Rice, Oil seeds, Lentil	Sugar, Spices Vegetable	3
Sultanpur	Ice cream, Menthol, Gur	Chillies, Garlic, Corinder	Edible oil, Sugar Salt	1

TOURISM

Wildlife lovers could not find the sprawling jungle at its best, other than Corbett Park, popularly known as Tiger Country. This wildlife sanctuary is set in 125 sq. kms. of the Kumaon foothills. Tiger, leopard and black bear, elephant, huge river tortoise and several varieties of deer are more common animals. There are watch-towers (machans) to facilitate a deer peep of jungle, which is full of green foliage that provides luxurious shelter to the beasts allowing them to roam freely. These are conducted tours to the park via Dhikula, that includes, entrance, guide charges and transport, tin accommodation etc. Named after a British hunter, who was in acute love with jungles of Kumaon and also splendid writer of Shikar-literature, this abode of deadly and mysterious jungle cries has a haunting appeal to naturalists and for a lay tourist in general.

HOTEL

Hotel Sonia, (Government Approved) 2 star.

Access: 16 kms. from Airport, 2 kms. from Railway station, 1.5 kms. from Bus stand.

Rooms: 21

FAIRS AND FESTIVALS

Important fairs and festivals organised in different parts of the district are mentioned below:

Janam Ashtmi, Chitrasila, Sita Bani, Shivratri, Bal Sundary Devi, Zahar Aulia, Chamunda Devi, Gudashi, Ganga Baba, Naumi Mela, Budha Babu, Kartika Purnima, Moteshwar, Muharram, Poornagiri, Attaria, Uldhan, Bale Miyan, Chellum, Sarwarpir, Ghat Fair, Sisla, Jharni Mahadeo, Bhimeshwar, Nanda Ashtmi, Kailash.

EDUCATION

According to 2001 Census, the population of the total literates (excluding the population in the age group of 0-6 years) is 671880 persons. Of these 409623 are males and 262057 are females. In the rural areas of the district 428933 persons (265777 males and 163156 females) are literates and in urban areas 242747 persons (143846 males and 98901 females) are literates. The rate of literacy of this population to the total population excluding 0-6 year age group according to 2001 census is shown as follows:

1991			2001		
Persons	*Males*	*Females*	*Persons*	*Males*	*Females*
49.29	60.47	36.02	65.76	76.20	54.16

The following table provides information on various types of educational institutions available in the towns of this district, including the number of stadia and public libraries:

Name of the towns	*Educational Institutions*	*Stadia*	*Public Libraries including reading rooms*
Bazpur	Higher Secondary/Intermediate School (1), Secondary/Matriculation Schools (2), Junior Secondary and Middle School (1), Primary Schools (5)	–	–
Gadarpur	Higher Secondary/Inter mediate School (1), Secondary/Matriculation School (2), Junior Secondary and Middle Schools (2), Primary Schools (4)	–	PL:1
Jashpur	Higher Secondary/Intermediate School (1), Sec ondary/Matriculation Schools (2), Junior Secondary and Middle Schools (4), Primary Schools (3)	–	–
Kashipur	Arts, Science and Commerce College (1), Polytechnics (1), Higher Secondary/Intermediate Schools (3), Secondary/Matriculation School (1), Junior Secondary and Middle School (6), Primary Schools (16)	1	PL:1
Khatima	Higher Secondary/Intermediate School (1), Secondary/Matriculation School (1), Junior Secon-		

	dary and Middle Schools (2), Primary Schools (3)	–	–
Kichha	Secondary/Matriculation School (2), Junior Secondary and Middle Schools (1), Primary Schools (7)	–	–
Rudrapur	Arts and Science College (1), Higher Secondary/ Intermediate School (1), Secondary/Matriculation School (1), Junior Secondary and Middle Schools (2), Primary Schools (5)	–	–
Sitarganj	Higher Secondary/ Intermediate School (1), Secondary/Matriculation Schools (2), Junior Secondary and Middle School (1), Primary Schools (8)		
Sultanpur	Higher Secondary/ Intermediate School (1), Secondary/Matriculation School (1), Junior Secondary and Middle School (1), Primary Schools (3)	–	–
Tanakpur	Arts, Science and Commerce College (1), Polytechnics (1), Higher Secondary/Intermediate Schools (2), Primary Schools (5)	–	–

COLLEGES

Ganna Krishak Girls Degree College, Kichha, (Established 1995).

Government Kishan Degree College, Bazpur, (Established 1995), Enrolment 273.

Government Postgraduate College, Rudrapur (1974), Enrolment 2885.

Government Degree College Khatima, (1987) Enrolment 1374.

Guru Nanak Girls Degree College, Nanakmata, Udham Singh

Nagar (1998), Enrolment 61.

R.H. Government Postgraduate College, Kashipur (1969), Enrolment 3691. Teachers 40.

Sanatan Dharma Girls Degree College, Rudrapur (1998), Enrolment 66, Teachers 6.

(Above named colleges belong to Kumaon University (Established 1973).

MEDICAL

The table given below provides town-wise break-up of medical institutions found in the towns alongwith the beds facility available therein:

Name of the Towns	*Medical institutions (alongwith bed facilities)*	
Bazpur	Dispensary (1)	–
	Hospital (1)	24
	T.B. Clinic (1)	–
Gadurpur	Dispensary (1)	–
	Hospital (1)	6
Jaspur	Hospital (1)	24
	Primary Health Centre (1)	6
Kashipur	Hospital (2)	101
	Family Planning Centre (1)	–
	Dispensary (2)	–
	Others (2)	–
Khatima	Primary Health Centre (1)	4
Kichha	T.B. Clinic (1)	–
	Hospital (1)	–
	Primary Health Centre (1)	8
Rudrapur	Hospital (2)	80
Sitarganj	Dispensary (1)	4
Sultanpur	Health Centre (1)	–
Tanakpur	Hospital (3)	18

NEWSPAPERS

Dabish, a Urdu weekly from Udham Singh Nagar.

New Uttaranchal Vikas Times, Hindi Fortnightly, published from Udham Singh Nagar.

B.S. Frontier, Hindi weekly, published from Udham Singh Nagar.

Udham Singh Nagar Ka Darpan, Hindi weekly, published from Udham Singh Nagar.

ADMINISTRATION

(i) Administrative Divisions:

Tehsils: Kashipur, Kichha, Sitarganj, Khatima.

Towns with their Population, Urban Status and Literates (2001)

City/Town	*Urban Status*	*Population*			*Literates*		
		Person	*Male*	*Female*	*Person*	*Male*	*Female*
Bazpur	MB	21782	11923	9859	14311	8534	5777
Bandia	CT	8897	5007	3890	4909	3151	1758
Dineshpur	NP	8856	4597	4259	5004	2972	2032
Gadarpur	MB	13638	7305	6333	8795	5031	3764
Jaspur	MB	39048	20589	18459	23364	13768	9596
Kachnal Gas	CT	4199	2393	1806	3026	1896	1130
Kashipur	MB	92978	48933	44045	63124	35780	27344
Kela Khera	NP	7783	4118	3665	2684	1790	894
Khatima	MB	14378	7787	6591	9520	5686	3834
Kichha	MB	30517	16223	14294	17160	10146	7014
Mahua Dabra	NP	6110	3207	2903	3582	2172	1410
Mahua Kher	NP	8859	4699	4160	3809	2558	1251
Nagla	CT	22944	12655	10289	16172	9904	6268
Rudrapur	MB	88720	47277	41443	48518	29097	19421
Shaktigarh	NP	4776	2489	2287	2903	1725	1178
Sitarganj	MB	21943	11547	10396	11877	7044	4833
Sultanpur	NP	7713	4109	3604	3989	2592	1897

(ii) Parliamentary Constituency and Assembly Segments:

No. and Name of Parliamentary Constituency. 4-NAINITAL

Assembly Constituency: 57. Jaspur

TEHSIL—KASHIPUR

Jashpur—1. Angadpur; 2. Raipur; 3. Rajpur; 4. Manduwakhera; 5. Ramnagar, Jaspur; 6. Badionwala; 7. Patrampur; 8. Mahuadabara; 9. Jaspur. ***Kunda***—10. Talabpur; 11. Daduwala; 12. Jagatpur Patti; 13. Lalpur; 14. Kunda;

15. Betwala; 16. Garhi Negi; 17. Bailjuri. ***Painga***—19. Painga; 23. Baskhera; 24. Basai. **Forest Area:** Forest Area. **Urban Area:** Jaspur MBH; Mahuadabra Haripur; NAC.

Assembly Constituency: 58. Kashipur

TEHSIL—KASHIPUR

Kashipur—25. Dhakiyakala; 26. Maheshpura; 27. Dhanauri Patti; 28. Gopipura; 29. Gangapur Gosai; 30. Manpur; 31. Pratappur; 32. Kundeshwari. ***Painga***—18. Rajpura Rani; 20. Barkhera Pandey; 21. Dabhaura; 22. Khokhratal. **Urban Area:** Kashipur MB; Mahuakheraganj NAC.

Assembly Constituency: 59. Bajpur

TEHSIL—KASHIPUR

Bajpur-I—1. Kelakhera; 3. Chakarpur; 7. Mahauli Jungle; 13. Hajira; 14. Barhaini; 15. Haripura; 19. Beriya Daulat; 20. Bhajuanagala; 21. Barwala; 22. Ganeshpur; 23. Badripur. ***Bajpur-II***—2. Guljarpur; 4. Rampurashakar; 5. Sultanpur; 6. Faridpur; 8. Vikrampur; 9. Jogipura; 10. Biraha; 11. Mudiyakala; 12. Maheshpura; 16. Khushalpur; 17. Ratan Pura; 18. Betkheri. **Forest Area:** Forest Area; **Urban Area:** Bajpur MB; Kilakhera NAC; Sultanpur NAC.

Assembly Constituency: 60. Pantnagar

TEHSIL—KICHHA

Dineshpur—6. Kulha; 7. Dhanpur Vijaypur; 8. Barirai; 11. Mehtosh; 12. Chandayan; 13. Vijaynagar; 14. Amarpur. ***Gadarpur***—1. Roshanpur; 2. Masit; 3. Sakainiya; 4. Motiyapura; 5. Govindpur; 9. Barakhera; 10. Lucknow. ***Kichha***—13. Anandpur-Nagla. ***Rudrapur***—16. Fulbag; 21. Danpur; 22. Matkota; 23. Kalyanpur. **Urban Area:** Dineshpur NAC; Gadarpur MB.

Assembly Constituency: 61-Rudrapur

TEHSIL—KICHHA

Kichha. 1. Firojpur; 2. Bara; 3. Shahdaura; 4. Najimabad; 5. Bhanga; 6. Sirolikala; 11. Kichha; 12. Indrapur; 14. Kotkhra; 15. Jawahar Nagar. ***Rudrapur.*** 7. Chhinki; 8. Darau; 9. Kuraiya; 10.. Chukti; 17. Bhamraula; 18. Shimla Pistaur; 19. Kanakpur; 20. Dewriya; 24. Rampura. **Urban Area:** Kichha MB; Rudrapur MB

Assembly Constituency: 62. Sitarganj (SC)

TEHSIL—KHATIMA

Nanakmatta. 20. Pipliya Pistaur; 22. Balkheri.

TEHSIL—SITARGANJ

Nanakmatta. 14. Dohara; 15. Lambakhera; 17. Nagla; 18. Sarauja; 19. Sadhunagar; 21. Deokali; 23. Bhikampur. ***Sitarganj.*** 1. Kunwarpur; 2. Tiliyapur; 3. Nakaha; 4. Nakuliya; 5. Pindari; 6. Baruwabag; 7. Bijati; 8. Mainajhundi 9. Rampura; 10. Rudpur; 11. Nakatpura; 12. Sarkara; 13. Sitarganj. **Urban Area:** Saktigarh NAC; Sitarganj MB.

Assembly Constituency: 63. Khatima (ST)

TEHSIL—KHATIMA

Bigarabag. 17. Amaun; 18. Nadanna; 19. Bigarabag; 20. Shripur Bichuwa; 21. Bhurakisani; 22. Chhinki; 23. Bhara Bhuriya; 24. Sabaura; 25. Naugawanath; 26. Diya. ***Khatima.*** 1. Umarukhurd; 2. Sarpura; 3. Gurkhura; 4. Jhankat; 5. Pahaniya; 6. Jarsupratappur; 7. Nauguwathagu; 8. Mudeli; 9. Barianjaniya; 10. Fulaiya; 11. Sisaiya; 12. Majhola; 13. Nagla Tarai; 14. Jadopur; 15. Haldi; 16. Sunpahar. ***Nanakmatta.*** 16. Nanakmatta. **Forest Area:** Nanakmatta Forest Area. **Urban Area:** Khatima MB.

OBSERVATIONAL ORGANISATION

Surface Observatories

This facility is available at Pantnagar.

Pantnagar

Latitude : 29.1° North

Longitude : 79.46° East

Altitude : 233 m

Date of starting : 25-5-1962

Agricultural Meteorological Stations

This facility is available at Pantnagar at two places. The instrument lies in,

Latitude : 29.0° North

Longitude : 79.5° East

Altitude : 244 m

Date of starting : 3-6-1977

1-1-1956

DISASTROUS WEATHER EVENTS

Snowfall

From 28-30 December 1996, it was severe and several person died due to it.

ARCHAEOLOGICAL SITE

At Kashipur

In the *terai* region, with a large polygonal mound engirdiled by vegetation covered ramparts, ornamental bricks, with cut work of leaf, flower, lotus, exhibiting Gupta workmanship, found reused in all phases and arrangement of windows. A terracotta bulla, perhaps used as a pendant. Shoeos two human figures as on some Pauri-Kushan coins. Copper coins range from those of the Mathura rulers to the bull and horseman type.

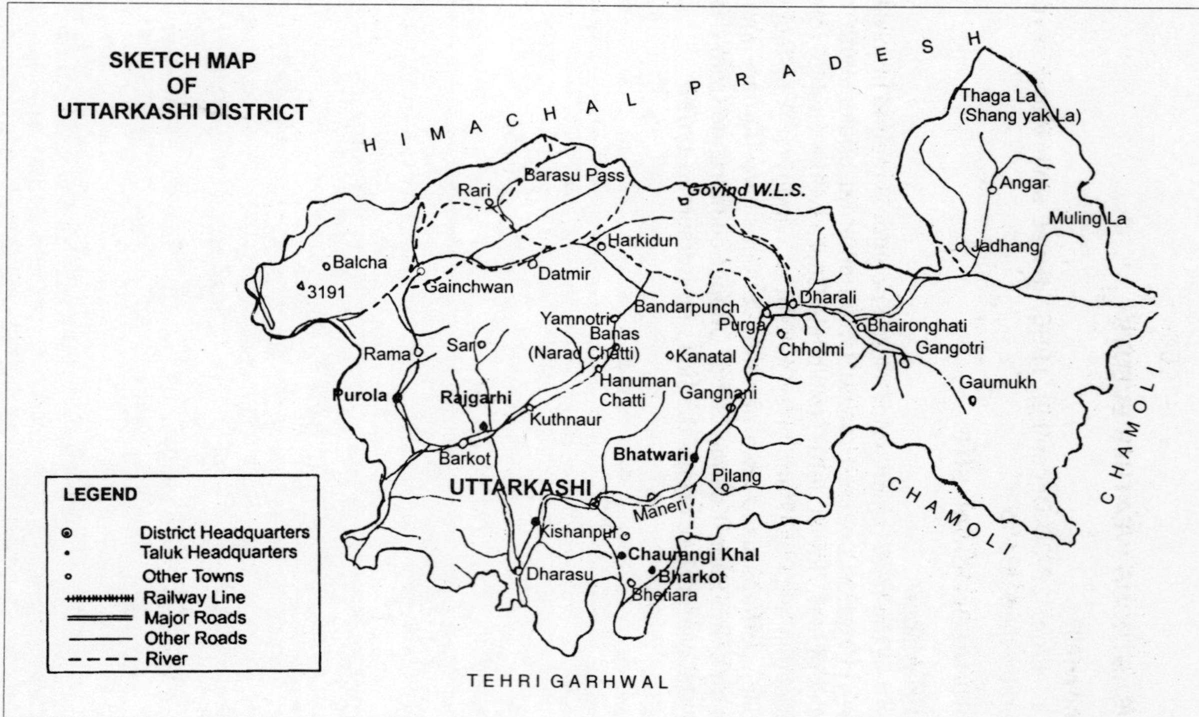
SKETCH MAP
OF
UTTARKASHI DISTRICT
HIMACHAL PRADESH
Thaga La
(Shang yak La)
Angar
Muling La
Jadhang
Barasu Pass
Rari
Govind W.L.S.
Harkidun
Balcha
3191
Gainchwan
Datmir
Dharali
Bandarpunch
Yamnotri
Banas
(Narad Chatti)
Purga
Chholmi
Bhaironghati
Gangotri
Gaumukh
Rama
Sari
Kanatal
Hanuman
Chatti
Gangnani
Purola
Rajgarhi
Kuthnaur
Barkot
Bhatwari
Pilang
UTTARKASHI
Maneri
Kishanpur
Chaurangi Khal
Dharasu
Bharkot
Bhetiara
CHAMOLI
CHAMOLI
TEHRI GARHWAL
LEGEND
District Headquarters
Taluk Headquarters
Other Towns
Railway Line
Major Roads
Other Roads
River

UTTAR KASHI

LOCATION AND AREA

Latitude	:	30.7° North to 31.5° North
Longitude	:	77.9° East to 79.2° East
Altitude	:	1200 m

Uttarkashi district was created on February 24, 1960 out of what then constituted the parganas of Rawain and Uttarkashi of Rawain tehsil of erstwhile Tehri Garhwal district. It sprawls in the extreme north-west corner of the state over an area of 7950 sq. kms. in the rugged terrain of the mystic Himalayas. On its north lie Himachal Pradesh State and the territory of Tibet while on its south touch the districts of Rudraprayag and Tehri Garhwal. Himachal Pradesh and the district of Dehradun bound it in the west and the territory of Tibet and the district of Chamoli in the east.

The district is named after its headquarters town Uttarkashi, an ancient place with rich cultural heritage and as the name suggests is the the Kashi of north (Uttara) held almost as high a veneration as Kashi of the plain (Varanasi). Both the Kashi of the plain (Varanasi) as well as the Kashi of north are situated on the banks of the river Ganga (Bhagirathi). The area which is held sacred and known as Uttarkashi, lies between the rivers Syalam Gad also known as the Varuna and Kaligad also known as the Asi. The Varuna and the Asi are also the names of the rivers between which the Kashi of the plain lies. One of the holiest Ghats in Uttarkashi is Manikarnika so is the one by the same name in Varanasi. Both have temples dedicated to Vishwanath.

HISTORY

The terrain and climate of Uttarkashi district provide uncongenial physical environment for human settlement. Yet undaunted by hazards and hardships this land was inhabited by hill tribes since ancient times bringing out the best in man his adaptive talents. The hill tribes namely Kiratas, Uttara Kurus, Khasas, Tanganas, Kunindas and Partanganas find references in the Upayana Parva of Mahabharata. The land of Uttarkashi district has been held sacred by Indians since ages where the seers and sages had found solace and spiritual aspirations and performed penances and where devas performed their sacrifices and Vedic language was better known and spoken than elsewhere. People came here for learning Vedic language and speech. According to an account given in the Mahabharata, Jada Bharata a great sage performed penances at Uttarkashi. The Kedar Khand of Skanda Purna refers Uttarkashi and the rivers Bhagirathi, Jahanavi and Bheel Ganga.

The district of Uttarkashi was part of Garhwal Kingdom ruled by Garhwal dynasty that carried the congnomen 'Pal' which was changed to Sah during 15th century conferred by Sultan of Delhi perhaps Bahlul Lodi. In 1803 Gorkhas of Nepal invaded Garhwal and Amar Singh Thapa was made Governor of this region. The Gorkhas came into contact with the British power in 1814 as their frontier in Garhwal became determinous with those of the British. The border troubles prompted the Britishers to invade Garhwal. In April, 1815 Gorkhas were ousted from Garhwal region and Garhwal was annexed as British district and was split up into eastern and western Garhwal. The eastern Garhwal was retained by the British Government. The western Garhwal, lying to the west of the Alaknanda river with the exception of the Dun was made over to the heir of Garhwal dynasty Sudarshan Sah. This state came to be known as Tehri Garhwal and it was merged with the state of Uttar Pradesh in 1949 after India attained independence in 1947.

POPULATION (GENERAL, SC/ST)

Total population of the district according to 2001 Census is 294179 persons, comprising of 151599 males and 142580 females. Rural population of the district is 227255 persons (138328 males and 132927 females) and urban population is 22924 persons (13271 males and 9653 females).

The Scheduled Castes and Scheduled Tribes population of the district as per 1991 Census is 54594 persons and 2300 persons respectively. The rural-urban breakup of this population is indicated below:

Rural	(i) Scheduled Castes	:	52355
	(ii) Scheduled Tribes	:	2240
Urban	(i) Scheduled Castes	:	2239
	(ii) Scheduled Tribes	:	60

The decennial growth rate of population of the district as a whole in relation state between the period 1981-1991 and 1991-2001 is presented below:

State/District	*Decennial growth rate of population (per cent)*	
	1981-91	*1991-2001*
Uttaranchal	24.23	19.20
Bageshwar	25.54	22.72

LANGUAGES AND RELIGION

Main language spoken in the district is Hindi.

Religion-wise breakup of population as per 1991 Census (At District Level)

Hindus: 235550, Muslims: 2164, Christians: 89, Sikhs: 241, Buddhists: 1377, Jains: 284, Other religions and persuasions: 2, Religion not stated: 2.

GEOGRAPHY AND PHYSICAL FEATURES

Lying in the upper Himalayas, Uttarkashi contains within itself varying geographic environments ranging from snow free valleys and outer hills to the high peaks with perpetual snow and glaciers. The terrain runs into series of ridges and valleys. Each ridge leads to another coiling up in seemingly unending chains. Most of the terrain is mountainous consisting of high rise ridges, hills and plateaus and flat pieces of land are rare. The land in these areas is low in fertlity due to large content of out crops of boulders and gravels. Made-up of alluvial soil, valley is a stream bed. Generally forests occur on the upper ridges that bound the valleys. On their sloping hill sides lie a chain of sparsely populated settlements interspersed with terrace cultivation.

The nature expresses itself in breath-taking variations from beauteous landscape luxuriously decked with vegetations punctuated by streams, brooks and rivers to high rise awesome rocky ridges and mountains gently tapering off into lefty snow-capped peaks. The widely varying climate and topography produce a wide range of vegetations and serve as habitats to diverse species of wild life. Forests occupy a place of pride in the environment of the district not only for the sheer bulk of the area they occupy but also for the richness of variety of vegetations.

As much as 88 per cent of the total area of the district is administered by the Forest Department. Of 695784 hectares of area under forest department, 391525 hectares is covered with vegetations while the remaining is either snow covered or nude rocks. Pine forests occur between the altitude of 900-2000 metres, Deodar forests between 2000-3000 metres, Fix and Spruce forests over 3000 metres and Kharshu, Birch and Juniperus forests upto the height of 4000 metres. Above the Fir and Spruce forest zone, alpine pastures are found throughout the district between the height of 3500 metres to 4877 metres above sea level. Rich varieties of grass, shrubs and herbs come up during June-September while during the remaining part of the year these areas remain covered with snow. A large number of medicinal plants of great commercial value grow spontaneously in the forests. Some of these grow in the valleys, some insub-montane tracts while some other on higher altitudes.

Forestry too does play an important role in the economy of the district. It employs persons both in preservation and propagation of forests as well as in their exploitation. The production of timber is estimated to be of the order of 44 thousand cubic metres. Herbs are the most important minor forest produce. A large variety of herbs grow wild. They are of a great commercial importance for their rapeutic value. The herbs are collected through cooperatives. There are twelve such cooperative societies operating, which are likely to grow to 30 during the next decade. The herbs are collected worth Rs. two lakh annually. Afforestation programme covers 450 hectares annually.

RIVERS, CANALS AND WATERWAYS

It is the land of Uttarkashi district that gives rise to two great and reverent rivers of India the Bhagirathi, called the Ganga in the plains and the Yamuna. The Ganga coming up in the glaciers 'Gaumukh' traverses 128 kms. in Uttarkashi district before flowing down farther. Hardly ten kms. away from Gaumukh is the place 'Gangotri' of great pilgrimage importance. The Yamuna rises from the west of Bandarpunch peak and revered highly is the place 'Yamnotri' situated nearby visited by pilgrims. The third important river of this district is Tons besides host of tributaries that drain these areas.

TOWNS, VILLAGES AND AMENITIES

The district at present comprises of 4 tehsils and 6 Community Development Blocks. It has 3 towns and 686 villages (678 inhabited villages and 8 uninhabited villages). The urban population of the district as percentage of total population in the census year 2001 is indicated below. It also shows the sex ratio (females per 1000 males) and density (population per sq. km.) in the urban population of the district in relation to the state:

State/ District	*Urban population as percentage of total population*	*Sex ratio, (females per 1000 males*		*Density (Population per sq. km.)*	
	2001	*1991*	*2001*	*1991*	*2001*
Uttaranchal	25.59	936	964	133	159
Uttar Kashi	7.79	918	941	30	37

Amenities

Number (with percentage) of villages having one or more amenities in the district as per 1991 Census is given below:

Sl. No.	*Amenities*	*Number of inhabited villages*	*Percentage*
1.	Education	510	75.22
2.	Medical	100	14.75
3.	Drinking Water	678	100.00
4.	Post and Telegraph	126	18.58

5.	Market/Hat	62	9.14
6.	Communications	273	40.27
7.	Approach by Pucca Road	205	30.24
8.	Power Supply	542	79.94

COMMUNICATIONS

Uttarkashi district is not served by railways and communications depends solely on roads and pathways. A national highway does not pass through this district. The district is served by a total length of 667 kms. of roads giving a ratio of 8.32 kms. of roads per 100 sq. kms. of area that keeps the infrastructure of the area at a low key. Of the total road length 524 kms. falls under the category of main district roads entirely managed by the Public Works Department. Other district roads measure to mere ten kms. out of which 9 kms. is under the management of local bodies while State highways account for 133 kms. out of which only 10 kms. of roads is managed by the Public Works Department.

AGRICULTURE AND IRRIGATION

Agriculture in these areas suffer from many constraints. The availability of cultivable land itself is the greatest restricting factor on the development of agriculture. It can be seen from the fact that as much as 88 per cent of the area is either covered by forests or is barren and uncultivable. The land is low in fertility except in the valleys and even land is too few and far between. Shorter agricultural season, low temperature, high altitude, smallness of land holding, perpetual problem of soil erosion due to steep gradients etc. are other inhibiting factors effecting agriculture. The agriculture therefore, does not offer too much hope for bringing about well-being to the people of the area. Sheep rearing for production of wool and meat, orchard raising, spinning and weaving of wool and other cottage industries etc. offer much scope and their potential be exploited to the fullest extent.

The cultivation in these areas are carried on largely by making terraces on the sloping hillsides. Some cultivation is done on steep hills also where terracing and tilling cannot be done and the place is cleared by burning scrubs and bushes.

The seeds are sown with the help of a hoe. This practice of cultivation is known as 'Katil'.

Both Rabi as well as Kharif crops are harvested. The main Kharif crops are paddy, small millets and potato and chief Rabi crops are wheat and barley. These crops account for over 80 per cent of the total cropped area. The largest area is under wheat (14222 hectares) followed by small millets (12410 hectares), paddy (9817 hectares), barley (1001 hectares) and potato (631 hectares). The cultivation of potato offers good commercial prospect. Efforts are under way to double the present production of 2500 tonnes by increasing the yield per hectare of land. The last decade has witnessed greater application of improved agricultural practices. The area under improved seeds increased from 1.78 thousand hectares to 11.56 thousand over the last decade.

Horticulture is another field that can boost up the economy of the district. However, it has not made much headway due to difficulties in marketing the produce, due to poor communications and remoteness of areas. Orchhards occupy almost seven thousand hectares of area out of which five thousand hectares is undder apples. The area under orchards is to be raised to twelve thousand hectares during sixth plan. The production of fruits account for 21 thousand tonnes worth Rs. two crores.

ANIMAL HUSBANDRY

Animal husbandry is an important source of supplementing income of the rural population. Of the total live-stock, bovine population and that of sheep accounted for almost one-third each. The production of milk per milch animal is very low. Efforts are under way for introducing high yielding strain. Sheep rearing is an important industry in the district. Yet it does not provide full time employment and it is only avocation for those who are engaged in its pursuit. The production of wool is estimated to be 200 tonnes. As many as sixteen sheep development centres are functioning.

INDUSTRIES

The knowledge regarding occurrences of minerals in the district is scanty. As per stray surveys, soap stones, iron, graphite, lime stone, kyanite and mica deposits occur in the district.

There has been hardly any industrial development in the district. There is only one factory registered under Factory Act, 1948. The cottage and village industries play an important role in the economy of the district. The most important cottage industry is the production of wool and woolen goods. Sheep are reared in a large number and the industry flourished at an altitude between 1525 metres and 2440 metres. Carpets (namdas), tweeds, blankets etc. are produced. Other cottage industries are basket-making mat weaving and wood craft.

The potentials of forest and horticulture can be better exploited by locating forest and horticulture based industries within the district. This will bring down transportation cost as a proportion to the selling price of the products, making them competitive in the market.

Tourist industry possesses tremendous possibilities of development. The terrain produces some of the rarest spectacles contrasting between awesome ruggedness and breathtakingly beautiful landscape which have charmed and challenged man since ages. The location of Hindu religious places takes it beyond the pale of connoiseur and lovers of nature to the common man who throngs for religious satiety. For the development of tourism it is important to connect some of the places of tourist interest like Deorhital, Hari Ki Duna and Gaumukh by roads.

TRADE, COMMERCE AND EXPORT

The following table gives the most important commodity exported, manufactured and imported in the towns of the district:

Name of the towns	*Most important commodity*		
	Manufactured	*Exported*	*Imported*
1	*2*	*3*	*4*
Barkot	—	Potato	Rice
Uttarkashi	Woollen Cloth	Potato	Wheat

As it can be seen from the above table, the important commodity exported from the district is potato while wheat and rice are imported from other districts.

TOURISM

Gangotri (Tehsil Bhagwari). Niched in Hindu mythology, Gangotri is a place highly revered and one of the greatest places of Hindu pilgrimage. It is said to be the place where the river Bhagirathi, also known as the Ganga first descended on the earth. It is situated on the bank of the river Bhagirathi in the serene setting of picturesque terrain. There is a temple dedicated to Bhagirathi which remains open between May and mid of November.

Situated nearby is Kedar Prayag the confluence of the rivers Bhagirathi and Kedar Ganga. A short distance away down stream the Bhagirathi falls into what is known as Gouri Kund. The water before fall is considered extremely holy and is collected for use at the worship of Shiva at Rameshwaram in the extreme south of India.

Gaumukh (Tehsil Bhatwari). Gaumukh, situated hardly ten kms. away from Gangotri is the junction of 15 glaciers and the cave formed thus resembles the mouth of a cow. The river Bhagirathi rises from these glaciers. The grandeur of nature unfolds itself in beauteous scenic settings with serenity and calm that gives solace to the visitors and elevates them spiritually. This is one of the places of great importance of pilgrimage of India and is visited by many undeterred by the difficulties of uncongenial terrain and difficult approach.

Uttarkashi (Tehsil Bhatwari). Uttarkashi is the district headquarters situated 663 kms. away from Lucknow. It is also an important place of pilgrimage only next to Gangotri. The place is perched on the bank of Bhagirathi in picturesque surroundings against the back drop of hills. Like Varanasi the Kashi of the plain, Uttar Kashi is the town of temples. The most important temple is dedicated to Shiva by name of Vishwanath as it is at Varanasi. The other temples of importance are those dedicated to Pershurama Duttatraya, Annapurna, Bhaiarava and Ekadashrudra. The temple Lakeshwar is associated with the Lac House built by Duryodhana to kill Pandavas. Many persons who have renounced the world or retired otherwise from life have settled down here.

Yamnotri. Yamnotri is yet another place of importance situated at the bank of river Yamuna near its source Bandarpunch.

The famous Yamuna temple is dedicated to the goddess Yamuna. The place is famous for its hot springs and varying temperature. These numerous springs are associated with twelve Rishis who followed Mahadeva from Lanka to Yamnotri.

FAIRS AND FESTIVALS

Important fairs and festivals organised in different parts of the district are mentioned below:

Vishwat Shankranti, Moltari, Bishu, Mawi, Thala, Odas Jakhandi Devta-ka-Mela, Jattar, Bhadra Kali Devi-ka-Mela, Jagra, Jatra, Thaul, Davrana, Molthat, Tansa, Tanger, Thaul, Chhilora, Durwashimi, Dewlong Gangani, Dhanari Pujar-gaon, Bishtpatti Nagun, Gauri Ravantal, Barsali Garh, Gajnakhathur Thati, Ramoli, Gajnakhathur Narpar, Fulali, Bhadranj, Baliraj, Makar Sankranti, Basant Panchami.

EDUCATION

According to 2001 Census, the population of total literates (excluding the population in the age group of 0-6 years) is 163501 persons. of these, 107016 are males and 56485 are females. In the rural areas of the district 145787 persons (95958 males and 49829 females) are literates and in urban areas 17714 persons (11058 males and 6656 females) are literates. The rate of literacy of this population to the total population, excluding 0-6 years age group according to 2001 Census is shown below:

1991			*2001*		
Persons	*Males*	*Females*	*Persons*	*Males*	*Females*
47.23	68.74	23.57	66.58	84.52	47.48

There are seven Primary Schools, two Middle Schools, three High Schools and three Intermediate Colleges per 10000 of population. The ratio is higher in smaller towns.

COLLEGES

Government Degree College Purola (Established 1990).

Government Degree College, Barkot (Established 1990)

Government P.G. College, Uttar Kashi (Established 1969). Enrolment 1200, Teachers 35.

(Above named colleges belong to Hemwati Nandan Bahuguna Garhwal University (Established 1973)

MEDICAL

Seven beds are available in urban areas of Uttarkashi district per 1000 population in medical institutions. The availability of about eight beds per 1000 population is the highest in Uttarkashi M.B. among three towns of the district.

ADMINISTRATION

(i) Administrative Divisions:

Tehsils. Puraula, Barkot, Dunda, Bhatwari.

Community Development Blocks: Mori, Purola, Naugaon, Dunda, Chinyalisaor, Bhatwari.

Towns with their Populations, Urban Status, and Literates (2001)

City/Town	Urban Status	Population			Literates		
		Person	Male	Female	Person	Male	Female
Gangotri	NP	606	581	25	539	527	12
Bandia	CT	16220	9252	6968	12694	7718	4976
Barkot	NP	6098	3438	2660	4481	2813	1668

(ii) Parliamentary constituencies and assembly segments:

No. and Name of Parliamentary Constituency: 1. TEHRI GARHWAL

No. and Name of Assembly Segments of Tehri Garhwal Parliamentary Constituencies which lies within the Jurisdiction of Uttarkashi District.

Assembly Constituency: 1. Purola

TEHSIL—BARKOT

Assembly Constituency: 28. Paunti and Forest Area

TEHSIL—PUROLA

Gundiyatgaon. 11. Gadugad; 12. Gundiyatgaon; 13. Mahargaon; 14. Badiyar (Digari); 15. Sunali. ***Naitwar (Kotgaon).*** 1. Jakhol; 2. Phitari; 3. Gangar; 4. Kotgaun; 5. Doni; 6. Naitwar. ***Naugaon.*** 29. Tunalka; 30. Kotiyalgaon; 31. Naugaon; 32. Tiyan; 33. Darsaun. ***Purola.*** 16. Devdhung; 17. Purola; 18. Chandeli; 19. Hudoli; 20. Bankoli; 21. Khawalisera. ***Rajgarhi.*** 39. Gadoli; 40. Gulari; 41. Gair (Banal); 42. Rajgarhi; 43. Chaptari; 44.

Gangtari; 45. Nagangaon; 7. Gurari; 8. Mori; 9. Bhutanu; 10. Tikochi. ***Forest Area.*** Forest area.

Assembly Constituency: 2. Gangotri

TEHSIL—BHATWARI

Bhatwari. 79. Mukhawa (Harsil); 80. Jhala; 81. Barsu; 82. Kyark; 83. Bhatwari; 84. Lata; 85. Bhelatipri. ***Joshiyara.*** 92. Sald; 93. Tekhala; 94. Joshiyara; 95. Bonga; 96. Mustiksaur.

Maneri. 86. Saura; 87. Didsari; 88. Sainj; 89. Gajoli; 90. Bhankoli; 91. Netala. **Forest Area:** Forest Area; **Urban Area:** Uttarkashi.

TEHSIL—DUNDA

Bhatwari. 71. Dhungi; 72. Thati; 73. Hitanu; 74. Bhatwari (Dhanari); 75. Kamad; 76. Dhauntri; 77. Nyusari; 78. Bareth (Gajana). ***Dunda.*** 46. Barethi (Barsali); 47. Matali; 48. Nakuri (Barsali).

Assembly Constituency: 3. Yamunotri (SC)

TEHSIL—BARKOT

Barkot. 22. Kharsari; 23. Ranageeth (Rana); 24. Kuthnaur; 25. Kharadi; 26. Barkot; 27. Chakragaon.

Barnigard. 34. Kuwan; 35. Garh; 36. Gatu; 37. Kandari; 38. Damta.

TEHSIL—DUNDA

Barethi. 55. Ramoli (Dasnagi); 56. Kyari; 57. Chaijyula; 58. Bangaon; 59. Banchaura (Dharkot); 60. Garath; 61. Jestwari; 62. Morgi; 63. Indra; 64. Barethi (Bist). ***Dunda.*** 49. Beerpur (Dunda); 50. Kalyani; 51. Jineth; 52. Genwala (Bhandarsyun); 53. Khurmola; 54. Junga. ***Sunargaon.*** 65. Jogat 66. Baldogi 67. Badhangaon 68. Kawagadi 69. Sunargaon 70. Jaspur. **Forest Area:** Forest Area.

MINERALS AND ORES OCCURRENCES

Auden reports the occurrence of medicinal clay at an altitude of 10,000 ft. along the track between Bhaironghati and Nilang of the Gartang *nala* with the Jadh Ganga (31.1, 78.9). A non-bedded silty clay, though resting on granite is thought to be fluvio-glacial origin and not a disintegration product of the granite in spite of its lack of bedding. The clay is said to be a remedy for flatulence.

Copper—Numerous boulders containing veins of chalcopyrite, quartz and felspar were found by Auden on a moraine descending from a South west branch of the Mana glacier (31.1, 79.2). The veins occur in granite which is intrusive into states and pellic quartzites of the Haimantha series.

Pebbles of chalcopyrite near Lhelta (30.6, 78.8). Malachite impregnated quartzite was seen as a boulder in the Jadh Ganga just below Dasumundu (31.1, 79.1).

Lead and Silver—Galena occurs at Pindki (30.9, 78.4) in a quartz vein about 15 ft. long with a maximum thickness of a 3 ft. 6 ins. at the centre.

Limestone—An occurrence of limestone has been reported Guinota (30.7, 78.2) Barahat (30.7, 78.4).

Mineral Waters—At Palla or Wazirgarh (30.9, 78.4), several springs occur here. Water is tepid, clear, impregnated with sulphuretted hydrogen and iron.

At Jamnotri (31.0, 78.5) numerous springs are recorded here. Temperature of water is 89°C. Discharge is very copious. Water deposits a thin calcareous and ferruginous sediment.

Pyrites—Pyrites occur in small quantities at (30.9, 78.4)

OBSERVATIONAL ORGANISATION

Hydrometeorological stations for climatological purposes:

This instrument facility is available at three places in the district, i.e., Beef, Bhaironghati and Maneri. These places lie in

Beef

Latitude	:	30.9° North
Longitude	:	78.4° East
Altitude	:	2595 m
Date of starting	:	21–10–1984

Bhairoghati

Latitude	:	31.1° North
Longitude	:	78.9° East

Altitude : 2865 m

Date of starting : 11–11–1977

Maneri

Latitude : 30.7° North

Longitude : 78.7° East

Altitude : 1303 m

Date of starting : 16–11–1977

DISASTER WEATHER EVENTS

Snowfall

From 28-30 December 1996, it was severe and several people died due to it.

Floods and Heavy Rains

On 3rd July 1993, there was heavy rains, several people died, houses damaged.

DISTRIBUTION OF *SCHEDULED CASTE* POPULATION BY SEX (1991)

	POPULATION Total	Males	Females
UTTARKASHI			
	54,594	28,082	26,512
Agariya	73	38	35
Badi	161	65	96
Baheliya	30	8	22
Baiga	44	32	12
Baiswar	78	29	49
Bajaniya	23	13	10
Bajgi	5,669	2,817	2,852
Balai	18	9	9
Balmiki	860	540	320
Bangali	10	0	10
Bansphor	10	1	9
Barwar	13	3	10
Basor	8	8	0
Beldar	2	2	0
Beriya	70	59	11
Bhantu	45	7	38
Chamar, Dhusia, Jhusia, Jatava	1,863	1,059	804
Chero	3	3	0
Dabgar	2	2	0
Dhangar	19	19	0
Dhanuk	5	5	0
Dharkar	1	1	0
Dhobi	74	72	2
Dom	3,908	1,895	2,013
Dusadh	1	1	0
Gond	15	5	10
Gual	41	35	6
Hela	16	16	0
Kalabaz	1	0	1
Karwal	2	0	2
Khairaha	22	0	22
Kharwar (excluding Benbansi)	12	12	0
Khatik	45	31	14
Kol	2,617	1,200	1,417
Kori	2,850	1,438	1,412
Korwa	5	5	0
Lalbegi	1	1	0
Majhwar	16	16	0
Mazhabi	3	3	0
Musahar	27	16	11
Nat	71	33	38
Parahiya	13	3	10
Pasi, Tarmali	19	19	0
Patari	17	17	0
Rawat	18	16	2
Saharya	10	10	0
Sanaurhiya	37	19	18
Sansiya	20	2	18
Shilpkar	34,723	18,048	16,675
Turaiha	44	34	10
Unclassified	959	415	544

DISTRIBUTION OF *SCHEDULED TRIBE* POPULATION BY SEX (1991)

	POPULATION		
	Total	Males	Females
UTTARKASHI			
	2,300	1,205	1,095
Bhotia	1,768	886	882
Buksa	26	9	17
Jaunsari	505	309	196
Tharu	1	1	0